Assessment in Health Professions Education

The health professions, i.e., persons engaged in teaching, research, administration, and/or testing of students and professionals in medicine, dentistry, nursing, pharmacy, and other allied health fields, have never had a comprehensive text devoted specifically to their assessment needs.

Assessment in Health Professions Education is the first comprehensive text written specifically for this audience. It presents assessment fundamentals and their theoretical underpinnings, and covers specific assessment methods. Although scholarly and evidence-based, the book is accessible to non-specialists.

- This is the first text to provide comprehensive coverage of assessment in the health professions. It can serve as a basic textbook in introductory and intermediate assessment and testing courses, and as a reference book for graduate students and professionals.
- Although evidence-based, the writing is keyed to consumers of measurement topics and data rather than to specialists. Principles are presented at the intuitive level without statistical derivations.
- Validity evidence is used as an organizing theme. It is presented early (Chapter 2) and referred to throughout.

Steven M. Downing (PhD, Michigan State University) is Associate Professor of Medical Education at the University of Illinois at Chicago and is the Principal Consultant at Downing & Associates. Formerly he was Director of Health Programs and Deputy Vice President at the National Board of Medical Examiners and Senior Psychometrician at the American Board of Internal Medicine.

Rachel Yudkowsky (MD, Northwestern University Medical School, MHPE, University of Illinois at Chicago) is Assistant Professor of Medical Education at the University of Illinois at Chicago. She has been director of the Dr. Allan L. and Mary L. Graham Clinical Performance Center since 2000, where she develops standardized patient and simulation-based programs for the instruction and assessment of students, residents, and staff.

Assessment in Health Professions Education

Edited by
Steven M. Downing, PhD
Rachel Yudkowsky, MD MHPE

Routledge
Taylor & Francis Group

NEW YORK AND LONDON

First published 2009
by Routledge
270 Madison Ave, New York, NY 10016

Simultaneously published in the UK
by Routledge
2 Park Square, Milton Park, Abingdon, Oxon OX14 4RN

Routledge is an imprint of the Taylor & Francis Group, an informa business

© 2009 Taylor and Francis

Typeset in Caslon by Swales & Willis Ltd, Exeter, Devon

Library of Congress Cataloging-in-Publication Data
Assessment in health professions education / edited by Steven M. Downing,
Rachel Yudkowsky.
     p. ; cm.
    Includes bibliographical references and index.
    1. Medicine—Study and teaching. 2. Educational tests and measurements.
    I. Downing, Steven M. II. Yudkowsky, Rachel.
    [DNLM: 1. Health Occupations—education. 2. Educational Measurement—
methods. W 18 A83443 2009]
    R834.5.A873 2009
    610.71—dc22

                                                              2008042218

ISBN 10: 0–8058–6127–0 (hbk)
ISBN 10: 0–8058–6128–9 (pbk)
ISBN 10: 0–203–88013–7 (ebk)

ISBN 13: 978–0–8058–6127–3 (hbk)
ISBN 13: 978–0–8058–6128–0 (pbk)
ISBN 13: 978–0–203–88013–5 (ebk)

To my husband Moshe
Looking forward to the next billion seconds and more

To our children Eliezer and Channah
Who bring us much pride and joy

And in memory of our son Yehuda Nattan
May his memory be a blessing to all who loved him

~ RY

Contents

List of Figures

List of Tables

Preface

The purpose of this book is to present a basic yet comprehensive treatment of assessment methods for use by health professions educators. While there are many excellent textbooks in psychometric theory and its application to large-scale standardized testing programs and many educational measurement and assessment books designed for elementary and secondary teachers and graduate students in education and psychology, none of these books is entirely appropriate for the specialized educational and assessment requirements of the health professions. Such books lack essential topics of critical interest to health professions educators and may contain many chapters that are of little or no interest to those engaged in education in the health professions.

Assessment in Health Professions Education presents chapters on the fundamentals of testing and assessment together with some of their theoretical and research underpinnings plus chapters devoted to specific assessment methods used widely in health professions education. Although scholarly, evidence-based and current, this book is intended to be readable, understandable, and practically useful for the non-measurement specialist. Validity evidence is an organizing theme and is the conceptual framework used throughout the chapters of this book, because the editors and authors think that all assessment data require some amount of scientific evidence to support or refute the intended interpretations of the assessment data and that validity is the single most important attribute of all assessment data.

The Fundamentals

Chapters 1 to 6 present some of the theoretical fundamentals of assessment, from the special perspective of the health professions educator. These chapters are basic and fairly non-technical but are intended to provide health professions instructors some of the essential background needed to understand, interpret, develop, and successfully apply many of the specialized assessment methods or techniques discussed in Chapters 7 to 12.

In Chapter 1, Downing and Yudkowsky present a broad overview of assessment in the health professions. This chapter provides the basic concepts and language of assessment and orients the reader to the conceptual framework for this book. The reader who is unfamiliar with the jargon of assessment or is new to health professions education will find this chapter a solid introduction and orientation to the basics of this specialized discipline.

Chapter 2 (Downing & Haladyna) discusses validity and the classic threats to validity for assessment data. Validity encompasses all other topics in assessment and thus this chapter is placed early in the book to emphasize its importance. Validity is the organizing principle of this book, so the intention of this chapter is to provide readers with the interpretive tools needed to apply this concept to all other topics and concepts discussed in later chapters.

Chapters 3 and 4 both concern reliability of assessment data, with Chapter 3 (Axelson & Kreiter) discussing the general principles and common applications of reliability. In Chapter 4, Kreiter presents the fundamentals of an important special type of reliability analysis, Generalizability Theory, and applies this methodology to health professions education.

In Chapter 5, Downing presents some basic information on the statistics of testing, discussing the fundamental score unit, standard scores, item analysis, and some information and examples of practical hand-calculator formulas used to evaluate test and assessment data in typical health professions education settings.

Standard setting or the establishment of passing scores is the topic presented by Yudkowsky, Downing, and Tekian in Chapter 6.

Defensibility of absolute passing scores—as opposed to relative or normative passing score methods—is the focus of this chapter, together with many examples provided for some of the most common methods utilized for standard setting and some of the statistics used to evaluate those standards.

The Methods

The second half of the book—Chapters 7 to 12—cover all the basic methods commonly used in health professions education settings, starting with written tests of cognitive knowledge and achievement and proceeding through chapters on observational assessment, performance examinations, simulations, oral exams and portfolio assessment. Each of these topics represents an important method or technique used to measure knowledge and skills acquisition of students and other learners in the health professions.

In Chapter 7, Downing presents an overview of written tests of cognitive knowledge. Both constructed-response and selected-response formats are discussed, with practical examples and guidance summarized from the research literature. Written tests of all types are prevalent, especially in classroom assessment settings in health professions education. This chapter aims to provide the instructor with the basic knowledge and skills needed to effectively test student learning.

Chapter 8, written by McGaghie and colleagues, overviews observational assessment methods, which may be the most prevalent assessment method utilized, especially in clinical education settings. The fundamentals of sound observational assessment methods are presented and recommendations are made for ways to improve these methods.

Yudkowsky discusses performance examinations in Chapter 9. This chapter provides the reader with guidelines for performance assessment using techniques such as standardized patients and Objective Structured Clinical Exams (OSCEs). These methods are extremely useful in skills testing, which is generally a major objective of clinical education and training at all levels of health professions education.

High-tech simulations used in assessment are the focus of Chapter 10, by McGaghie and Issenberg. Simulation technology is becoming ever more important and useful for teaching and assessment, especially in procedural disciplines such as surgery. This chapter presents the state-of-the art for simulations and will provide the reader with the tools needed to begin to understand and use these methods effectively.

Chapters 11 and 12, written by Tekian and Yudkowsky, provide basic information on the use of oral examinations and portfolios. Oral exams in various forms are used widely in health professions education worldwide. This chapter provides information on the fundamental strengths and limitations of the oral exam, plus some suggestions for improving oral exam methods. Portfolio assessment, discussed in Chapter 12, is both old and new. This method is currently enjoying a resurgence in popularity and is widely applied in all levels of health professions education. This chapter presents basic information that is useful to those who employ this methodology.

Acknowledgments

As is often the case in specialized books such as this, the genesis and motivation to edit and produce the book grew out of our teaching and faculty mentoring roles. We have learned much from our outstanding students in the Masters of Health Professions Education (MHPE) program at the University of Illinois at Chicago (UIC) and we hope that this book provides some useful information to future students in this program and in the many other health professions education graduate and faculty development programs worldwide.

We are also most grateful to all of our authors, who dedicated time from their over-busy professional lives to make a solid contribution to assessment in health professions education.

We thank Lane Akers, our editor/publisher, at Routledge, for his encouragement of this book and his patience with our much delayed writing schedule. We also wish to acknowledge and thank all our reviewers. Their special expertise, insight, and helpful comments have made this a stronger publication.

Brittany Allen, at UIC, assisted us greatly in the final preparation of this book and we are grateful for her help. We also thank our families, who were most patient with our many distractions over the long time-line required to produce this book.

Steven M. Downing
Rachel Yudkowsky
University of Illinois at Chicago, College of Medicine
July 2008

Chapter-specific Acknowledgments

Chapter 2 Acknowledgments

This chapter is a modified and expanded version of two papers which appeared in the journal, *Medical Education*. The full references are:

Downing, S.M. (2003). Validity: On the meaningful interpretation of assessment data. *Medical Education*, 37, 830–837.
Downing, S.M., & Haladyna, T.M. (2004). Validity threats: Overcoming interference with proposed interpretations of assessment data. *Medical Education*, 38, 327–333.

Chapter 5 Acknowledgments

The author is grateful to Clarence D. Kreiter, PhD for his review of this chapter and helpful suggestions.

Chapter 6 Acknowledgments

This chapter is an updated and expanded version of a paper that appeared in *Teaching and Learning in Medicine* in 2006:

Downing, S., Tekian, A., & Yudkowsky, R. (2006). Procedures for establishing defensible absolute passing scores on performance examinations in health professions education. *Teaching and Learning in Medicine*, 18(1), 50–57.

The authors are grateful to the publishers Taylor and Francis for permission to reproduce here material from the paper. The original paper is available at the journal's website www.informaworld.com.

Chapter 7 Acknowledgments

The author is most grateful to Thomas M. Haladyna, PhD for his review of and constructive criticisms and suggestions for this chapter.

Chapter 12 Acknowledgments

Our thanks to Mark Gelula, PhD for reviewing this chapter and for his helpful comments and suggestions.

Introduction to Assessment in the Health Professions

Steven M. Downing and Rachel Yudkowsky

Assessment is defined by the *Standards for Educational and Psychological Testing* (AERA, APA, & NCME, 1999, p. 172) as: "Any systematic method of obtaining information from tests and other sources, used to draw inferences about characteristics of people, objects, or programs." This is a broad definition, but it summarizes the scope of this book, which presents current information about both assessment theory and its practice in health professions education. The focus of this book is on the assessment of learning and skill acquisition in *people*, with a strong emphasis on broadly defined achievement testing, using a variety of methods.

Health professions education is a specialized discipline comprised of many different types of professionals, who provide a wide range of health care services in a wide variety of settings. Examples of health professionals include physicians, nurses, pharmacists, physical therapists, dentists, optometrists, podiatrists, other highly specialized technical professionals such as nuclear and radiological technicians, and many other professionals who provide health care or health related services to patients or clients. The most common thread uniting the health professions may be that all such professionals must complete highly selective educational courses of study, which usually include practical training as well as classroom instruction; those who successfully complete these rigorous courses of study have the serious responsibility of taking care of patients—sometimes in life and death situations. Thus health professionals usually require a specialized license or other type of certificate to practice. It is important to base our health professions education assessment practices and methods on the best research evidence available, since many of the decisions made about our students ultimately have impact on health care delivery outcomes for patients.

The *Standards* (AERA, APA, & NCME, 1999) represent the consensus opinion concerning all major policies, practices, and issues in assessment. This document, revised every decade or so, is sponsored by the three major North American professional associations concerned with assessment and its application and practice: The American Educational Research Association (AERA), the American Psychological Association (APA), and the National Council on Measurement in Education (NCME). The *Standards* will be referenced frequently in this book because they provide excellent guidance based on the best contemporary research evidence and the consensus view of educational measurement professionals.

This book devotes chapters to both the contemporary theory of assessment in the health professions and to the practical methods typically used to measure students' knowledge acquisition and their abilities to perform in clinical settings. The theory sections apply to nearly all measurement settings and are essential to master for those who wish to practice sound, defensible, and meaningful assessments of their health professions students. The methods section deals specifically with common procedures or techniques used in health professions education—written tests of cognitive achievement, observational methods typically used for clinical assessment, and performance examinations such as standardized patient examinations.

George Miller's Pyramid

Miller's pyramid (Miller, 1990) is often cited as a useful model or taxonomy of knowledge and skills with respect to assessment in health professions education. Figure 1.1 reproduces the Miller pyramid, showing schematically that cognitive knowledge is at the base of a pyramid upon which foundation all other important aspects or features of learning in the health professions rests. This is the "knows"

level of essential factual knowledge, the knowledge of biological process and scientific principles on which most of the more complex learn-
ings rest. Knowledge is the essential prerequisite for most all other
types of learning expected of our students. Miller would likely agree
that this "knows" level is best measured by written objective tests, such
as selected- and constructed-response tests. The "knows how" level of
the Miller pyramid adds a level of complexity to the cognitive scheme,
indicating something more than simple recall or recognition of factual knowledge. The "knows how" level indicates a student's ability to
manipulate knowledge in some useful way, to apply this knowledge,
to be able to demonstrate some understanding of the relationships
between concepts and principles, and may even indicate the student's
ability to describe the solution to some types of novel problems. This
level can also be assessed quite adequately with carefully crafted written tests, although some health professions educators would tend to
use other methods, such as oral exams or other types of more subjective, observational procedures. The "knows how" level deals with cognitive knowledge, but at a somewhat more complex or higher level
than the "knows" level. The first two levels of the Miller pyramid are
concerned with knowledge that is verbally mediated; the emphasis
is on verbal-type knowledge and the student's ability to describe this
knowledge verbally rather than on "doing."

The "shows how" level moves the methods of assessment toward
performance methods and away from traditional written tests of knowledge. Most performance-type examinations, such as using simulated
patients to assess the communication skills of medical students, demonstrate the "shows how" level of the Miller pyramid. All such performance exams are somewhat artificial, in that they are presented in
a standard testing format under more-or-less controlled conditions.
Specific cases or problems are pre-selected for testing and special
"standardized patients" are selected and trained to portray the case
and rate the student's performance using checklists and/or rating
scales. All these standardization procedures add to the measurement
qualities of the assessment, but may detract somewhat from the
authenticity of the assessment. Miller's "does" level indicates the
highest level of assessment, associated with more independent and

free-range observations of the student's performance in actual patient or clinical settings. Some standardization and control of the assessment setting and situation is traded for complete, uncued authenticity of assessment. The student brings together all the cognitive knowledge, skills, abilities, and experience into a performance in the real world, which is observed by expert and experienced clinical teachers and raters.

Miller's pyramid can be a useful construct to guide our thinking about teaching and assessment in the health professions. However, many other systems or taxonomies of knowledge structure are also discussed in the literature. For example, one of the oldest and most frequently used taxonomies of cognitive knowledge (the "knows" and "knows how" level for Miller) is Bloom's Cognitive Taxonomy (Bloom, Engelhart, Furst, Hill, & Krathwohl, 1956). The Bloom Cognitive Taxonomy ranks knowledge from very simple recall or recognition of facts to higher levels of synthesizing and evaluating factual knowledge and solving novel problems. The Bloom cognitive taxonomy, which is often used to guide written testing, is discussed more thoroughly in Chapter 7. For now, we suggest that for meaningful and successful assessments, there must be some rational system or plan to

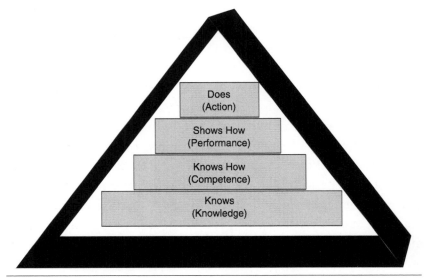

Figure 1.1 George Miller's Pyramid (Miller, 1990).

connect the content tested to the knowledge, skills and abilities that we think important for learning.

Four Major Assessment Methods

In health professions education, almost all of the assessments we construct, select, and administer to our students can be classified into one (or more) of these four categories: Written tests, performance tests, clinical observational methods, and a broad "miscellaneous" category consisting of many other types of assessments, such as oral examinations ("vivas" or live patient exams in the classic long and short-cases), portfolios, chart-stimulated recall type assessments, and so on. These methods fit, more or less, with the Miller Pyramid shown in Figure 1.1. This section provides an overview of these methods, each of which will be considered in detail in other chapters.

Written Tests

Most of the formal assessment in health professions education includes some type of written testing. This simply means that the tests consist of written questions or stimuli, to which students or trainees must respond. There are two major types of written tests: Constructed-response (CR) tests and selected-response (SR) tests. Both of these formats can be presented in either the traditional paper-and-pencil format or in the newer computer-based formats, in which computer screens are used to present the test stimuli and record examinee responses or answers. For constructed-response tests, questions or stimuli are presented and examinees respond by writing or typing responses or answers. There are many varieties of constructed-response formats, including "fill-in-the-blanks" type items and short- and long-answer essays. Selected-response tests, on the other hand, present a question or stimulus (referred to as a stem), followed by a number of option choices. The multiple-choice (MC) item is the prototype for selected-response formats, but there are many variations on the theme, such as true-false and alternate-choice items, matching items, extended matching items, and many other innovative formats (Sireci & Zenisky, 2006) used primarily in computer-based tests (CBTs). While the constructed-response format is probably the most widely used worldwide, the selected-response format is the true "workhorse" of the testing world, especially in North America. This format has many practical advantages and at least 90 years of research to support its validity (Downing, 2002; Welch, 2006). Chapter 7 discusses both constructed and selected response written tests.

Observational of Clinical Performance

Assessment of clinical performance during clinical training is a very common form of assessment in health professions education. These types of assessment range from informal observations of students in clinical settings to very formal (and sometimes complex) systems of data gathering from multiple raters about the performance of health professions students in actual clinical settings, with real patients over lengthy periods of time. Typically, many of these observational assessment methods rely on checklists and rating forms, completed by faculty and other instructors in clinical settings.

Many of these observational assessments carry major weight in overall or composite grading schemes, such that the stakes associated with these observations of clinical behavior are high for the student. Health professions educators rely heavily on these types of observational assessments, but the shortcomings of these methods are well known and are difficult to remediate (e.g., Williams, Klamen, & McGaghie, 2003). Validity problems are common in data obtained from observational methods, yet these methods are highly valued in health professions education because of strong traditions and (often false) beliefs concerning the quality of the data obtained. Chapter 8 is devoted to a discussion of the issues concerning assessments based on observation of clinical performance in real-life settings and Chapter 12 discusses other types of observational methods in the context of portfolios, noting their strengths and limitations.

Performance Tests

The term "performance test" is the generic term used to describe many types of formal testing with the primary purpose of measuring "what students can do," rather than simply "what they know." Health professions education has always valued the assessment of student performance, with a traditional reliance on "live patient oral examinations," and so-called "vivas," during which students were orally questioned in the classic long and short cases. Systematic, formal performance testing began fairly recently, with the introduction of the Objective Structured Clinical Examination (OSCE) by Hart and Harden in the late 1970s (e.g., Harden, Stevenson, Downie, & Wilson, 1975). Medical education in particular has adopted performance testing at all levels of training, from early in the medical school curriculum through graduate or residency training, including its use as one component of the United States Medical Licensure Examination (NBME, 2006) and post-graduate licensure examinations in Canada (Medical Council of Canada).

For simplicity, we categorize simulations as a type of performance examination, but many authors and researchers classify all types of simulations, used for both teaching and assessment, as a separate category. The term "simulation" refers to a testing method that utilizes a representation of a real-world task. Simulations cover a wide-range of methods and modalities, from fairly simple structured oral exams to very sophisticated and intricate computer simulations of complex patient clinical cases such as Primum® Computer-Based Case Simulations (CCS), one component of the United States Medical Licensure Examination (USMLE) Step II medical licensing test (NBME, 2006). Simulated or standardized patient exams, often used in OSCE stations, are utilized for both teaching and assessment and now comprise a major category of performance testing in many areas of health professions education. Simulated patient examinations date back to the early 1960's, pioneered by Howard Barrows (Barrows and Abrahamson, 1964), with the term "standardized patient" credited to Geoff Norman at McMaster University (Wallace, 1997). Some 30 years of research evidence now supports the validity of the standardized patient method and the many different facets of this testing modality (e.g., Anderson & Kassebaum, 1993).

Performance examinations can also utilize mechanical simulators. These range from single-task trainers that present heart sounds to students for identification or provide a "skin surface" for suturing to complex teaching-testing manikins such as Harvey® (Gordon, 1999) and high-fidelity human simulator models such as Sim-Man® (Laerdal) and the Human Patient Simulator® (METI).

Chapters 9 and 10 address the measurement issues and special problems of performance examinations, with a focus on standardized patients and other types of simulations.

Other Assessment Methods

This "miscellaneous" category includes many different types of assessments traditionally used in health professions education settings globally. These are methods such as the formal oral exam, the less formal bedside oral, portfolios of student experiences and work products, vivas (the so-called "long case" and "short case" assessments) and some other traditional variations. There are some strengths associated with these non-standardized assessment methods, but because of the pervasive subjectivity associated with such methods the threats to validity are strong. There are serious limitations and challenges to many of these methods, particularly for use in high-stakes assessment settings from which serious consequences are possible. Nonetheless there is a strong tradition supporting their use in many health professions settings, especially in the emerging world. Chapters 11 and 12 review these methods with an eye to their shortcomings and methods to enhance their validity.

Assessment Toolbox

There are many other ways to categorize and classify various assessment methods. In the United States, the Accreditation Council for Graduate Medical Education (ACGME) and the American Board of

Medical Specialties (ABMS) recently collaborated in a wide-ranging assessment project known as Outcomes Project (ACGME, 2000). The ACGME General Competencies are a product of this collaboration, mandating that residency training programs assess and document their residents' competence in six domains: Patient care, Medical knowledge, Practice-based learning and improvement, Interpersonal and communication skills, Professionalism, and Systems-based practice (ACGME, 2000). The Outcomes Project also produced a Toolbox of Assessment Methods (ACGME & ABMS, 2000), which describes thirteen methods that can be used to measure the six general competencies. This document is a handy summary of what is known about the strengths and limitations of each method for measuring various aspects of what might be called "competence" in health professions education. Both the Competencies and the Toolbox are sufficiently general to be useful in many different areas of health professions education, and at all levels of training. We recommend that you download these documents and become familiar with their content. Table 1.1 summarizes the thirteen assessment methods included in the Toolbox. Many of the methods noted in the Toolbox (Table 1.1) will be discussed at some depth in this book.

Instruction and Assessment

While the major focus of this book is on assessment, it is important to remember that assessment and instruction are intimately related. Teaching, learning, and assessment form a closed circle, with each entity tightly bound to the other. Assessments developed locally (as opposed to large-scale standardized testing) must be closely aligned with instruction, with adequate, timely, and meaningful feedback provided to learners wherever possible. Just as we provide students with many different types of learning experiences from classroom to clinic, we must also utilize multiple methods to assess their learning across competencies, from "knows" to "does." An exclusive reliance on a single method such as written tests will provide a skewed view of the student. Since assessment ultimately drives learning, judicious use of assessment methods at different levels of the Miller triangle can help

Table 1.1 ACGME Toolbox Assessment Methods (ACGME and ABMS, 2000)

Type of Assessment	Definition	Chapter
1. 360-Degree Evaluation	Rating forms completed by multiple evaluators, such as peers, patients, instructors	Chapter 8: Observational Assessment
2. Chart Stimulated Recall (CSR)	Standardized oral exam using examinees' written patient records	Chapter 11: Oral Examinations
3. Checklist Evaluations	Observational methods used to rate performance in real-world settings; generally "yes–no" items	Chapter 9: Performance Tests
4. Global Ratings	Ratings scales used to rate performance in real-world settings; generally scaled 0 or 1 to N	Chapter 9: Performance Tests
5. Objective Structured Clinical Exams (OSCEs)	Structured, standardized performance assessments, administered in sequential stations	Chapter 9: Performance Tests
6. Logs	Written records of procedures or cases completed	Chapter 12: Assessment Portfolios
7. Patient Surveys	Satisfaction questionnaires completed by patients or clients	Chapter 8: Observational Assessment
8. Portfolios	Systematic collections of educational products	Chapter 12: Assessment Portfolios
9. Record Review	Systematic review of written records by trained evaluators	Chapter 12: Assessment Portfolios
10. Simulations and Models	Low- to high-technology performance exams that closely match real-life	Chapter 10: Simulations
11. Standardized Oral Exam	Highly structured oral examinations in which examiners ask pre-defined questions, with model answers	Chapter 11: Oral Examinations
12. Standardized Patient Exam (SP)	Simulated patients, highly trained to portray specific cases and rate performance	Chapter 9: Performance Tests
13. Written Exam	Selected-response type tests of cognitive knowledge; constructed-response (essay) type tests of knowledge	Chapter 7: Written Tests

ensure that our students focus their learning in ways that are most valuable for their future practice.

Some Basic Terms and Definitions

As we begin this journey, some basic terms and definitions may be helpful.

The terms and concepts discussed here will be used throughout this book and will be important to many other topics in the book.

Assessment, Measurement, and Tests

The *Standards* (AERA, APA, & NCME, 1999) define "assessment" very broadly to include about any method, process, or procedure used to collect any type of information or data about people, objects or programs. The focus of this book is on the assessment of student learning, and not on the evaluation of educational programs or educational products. We use the term *assessment* to cover almost everything we do to measure the educational learning or progress of our students or other trainees. The term "measurement" refers to some type of quantification used as an assessment. *Measurement* implies the assignment of numbers, based on some systematic rules and specific assessment process. While the measurement process may include some types of qualitative assessment, the major emphasis in this book is on quantitative measurement.

A "test" is a specific type of assessment used to measure or quantify the achievement of specific learning objectives. The term *test* generally refers to a specific assessment method designed to elicit and measure specific cognitive behavior (in contrast to observation of day-to-day activity, in vivo). (*Test* is typically used to indicate a cognitive assessment, such as an achievement test in gross anatomy; *instrument* usually indicates a non-cognitive assessment, such as a psychological inventory.) The term "examination" is used synonymously with the term "test," although educational measurement professionals tend to prefer the term "test."

Types of Numbers

Since a book on assessment in the health professions must deal with quantitative matters and numbers, it seems appropriate to begin with a brief overview of the types of number scales commonly used. There are four basic types of number scales that will be familiar to many readers (e.g., Howell, 2002). The most basic number scale is the *nominal scale*, which uses numbers only as arbitrary symbols. Coding a questionnaire demographic question about gender as a nominal response such as 1 = Female and 2 = Male is an example of a nominal number scale. The numbers have no inherent meaning, only the arbitrary meaning assigned by the researcher. The key point is that we can do only very limited mathematical procedures, such as counting, on nominal numbers. We cannot legitimately compute averages for nominal numbers, since the average "score" has no meaning or interpretation.

An *ordinal* number has some inherent meaning, although at a very basic level. Ordinal numbers designate the order or the rank-order of the referent. For example, we can rank the height in meters of all students in an entering pharmacy class, designating the rank of 1 as the tallest student and the last number rank as the shortest student. The distance or interval between rank 4 and rank 5 is not necessarily the same as the distance between ranks 6 and 7, however. With ordinal numbers, we can compute averages or mean ranks, take the standard deviation of the distribution of ranks, and so on. In other words, ordinal numbers have some inherent meaning or interpretation and, therefore, summary statistics are useful and interpretable.

Interval numbers are a bit more sophisticated than ordinal numbers in that the distance between numbers is meaningful and is considered equal. This means that the meaning or interpretation associated with the score interval 50 to 60 (ten points) is the same as the interval or distance between scores 30 and 40. This is an important characteristic, since the interval nature of these numbers permits all types of statistical analyses, the full range of what are called parametric statistics.

A *ratio* scale of numbers is the most sophisticated number scale, but is rarely if ever possible to obtain in educational measurement or the social sciences. A true ratio scale has a meaningful zero point, so that zero means "nothingness." This mean that if we could devise a legitimate ratio testing instrument for measuring the achievement of nursing students in biochemistry, students scoring 0 would have absolutely no knowledge of the biochemistry objectives tested. This is not possible in educational measurement, obviously, since even the least capable student will have some minimal knowledge. (True ratio scales are often found in the physical sciences, but not in the social sciences.)

The main point of this discussion of number-types is that most of the assessment data we obtain in health professions education is considered or assumed to be interval data, so that we can perform nearly all types of statistical analyses on the results. For instance, data from a multiple-choice achievement test in pharmacology is always assumed to be interval data, so that we can compute summary statistics for the distribution of scores (means, standard deviations), correlations between scores on this test and other similar tests or subtests, and may even perform a paired t-test of mean pre-post differences in scores. If these data were ordinal, we would have some limitations on the statistical analyses available, such as using only the Spearman rank-order correlation coefficient. All psychometric models of data used in assessment, such as the various methods used to estimate the reproducibility or reliability of scores or ratings, are derived with the underlying assumption that the data are interval in nature.

Fidelity to the Criterion

Another familiar concept in assessment for the health professions is that of "fidelity." The full term, as used by most educational measurement professionals, is "fidelity to the criterion," implying some validity-type relationship between scores or ratings on the assessment and the ultimate "criterion" variable in real life. "Fidelity to the criterion" is often shortened to "fidelity." What does this actually mean? Think of a dichotomy between a high fidelity and a low fidelity assessment. A simulation of an actual clinical problem, presented to pharmacy students by highly trained actors, is thought to be "high fidelity," because the test appears to be much like an authentic, real-life situation that the future pharmacists may encounter with a real patient. On the other hand, a multiple-choice test of basic knowledge in chemistry might be considered a very low-fidelity simulation of a real-life situation for the same students. High-fidelity assessments are said to be "more proximate to the criterion," meaning that the assessment itself appears to be fairly lifelike and authentic, while low-fidelity assessments appear to be far removed from the criterion or are less proximate to the criterion (Haladyna, 1999). Most highly structured performance exams, complex simulations, and less well structured observational methods of assessment are of higher fidelity than written exams, and are all intended to measure different facets of learning.

The concept of fidelity is important only as a superficial trait or characteristic of assessments. Fidelity may have little or nothing to do with true scientific validity evidence and may, in fact, actually interfere with objectivity of measurement, which tends to decrease validity evidence (Downing, 2003); this topic will be explored in some depth in Chapter 2. Students and their faculty, however, often prefer (or think they prefer) more high-fidelity assessments, simply because they look more like real-life situations. One fact is certain: the higher the fidelity of the assessment, the higher the cost and the more complex are the measurement issues of the assessment.

Formative and Summative Assessment

The concepts of formative and summative assessment are pervasive in the assessment literature and date to the middle of the last century; these concepts originated in the program evaluation literature, but have come to be used in all areas of assessment (Scriven, 1967). These useful concepts are straightforward in meaning. The primary purpose of formative testing is to provide useful feedback on student strengths and weaknesses with respect to the learning objectives. Classic formative assessment takes place *during* the course of study, such that student learners have the opportunity to understand what content they have already mastered and what content needs more study (or for the instructor, needs more teaching). Examples of formative assessments include weekly short quizzes during a microbiology course, shorter written tests given at frequent intervals during a two semester-long course in pharmacology, and so on.

Summative assessment "sums up" the achievement in a course of study and typically takes place at or near the end of a formal course of study, such as an end of semester examination in anatomy which covers the entire cumulative course. Summative assessments emphasize the final measurement of achievement and usually count heavily in the grading scheme. Feedback to students may be one aspect of the summative assessment, but the primary purpose of the summative assessment is to measure what students have learned during the course of instruction. The ultimate example of a summative assessment is a test given at the conclusion of long, complex courses of study, such as a licensure test in nursing which must be taken and passed at the very end of the educational sequence and before the newly graduated nurse can begin professional work.

Norm- and Criterion-Referenced Measurement

The basic concept of norm- and criterion-referenced measurement or assessment is also fairly simple and straightforward. Norm-referenced test scores are interpreted relative to some well-defined normative group, such as all students who took the test. The key word is *relative*; norm-referenced scores or ratings tell us a lot about how well students score or are rated relative to some group of other students, but may tell us less about what exact content they actually know or can do. Criterion-referenced scores or ratings, on the other hand, tell us how much of some specific content students actually know or can do. Criterion-referenced testing has been popular in North America since the 1970s (Popham & Husek, 1969). This type of assessment is most closely associated with competency or content-based teaching and testing. Other terms used somewhat interchangeably with criterion-referenced testing are "domain-referenced," "objectives-referenced," "content-referenced," and "construct-referenced." There are some subtle differences in the usage of these terms by various authors and researchers, but all have in common the strong interest in the content actually learned or mastered by the student and the lack of interest in rank-ordering students by test scores.

Mastery testing is a special type of criterion-referenced testing, in that the assessments are constructed to be completed nearly perfectly by almost all students. For mastery tests, the expected score is 100 percent-correct. Mastery teaching strategies and testing methods imply that all students can learn up to some criterion of "mastery," and the only difference may be in the time needed to complete the mastery learning and testing. Some special theories and methods of assessment are required for true mastery testing, since almost all of testing theory is based on norm-referenced testing. Many norm-referenced testing statistics are inappropriate for true mastery tests.

A final note on this important topic. Any assessment score or rating can be interpreted in either a norm-referenced or criterion-referenced manner. The test, the methods used to construct the test, and the overarching philosophy of the instructor about testing and student learning and achievement determine the basic classification of the test as either norm- or criterion-referenced. It is perfectly possible, for example, to interpret an inherently normative score, like a percentile or a z-score, in some absolute or criterion-referenced manner. Conversely, some criterion-referenced tests may report only percent-correct scores or raw scores but interpret these scores relative to the distribution of scores (i.e., in a normative or relative fashion).

The concepts of norm- and criterion-referenced testing will be revisited often in this book, especially in our treatment of topics like standard setting or establishing effective and defensible passing scores. For the most part, the orientation of this book is criterion-referenced. We are most interested in assessing what our students have learned and achieved and about their competency in our health professions disciplines rather than ranking them in a normative distribution.

High-stakes and Low-stakes Assessments

Other terms often used to describe assessments are high- and low-stakes assessments. These terms are descriptive of the consequences of testing. If the results of a test can have a serious impact on an examinee, such as gaining or loosing a professional job, the stakes associated with the test are clearly high. High-stakes tests require a much higher burden, in that every facet of such tests must be of extremely high quality, with solid research-based evidence to support validity of interpretations. There may even be a need to defend such high-stakes tests legally, if the test is perceived to cause some individuals or groups harm. Examinations used to admit students to professional schools and tests used to certify or license graduates in the health professions are good examples of very high-stakes tests. Assessments used to determine final grades in important classes required for graduation or final summative exams that must be passed in order to graduate are also high stakes for our students.

A low- to moderate-stakes test carries somewhat lower consequences. Many of the formative-type assessments typically used in health professions education are low to moderate stakes. If the consequences of failing the test are minor or if the remediation (test retake) is not too difficult or costly, the exam stakes might be thought of as low or moderate.

Very high-stakes tests are usually professionally produced by testing experts and large testing agencies using major resources to ensure the defensibility of the resulting test scores and pass-fail decisions. Lower stakes tests and assessments, such as those used by many health professions educators in their local school settings, require fewer resources and less validity evidence, since legal challenges to the test outcomes are rare. Since this book focuses on assessments developed at the local (or classroom) level by highly specialized content experts, the assessments of interest are low to moderate stakes. Nevertheless, even lower stakes assessments should meet the basic minimum standards of quality, since important decisions are ultimately being made about our students from our cumulative assessments over time.

Large-scale and Local or Small-scale Assessments

Another reference point for this book and its orientation toward assessment in the health professions is the distinction between large- and small-scale assessments. Large-scale assessments refer to standardized testing programs, often national or international in scope, which are generally designed by testing professionals and administered to large numbers of examinees. Large-scale tests such as the Pharmacy College Admissions Test (PCAT) and the Medical College Admissions Test (MCAT) are utilized to help selected students for pharmacy and medical schools. Tests such as the National Council Licensure Examination (NCLEX®) for Registered Nurses is another example of a large-scale test, which is used for licensure of registered nurses by jurisdictions in the United States.

Small-scale or locally developed assessments—the main focus of this book—are developed, administered, and scored by "classroom" instructors, clinical teaching faculty, or other educators at the local school, college, or university level. Too frequently, health professions educators "go it alone" when assessing their students, with little or no formal educational background in assessment and with little or no support from their institutions for the critically important work of assessment. This book aims to provide local instructors and other health professions educators with sound principles, effective tools, and defensible methods to assist in the important work of student assessment.

Summary

This introduction provided the general context and overview for this book. Most of the concepts introduced in this chapter are expanded and detailed in later chapters. We hope that this introductory chapter provides even the most novice assessment learner with the basic vocabulary and some of the most essential concepts and principles needed to comprehend some of the more technical aspects of following chapters.

Christine McGuire, a major contributor to assessment theory and practice in medical education, once said: "Evaluation is probably the most logical field in the world and if you use a little bit of logic, it just fits together and jumps at you. . . . It's very common sense." (Harris & Simpson, 2005, p. 68). We agree with Dr. McGuire's statement. While there is much technical nuance and much statistical elaboration to assessment topics in health professions education, we should never lose sight of the mostly commonsense nature of the enterprise. On the other hand, Voltaire noted that "Common sense is very rare" (Voltaire, 1962, p. 467), so the goal of this book is to bring state-of-the art assessment theory and practice to health professions educators, so that their students will benefit from quality assessments that become "common" in their curricula.

References

Accreditation Council for Graduate Medical Education. (2000). ACGME Outcome Project. Retrieved December 2, 2005, from http://www.acgme.org/outcome/assess/assHome.asp/

Accreditation Council for Graduate Medical Education & American Board of Medical Specialties. (2000). Toolbox of assessment methods. Retrieved December 2, 2005, from http://www.acgme.org/outcome/assess/toolbox.asp/

American Educational Research Association, American Psychological Association, & National Council on Measurement in Education. (1999). *Standards for educational and psychological testing*. Washington DC: American Educational Research Association.

Anderson, M.B., & Kassebaum, D.G. (Eds.). (1993). Proceedings of the AAMC's consensus conference on the use of standardized patients in the teaching and evaluation of clinical skills. *Academic Medicine*, 68, 437–483.

Barrows, H.S., & Abrahamson, S. (1964). The programmed patient: A technique for appraising student performance in clinical neurology. *Journal of Medical Education*, 39, 802–805.

Bloom, B.S., Engelhart, M.D., Furst, E.J., Hill, W.H., & Krathwohl, D.R. (1956). *Taxonomy of educational objectives*. New York: Longmans Green.

Downing, S.M. (2002). Assessment of knowledge with written test forms. In G.R. Norman, C.P.M. Van der Vleuten, & D.I. Newble (Eds.), *International handbook for research in medical education* (pp. 647–672). Dordrecht, The Netherlands: Kluwer Academic Publishers.

Downing, S.M. (2003). Validity: On the meaningful interpretation of assessment data. *Medical Education*, 37, 830–837.

Gordon, M.S. (1999). Developments in the use of simulators and multimedia computer systems in medical education. *Medical Teacher*, 21(1), 32–36.

Haladyna, T.M. (1999, April). When should we use a multiple-choice format? A paper presented at the annual meeting of the American Educational Research Association, Montreal, Canada.

Harden, R., Stevenson, M., Downie, W., & Wilson, M. (1975). Assessment of clinical competence using objective structured examinations. *British Medical Journal*, 1, 447–451.

Harris, I.B., & Simpson, D. (2005). Christine McGuire: At the heart of the maverick measurement maven. *Advances in Health Sciences Education*, 10, 65–80.

Howell, D.C. (2002). *Statistical methods for psychology* (5th ed.). Pacific Grove, CA: Duxbury-Wadsworth Group.

Miller, G. (1990). The assessment of clinical skills/competence/performance. *Academic Medicine*, 65, S63–S67.

National Board of Medical Examiners. (2006). USMLE Bulletin of Information. Federation of State Medical Boards and National Board of Medical Examiners. Retrieved December 2, 2005, from http://www.usmle.org/bulletin/2006/2006bulletin.pdf/

Popham, W.J., & Husek, T.R. (1969). Implications of criterion-referenced measurement. *Journal of Educational Measurement*, 7, 367–375.

Scriven, M. (1967). The methodology of evaluation. In R. Tyler, R. Gagne, & M. Scriven (Eds.), *Perspectives of curriculum evaluation* (pp. 39–83). Chicago: Rand McNally.

Sireci, S.G., & Zenisky, A.L. (2006). Innovative item formats in computer-based testing: In pursuit of improved construct representation. In S.M. Downing & T.M. Haladyna (Eds.), *Handbook of test development* (pp. 329–348). Mahwah, NJ: Lawrence Erlbaum Associates.

Voltaire. (1962). *Philosophical dictionary* (P. Gay, Trans.). New York: Basic Books, Inc.

Wallace, P. (1997). Following the threads of an innovation: The history of standardized patients in medical education. *CADUCEUS*, 13 (2), 5–28.

Welch, C. (2006). Item and prompt development in performance testing. In S.M. Downing & T.M. Haladyna (Eds.), *Handbook of test development* (pp. 303–328). Mahwah, NJ: Lawrence Erlbaum Associates.

William, R.G., Klaman, D.A., & McGaghie, W.C. (2003). Cognitive, social, and environmental sources of bias in clinical performance ratings. *Teaching and Learning in Medicine*, 15(4), 270–292.

2

VALIDITY AND ITS THREATS

STEVEN M. DOWNING AND
THOMAS M. HALADYNA

Validity is the *sine qua non* of all assessment data, without which assessment data has little or no meaning. All assessments require validity evidence and nearly all topics in assessment involve validity in some way. Thus, validity gets to the heart or essence of all assessment and is the single most important topic in testing.

Many books on assessment place a chapter on validity toward the end of the text. The placement of this validity chapter early in the book emphasizes a major point: Validity is the single most important characteristic of assessment data. If you understand validity at some deep level, you will know most of what is important concerning assessments and their application in health professions educational settings.

The purpose of this chapter is to present an overview of contemporary validity theory, illustrated by specific examples from health professions education together with concrete examples of the various types of scientific data required as validity evidence. Threats to validity will also be discussed in some detail, since such threats abound.

In the absence of solid scientific evidence of validity, most assessment data has little or no meaning. For instance, if you are given a distribution of numbers, ranging from 3 to 100, for a class of pharmacy students, what do you know about these students? Obviously, very little without much more information. Unless you know what the numbers are supposed to represent, it's very difficult to assign a valid or meaningful interpretation to the numbers. You would need to know, for example: Do these numbers represent a count of the questions answered correctly on a multiple-choice test? Or, are these numbers some type of percent-correct score, on either a selected-response, constructed-response test or a performance test or on some observational rating scale? If the numbers represent a number-correct or percent-correct score, what content is measured by the written or performance test? How was this content sampled? How representative is the sampled content to the entire domain or universe of content? How scientifically sound was the measurement? Are the numbers/scores scientifically reproducible? And so on and on with inquiry of this type, posing and answering essential questions about the assessment, the answers to which help provide meaning to the numbers. This scientific inquiry aimed at establishing a certain meaning or interpretation for assessment data is the essence of validity.

What is Validity?

Validity refers to the evidence presented to support or to refute the meaning or interpretation assigned to assessment data or results (Messick, 1989). Kane discusses validity and validation thus: "To validate a proposed interpretation or use of test scores is to evaluate the claims being based on the test scores. The specific mix of evidence needed for validation depends on the inferences being drawn and the assumptions being made." (Kane, 2006a, p. 131) In common parlance, it is said that validity has to do with a test measuring what it is supposed to measure. This is a generally true statement, but a statement in need of considerable elaboration, which is the intended purpose of this chapter.

Validation as Scientific Research

Contemporary validity theory is primarily concerned with a process of scientific inquiry, based on sound theory and focused on hypotheses, which guides the gathering of scientific evidence from multiple sources, to either support or refute specific interpretations or meanings associated with assessment data, used for a specific purpose. Validity evidence is associated with scores or data resulting from tests or assessments, not the assessment forms or instruments which produce the data. Validity evidence is case and time specific; the data presented to support or refute a specific score interpretation or the arguments for a given score meaning are not good for all time, but rather only for the specific uses specified by the assessment user and the purpose of the assessment. Validity evidence used for one test administration does not necessarily apply to a different test administration; the argument for generalizing validity evidence must be made on a case-by-case basis.

Validity is the application of the scientific method to assessment data, for the purpose of establishing reasonable interpretations or legitimate meanings to data. In this conceptualization, assessment data are more or less valid for some very specific purpose, meaning or interpretation, at a specific point in time and only for some well defined population. The assessment itself is never said to be *valid* or *invalid*; rather one speaks of the scientifically sound evidence presented to either support or refute the specific proposed interpretation of assessment scores, at a particular time period in which the validity evidence was collected from some specific population.

Validity theory, like many theories in education and psychology, has evolved over time. The formal theory and practice of educational measurement is only about 100 years old, dating back to the early twentieth century in the United States with the introduction of the U. S. Army Alpha test, used to test large numbers of recruits for World War I (Ebel, 1972). The history of the evolution of validity theory in assessment is summarized succinctly by a review of successive editions of a document currently titled *Standards of Educational and Psychological Testing* (AERA, APA, & NCME, 1999). This *Standards* document represents the best consensus thinking about acceptable testing practice by the three North American organizations which are most involved with testing: the American Educational Research Association (AERA), the American Psychological Association (APA), and the National Council on Measurement in Education (NCME). The *Standards* are updated periodically, with the last update published in 1999. Previous editions of the *Standards* were published in 1955, 1966, 1974, and 1985; a careful reading of the *Standards*, over various editions, gives an historical overview of an evolving view of validity (Linn, 2006).

A complete overview of the evolution of validity theory is beyond the scope of this chapter, but it is important to understand that the theory, definitions, and methods of validity and validation research have changed considerably over the past fifty years or so. In earlier editions of the *Standards* (e.g., 1955 and 1966), validity was discussed as the trinitarian or three-level model of validity: content, criterion-related, and construct validity. Criterion-related validity was often thought of as either "concurrent" or "predictive," depending on the timing of data collection for the criterion variable (Cureton, 1951). Such a trinitarian view of validity is dated and is generally no longer used in educational measurement research and writing, given the evolution of validity theory in the late twentieth century.

Contemporary Validity Theory

In its contemporary conceptualization, validity is a unitary concept, which requires multiple sources of scientific evidence to support or refute the meaning associated with assessment data (e.g., AERA, APA, & NCME, 1999; Cronbach, 1988, 1989; Kane, 1992, 1994, 2006 a, b; Messick, 1989, 1995). These evidentiary sources are logically suggested by the desired types of interpretation or meaning associated with measures, firmly rooted in theory and the scientific method. All validity is construct validity in this framework, described most philosophically and eloquently by Messick (1989) and Kane (2006b) and embodied in the *Standards* (AERA, APA, & NCME, 1999).

Constructs

Why is construct validity now considered the sole type of validity? The complex answer is found in the philosophy of science from which, it is posited, there are many complex webs of inter-related inference associated with sampling content in order to make meaningful and reasonable inferences from a sample to a domain or larger population of interest. The more straightforward answer is: Nearly all assessments in the social sciences deal with *constructs*— intangible collections of abstract concepts and principles, which are inferred from behavior and explained by educational or psychological theory.

Cronbach and Meehl (1955) set the course for development of contemporary views of test validity as early as the mid-1950s, defining a construct as a hypothesized attribute assumed to be tested by the assessment. Note that their definition of a construct is fairly circular, but it captures the essence of the scientific point we attempt to establish with our work in validation.

Educational achievement is a construct, usually inferred from performance on assessments such as written tests over some well-defined domain of knowledge, oral examinations over specific problems or cases, or highly structured performance examinations such as standardized-patient examinations of history taking, communication or physical examination skills. The educational achievement construct is the primary assessment focus of this book. While constructs such as *ability* or *aptitude*, or *intelligence* are important in some educational settings, they are not the primary focus of this book.

Because constructs are necessarily intangible, validation of our assessment data requires an evidentiary chain which clearly links the interpretation of the assessment scores or data to an inter-related, complex network of theory, hypotheses and logic, which are presented to support or refute the reasonableness of some specific desired interpretations. Validity is an ongoing process of hypothesis generation, data collection and testing, critical evaluation, and logical inference.

The validity argument relates theory, predicted relationships, and empirical evidence in ways to suggest which particular interpretative meanings are reasonable and which are not reasonable for a specific assessment use or application (Kane, 1992, 1994, 2006 a, b). The notion of validity as argument is now prominent since the publication of the fourth edition of *Educational Measurement* in which Michael Kane's chapter discusses the validity model as a process of building logical, scientific and empirical arguments to support or refute very specific intended interpretations of assessment scores (Kane, 2006b). Kane's validity argument requires an overt linking of inferences, with all the interconnections and intermediate steps, which trace the specific content tested by items or performance prompts back to the content domain—or the population of knowledge, skills, or ability to which one wishes to make inferences or to generalize.

The Negative Case—Refuting the Intended Interpretation of Test Scores

Too often in validation research and in our thinking about validity theory, we forget or ignore the negative case for validity (Haladyna, 2006). We have discussed validity and validation research in terms of hypothesis driven research in search of hard scientific evidence to either support or refute specific interpretations or meanings associated with assessment data. The "negative case" refers to serious attempts to refute or falsify the hypothesis or overturn our expectations or beliefs about the interpretative meaning. "A proposition deserves some degree of trust only when it has survived serious attempts to falsify it." (Cronbach, 1980, p. 103.) Again, this sounds much like solid scientific research. Using experimental research methods, we set out to objectively test hypotheses. When research is conducted in a sound scientific manner, controlling for all important nuisance variables that could spoil the study, the researcher must always be open to negative findings. This is the essence of all scientific research; this is the major point of validation research. An alternate meaning or interpretation of assessment data may always be found, thus falsifying our hypotheses or our beliefs about the meaning or proper interpretation of our assessment data.

Meaningful Interpretation of Scores

In order to meaningfully interpret scores, some assessments, such as achievement tests of cognitive knowledge, may require only fairly straightforward content-related evidence of the adequacy of the content tested (in relationship to instructional objectives), statistical evidence of score reproducibility and item statistical quality and evidence to support the defensibility of passing scores or grades. Other types of assessments, such as complex performance examinations, may require both evidence related to content and considerable empirical data demonstrating the statistical relationship between the performance examination and other measures of ability or achievement, the generalizability of the sampled cases to the population of skills, the reproducibility of the score scales, the adequacy of the standardized patient training, and so on. There can never be too much validity evidence, but there is often too little evidence to satisfy the skeptic. Validation research for high-stakes tests is an on-going task, with data collected routinely over time to address specific validity questions (e.g., Haladyna, 2006).

The higher the stakes associated with assessments, the greater the requirement for validity evidence, from multiple sources, which are collected on an on-going basis and continually re-evaluated (Linn, 2002). The on-going documentation of validity evidence for a high-stakes testing program, such as a licensure or certification examination in any of the health professions, may require the allocation of many resources and the contributions of many different professionals with a variety of skills—content specialists, psychometricians and statisticians, test editors and administrators (Haladyna, 2006). For low-to-medium stakes assessment programs, such as formative classroom tests in the basic sciences, less validity evidence is required.

Five Sources of Validity Evidence

According to the *Standards*: "Validity refers to the degree to which evidence and theory support the interpretations of test scores entailed by proposed uses of tests" (AERA, APA, & NCME, 1999, p. 9). The *Standards* closely parallel Messick's seminal chapter in *Educational Measurement* (Messick, 1989), which considers all validity to be construct validity. Kane (1992, 1994, 2006 a, b) discusses validity as an investigative process through which constructs are carefully defined, data and evidence are gathered and assembled to form an argument, which either supports or refutes some very specific interpretation of assessment scores.

In this context, the validity hypothesis is tested as a series of propositions—usually interrelated—concerning the sufficiency of the evidence supporting or refuting a specific score interpretation.

The *Standards*

The *Standards* discuss five distinct sources or types of validity evidence, which are summarized in Table 2.1: Content, Responses, Internal structure, Relationship to other variables, and Consequences. Each source of validity evidence is associated with some examples of the types of data that might be collected to support or refute specific assessment interpretations (validity). Some assessment formats or types demand a stronger emphasis on one or more sources of evidence as opposed to other sources and not all sources of data or evidence are required for all assessments. For example, a written, objectively scored test covering several weeks of instruction in microbiology, might emphasize content-related evidence, together with some evidence of response quality, internal structure, and consequences, but very likely would not seek much or any evidence concerning relationship to other variables. On the other hand, a high-stakes summative Objective Structured Clinical Examination (OSCE), using standardized patients to portray and rate student performance on a examination that must be passed in order to proceed in the curriculum, might require all of these sources of evidence and many of the data examples noted in Table 2.2, to support or refute the proposed interpretation of the scores.

The construct validity model, using five major sources or aspects of validity evidence, is now being used in the health professions education settings. For example, several recent publications used this model to examine multiple sources of validity evidence for clinical teaching (Beckman & Cook, 2005), assessments of all types in internal medicine (Cook & Beckman, 2006), and for an integrated assessment system in an undergraduate clinical teaching setting (Auewarakul, Downing, Jaturatumrong, & Praditsuwan, 2005).

Examples: Sources of Validity Evidence

Each of the five sources of validity evidence are considered, in the context of a written assessment of cognitive knowledge or achievement and a performance examination in health professions education.

Table 2.1 Five Major Sources of Test Validity: Evidence Based on Messick (1989) and AERA, APA, & NCME (1999)

1. **Content**—relationship between test content and the construct of interest; theory; hypothesis about content; independent assessment of match between content sampled and domain of interest; solid, scientific, quantitative evidence.

2. **Response Process**—analysis of individual responses to stimuli; debriefing of examinees; process studies aimed at understanding what is measured and the soundness of intended score interpretations; quality assurance and quality control of assessment data

3. **Internal Structure**—data internal to assessments such as: reliability or reproducibility of scores; inter-item correlations; statistical characteristics of items; statistical analysis of item option function; factor studies of dimensionality; Differential Item Functioning (DIF) studies

4. **Relations to Other Variables**—data external to assessments such as: correlations of assessment variable(s) to external, independent measures; hypothesis and theory driven investigations; correlational research based on previous studies, literature
   a. Convergent and discriminant evidence: relationships between similar and different measures
   b. Test-criterion evidence: relationships between test and criterion measure(s)
   c. Validity generalization: can the validity evidence be generalized? Evidence that the validity studies may generalize to other settings.

5. **Evidence Based on Consequences of Testing**—intended and unintended consequences of test use; differential consequences of test use; impact of assessment on students, instructors, schools, society; impact of assessments on curriculum; cost/benefit analysis with respect to tradeoff between instructional time and assessment time.

Both example assessments are high-stakes, in that the consequences of passing or failing are very important to students, faculty, and ultimately the patients or clients of the health professions' provider.

The example written assessment is a summative comprehensive examination in the basic sciences—a test consisting of 250 multiple-choice questions (MCQs) covering all the pre-clinical instruction in the basic sciences—and a test that must be passed in order to proceed into clinical training. The performance examination example is a standardized patient (SP) examination, administered to students toward the end of their clinical training, after having completed all of their required clerkship rotations. The purpose of the SP examination is to comprehensively assess graduating students' ability to take a history and do a focused physical examination in an ambulatory primary-care setting. The SP examination consists of ten twenty-minute SP cases, presented by a lay, trained standardized patient who simulates the patient's presenting problem and rates the student's

Table 2.2 Some Sources of Validity Evidence for Proposed Score Interpretations and Examples of Some Types of Evidence

Source of Evidence	Content	Response Process	Internal Structure	Relationship to Other Variables	Consequences

Examples of Evidence	• Examination blueprint
	• Representativeness of test blueprint to achievement domain
	• Test specifications
	• Match of item content to test specifications
	• Representativeness of items to domain
	• Logical/empirical relationship of content tested to achievement domain
	• Quality of test questions
	• Item writer qualifications
	• Sensitivity review
		• Student format familiarity
		• Quality control of electronic scanning/scoring
		• Key validation of preliminary scores
		• Accuracy in combining different item format scores
		• Quality control/accuracy of final scores/marks/grades
		• Accuracy of applying pass–fail decision rules to scores
		• Quality control of score reporting to students/faculty
		• Understandable/accurate descriptions/interpretations of scores for students
			• Item analysis data
			• Item difficulty/discrimination
			• Item/test characteristic curves (ICCs/TCCs)
			• Inter-item correlations
			• Item–total correlations
			• Score scale reliability
			• Standard errors of measurement (SEM)
			• Subscore/subscale analyses
			• Generalizability
			• Dimensionality
			• Item factor analysis
			• Differential Item Functioning (DIF)
			• Psychometric model
				• Correlation with other relevant variables
				• Convergent correlations—internal/external
				  • Similar tests
				• Divergent correlations—internal/external
				  • Dissimilar measures
				• Test–criterion correlations
				• Generalizability of evidence
					• Impact of test scores/results on students/society
					• Consequences on learners/future learning
					• Positive consequences outweigh unintended negative consequences?
					• Reasonableness of method of establishing pass–fail (cut) score
					• Pass/fail consequences
					• P/F Decision reliability—Classification accuracy
					• Conditional standard error of measurement at pass score (CSEM)
					• False positives/negatives
					• Instructional/learner consequences

performance at the conclusion of the examination. The SP examination must be passed in order to graduate. (These examples from medical education generalize easily to all types of health professions education which have a classroom-type component and a practical or clinical teaching/learning component.)

Documentation of these five sources of validity evidence consists of the systematic collection and presentation of information and data to present a convincing argument that it is reasonable and defensible to interpret the assessment scores in accordance with the purpose of the measurement. The scores have little or no intrinsic meaning; thus the evidence presented must convince the skeptic that the assessment scores can reasonably be interpreted in the proposed manner.

Content Evidence

For our written assessment example, documentation of validity evidence related to the content tested is the most essential. The outline and plan for the test, described by a detailed test blueprint and test specifications (Downing, 2006b), clearly relates the content tested by the 250 MCQs to the domain of the basic sciences as described by the course learning objectives. This type of blueprinting and its documentation form the logical basis for the essential validity argument (Kane, 2006b).

Test Blueprint

The process of defining the content to sample on an assessment can be an exacting and complex process. The scientific methods used to study and define test content—especially for credentialing examinations—can be elaborate and entail complex research designs using specialized data analysis methods, all of which are beyond the scope of this book (e.g., Raymond & Neustel, 2006). As the test stakes increase, so must the scientific evidence linking the content on the assessment to the domain or population of interest. This is an essential validity requirement. Since all assessments are samples of knowledge or behavior, the unbiased methods used to sample content form an essential basis for content-related validity evidence. A test blue-print defines and precisely outlines the proportion of test questions or performance prompts allocated to each major and minor content area and the proportion of these stimuli designed to test which specific cognitive knowledge levels or performance skill levels (Linn, 2006).

Test specifications and the specific test blueprints arising from these detailed specifications form an exact sampling plan for the content domain to be tested. These documents and their rationales form a solid foundation for all systematic test development activities and for the content-related validity evidence needed to support score infer-ences to the domain of knowledge or performance and the meaningful interpretation of test scores with respect to the construct of interest.

The test blueprint should be sufficiently detailed to describe sub-categories and subclassifications of content and specifies precisely the proportion of test questions in each category and the cognitive level of those questions. At minimum, the blueprint documentation must show a direct linkage of the stimuli on the test to the instructional objectives and should clearly document the rationale for specific content selected. Independent content experts should evaluate the rea-sonableness of the test blueprint with respect to the course objectives and the cognitive levels tested. In our current example, the logical relationship between the content tested by the 250 MCQs and the major instructional objectives and teaching/learning activities of the course should be obvious and demonstrable, especially with respect to the proportionate weighting of test content to the actual emphasis of the basic science courses taught. Further, if most learning objectives were at the application or problem-solving level, most test questions should also be directed to these cognitive levels.

Test Item Quality

The quality of the test items is a source of content-related validity evidence. Do the MCQs adhere to the best-evidence-based principles of effective item writing (Haladyna, Downing, & Rodriguez, 2002)? Are the item writers qualified as content experts in the disciplines? Are there sufficient numbers of questions to adequately sample the large content domain? Have the test questions been edited for clarity, removing all ambiguities and other common item flaws? Have the test questions been reviewed for cultural sensitivity? (Zieky, 2006).

For the SP performance examination, some of the same content issues must be documented and presented as validity evidence. For example, each of the ten SP cases fits into a detailed content blueprint of ambulatory primary-care history and physical examination skills. There is evidence of faculty content-expert agreement that these specific ten cases are representative of primary-care ambulatory cases. Ideally, the content of the ten clinical cases is related to population demographic data and population data on disease incidence in primary-care ambulatory settings. Evidence is documented that expert clinical faculty have created, reviewed, and revised the SP cases together with the checklists and ratings scales used by the SPs, while other expert clinicians have reviewed and critically critiqued the SP cases. Exacting specifications detail all the essential clinical information to be portrayed by the SP. Evidence that SP cases have been competently edited and that detailed SP training guidelines and criteria have been prepared, reviewed by faculty experts, and implemented by experienced SP trainers are all important sources of content-related validity evidence.

There is documentation that during the time of SP administration, the SP portrayals are monitored closely to ensure that all students experience nearly the same case. Data is presented to show that a different SP, trained on the same case, rates student case performance in about the same manner, thus assuring the equivalence of the content tested. Many basic quality-control issues concerning performance examinations contribute to the content-related validity evidence for the assessment (Boulet, McKinley, Whelan, & Hambleton, 2003).

Response Process

As a source of validity evidence, *response process* may seem a bit strange or inappropriate. *Response process* is defined here as evidence of data integrity such that all sources of error associated with the test administration are controlled or eliminated to the maximum extent possible.

Response process has to do with aspects of assessment such as ensuring the accuracy of all responses to assessment prompts, the quality control of all data flowing from assessments, the appropriateness of the methods used to combine various types of assessment scores into one composite score, and the usefulness and the accuracy of the score reports provided to examinees. (Assessment data quality-control issues could also be discussed as content evidence.)

For evidence of *response process* for the written comprehensive examination, documentation of all practice materials and written information about the test and instructions to students is important. Documentation of all quality-control procedures used to ensure the absolute accuracy of test scores is also an important source of evidence: the final *key validation* after a preliminary scoring—to ensure the accuracy of the scoring key and eliminate from final scoring any poorly performing test items; a rationale for any combining rules, such as the combining into one final composite score of MCQ, multiple-true-false, and short-essay question scores.

Other sources of evidence may include documentation and the rationale for the type of scores reported, the method chosen to report scores, and the explanations and interpretive materials provided to fully explain the score report and its meaning, together with any materials discussing the proper use and any common misuses of the assessment score data.

For the SP performance examination, many of the same response process sources may be presented as validity evidence. For a performance examination, documentation demonstrating the accuracy of the SP rating is needed and the results of an SP accuracy study is a particularly important source of response-process evidence. Basic quality control of the large amounts of data from an SP performance examination is important to document, together with information on score calculation and reporting methods, their rationale, and, particularly, the explanatory materials discussing an appropriate interpretation of the performance-assessment scores (and their limitations).

Documentation of the rationale for using global versus checklist rating scores, for example, may be an important source of response evidence for the SP examination. Or, the empirical evidence and logical rationale for combining a global rating-scale score with check-list item scores to form a composite score may be one very important source of *response process evidence*.

Internal Structure

Internal structure, as a source of validity evidence, relates to the stat-istical or psychometric characteristics of the examination questions or performance prompts, the scale properties—such as reproducibility and generalizability, and the psychometric model used to score and scale the assessment. For instance, scores on test items or sets of items intended to measure the same variable, construct, or content area should be more highly correlated than scores on items intended to measure a different variable, construct, or content area.

Many of the statistical analyses needed to support or refute evidence of the test's internal structure are often carried out as routine quality-control procedures. Analyses such as statistical item analyses —which computes the difficulty (or easiness) of each test question (or performance prompt), the discrimination of each question (a statistical index indicating how well the question separates the high scoring from the low scoring examinees), and a detailed count of the number or proportion of examinees who responded to each option of the test question—are completed. Summary statistics are usually computed, showing the overall difficulty (or easiness) of the total test scale, the average discrimination, and the internal-consistency reliabil-ity of the test.

Reliability is one very important aspect or facet of validity evidence for all assessment data. Reliability refers to the reproducibility of the data or scores on the assessment; high score reliability indicates that if the test were to be repeated over time, examinees would receive about the same scores on retesting as they received the first time. Unless assessment scores are reliable and reproducible (as in an experiment) it is nearly impossible to interpret the meaning of those scores—thus, validity evidence is lacking (Axelson & Kreiter, Chapter 3, this volume).

There are many different types of reliability, appropriate to various uses of assessment scores. In both example assessments described above, in which the stakes are high and a passing score has been established, the reproducibility of the pass–fail decision is a very important source of validity evidence. That is, analogous to score reliability, if the ultimate outcome of the assessment (passing or failing) cannot be reproduced at some high level of certainty, the meaningful interpretation of the test scores is questionable and validity evidence is compromised.

For performance examinations, such as the SP example, a specialized type of reliability, derived from Generalizability Theory (GT) is an essential component of the internal structure aspect of validity evidence (Brennan, 2001; Crossley, Davies, Humphris, & Jolly, 2002; Kreiter, Chapter 4, this volume). GT is concerned with how well the specific samples of behavior (in this example, SP cases) can be generalized to the population or universe of behaviors. GT is also a useful tool for estimating the various sources of contributed error in the SP exam, such as error due to the SP raters, error due to the cases (case specificity), and error associated with examinees. Since rater error and case specificity are major threats to meaningful interpretation of SP scores, GT analyses are important sources of validity evidence for most performance assessments such as OSCEs, SP exams, and clinical performance examinations.

The measurement model itself can serve as evidence of the internal structure aspect of construct validity. For example, Item Response Theory (IRT) measurement models (e.g., Downing, 2003b; Embretson & Reise, 2000; van der Linden & Hambleton, 1997), might be used to calibrate and score our example comprehensive examination, in which case the factor structure, item-intercorrelation structure, and other internal statistical characteristics of the examination can all contribute to validity evidence.

Issues of bias and fairness also pertain to internal test structure and are important sources of validity evidence. All assessments, presented to heterogeneous groups of examinees, have the potential of validity threats from statistical bias. Bias analyses, such as Differential Item Functioning (DIF) analyses (e.g., Holland & Wainer, 1993; Penfield & Lam, 2000) and the sensitivity review of item and performance prompts are sources of internal structure validity evidence

(Baranowski, 2006; Zieky, 2006). Documentation of the absence of statistical test bias permits the desired score interpretation and therefore adds to the validity evidence of the assessment.

Relationship to Other Variables

This familiar source of validity evidence is statistical and correlational. The correlation or relationship of assessment scores to a criterion measure's scores is a typical design for a validity study, in which some newer (or simpler or shorter) measure is validated against an existing, older measure with well known characteristics.

This source of validity evidence embodies all the richness and complexity of the contemporary theory of validity in that the *relationship to other variables* aspect seeks both confirmatory and counterconfirmatory evidence. For example, it may be important to collect correlational validity evidence which shows a strong positive correlation with some other measure of the same achievement or ability *and* evidence indicating no correlation (or a negative correlation) with some other assessment that is hypothesized to be a measure of some completely different achievement or ability.

The concept of convergence or divergence of validity evidence (or discriminant validity evidence) is best exemplified in the classic research design first described by Campbell and Fiske (1959). In this multitrait-multimethod design, multiple measures of the same trait (achievement, ability, performance) are correlated with each other and with different measures of the same trait. The resulting pattern of correlation coefficients show the convergence and divergence of the different assessment methods on measures of the same and different abilities or proficiencies, thus triangulating appropriate interpretations of scores on measures.

In the written comprehensive examination example discussed here, it may be important to document the correlation of total and subscale scores with achievement examinations administered during the basic science courses. One could hypothesize that a subscale score for biochemistry on the comprehensive examination would correlate more highly with biochemistry course test scores than with behavioral science course scores. Additionally, the correlation of the written examination scores with the SP final examination may show a low (or no) correlation, indicating that these assessment methods measure some unique achievement, while the correlation of the SP scores with other performance examination scores during the students' clinical training may be high and positive.

As with all research, issues of the generalizability of the results of these studies and the limitations of data interpretation pertain. Interpretation of correlation coefficients, as validity coefficients, may be limited due to the design of the study, systematic bias introduced by missing data from either the test or the criterion or both, and statistical issues such as restriction of the range of scores (lack of variance).

Consequences

This aspect of validity evidence may be the most controversial, although it is solidly embodied in the 1999 *Standards*. The consequential aspect of validity refers to the impact on examinees from the assessment scores, decisions, and outcomes and the impact of assessments on teaching and learning. The consequences of assessments on examinees, faculty, patients, and society can be great and these consequences can be positive or negative, intended or unintended.

High-stakes examinations abound in North America, especially in health professions education. Extremely high-stakes assessments are often mandated as the final, summative hurdle in professional education. As one excellent example, the United States Medical Licensure Examination (USMLE) sequence, sponsored by the National Board of Medical Examiners (NBME), currently consists of three separate examinations (Steps 1, 2, and 3) which must be passed in order to be licensed by the state or jurisdiction as a physician. The consequences of failing any of these examinations is enormous, in that medical education is interrupted in a costly manner or the examinee is not permitted to enter graduate medical education or practice medicine. Likewise, most medical specialty boards in the United States mandate passing a high-stakes certification examination in the specialty or subspecialty, after meeting all eligibility requirements of post-graduate training.

The consequences of passing or failing these types of examinations are great, since false positives (passing candidates who should fail) may do harm to patients through the lack of a physician's specialized knowledge or skill and false negatives (failing candidates who should pass) may unjustly harm individual candidates who have invested a great deal of time and resources in graduate medical education.

Thus, consequential validity is one very important aspect of the construct validity argument. Evidence related to consequences of testing and its outcomes is presented to suggest that no harm comes directly from the assessment or, at the very least, more good than harm arises from the assessment. Much of this evidence is more judgmental, qualitative or subjective than other aspects of validity.

In both of our example assessments, sources of consequential validity may relate to issues such as passing rates (the proportion who pass), the subjectively judged appropriateness of these passing rates, data comparing the passing rates of each of these examinations to other comprehensive examinations such as the USMLE Step 1, and so on. Evaluations of false positive and false negative outcomes relate to the consequences of these two high-stakes examinations.

The passing score (or grade levels) and the process used to determine the cut scores, the statistical properties of the passing scores, and so on all relate to the consequential aspects of validity (Cizek, 2006; Norcini, 2003; Yudkowsky, Downing, & Tekian, Chapter 6, this volume). Documentation of the method used to establish a pass–fail score is key consequential evidence, as is the rationale for the selection of a particular passing score method. The psychometric characteristics of the passing score judgments and the qualification and number of expert judges—all may be important to document and present as evidence of consequential validity.

Other psychometric quality indicators concerning the passing score and its consequences—for both example assessments—include a formal, statistical estimation of the pass–fail decision reliability or classification accuracy (e.g., Subkoviak, 1988). and some estimation of the standard error of measurement at the cut score (Angoff, 1971)

Equally important consequences of assessment methods on instruction and learning have been discussed by Newble and Jaeger (1983).

The methods and strategies selected to evaluate students can have a profound impact on what is taught, how and exactly what students learn, how this learning is used and retained (or not) and how students view and value the educational process.

These five sources or facets of validity evidence provide a systematic and concrete structure for validity studies and validation research. At least two different categories of validity evidence are required for most measures, with more evidence needed for higher-stakes test and assessment data. As Haladyna notes: "Without research, a testing program will have difficulty generating sufficient evidence to validate its intended test score interpretations and uses" (Haladyna, 2006, p. 739). For on-going high-stakes testing programs, validation research is a fairly open-ended loop in that too much validity evidence can never be presented, but often too little data is offered to support the particular score interpretations desired.

Threats to Validity

There are many threats to validity; in fact, there may be many more threats to validity than there are sources of validity evidence. Any factors that interfere with the meaningful interpretation of assessment data are a threat to validity. Messick (1989) noted two major sources of validity threats: construct underrepresentation (CU) and construct-irrelevant variance (CIV). CU refers to the undersampling or biased sampling of the content domain by the assessment instrument. CIV is systematic error (rather than random error) introduced into the assessment data by variables unrelated to the construct being measured. Both CU and CIV reduce the ability to interpret the assessment results in the proposed manner and thus decrease evidence for validity.

Table 2.3 lists examples of some typical threats to validity for written assessments, performance examinations, such as Objective Structured Clinical Examinations (OSCEs) or standardized patient (SP) examinations, and clinical performance ratings. These threats to validity are organized by CU and CIV, following Mesick's model.

Table 2.3 Threats to Validity of Assessments

	Written Test	Performance Examination	Ratings of Clinical Performance
Construct Underrepresentation (CU)	Too few items to sample domain adequately	Too few cases/OSCEs for generalizability	Too few observations of clinical behavior
	Biased/unrepresentative sample of domain	Unstandardized patient raters	Too few independent raters
	Mismatch of sample to domain	Unrepresentative cases	Incomplete observations
	Low score reliability	Low reliability of ratings	Low reliability of ratings/Low generalizability
Construct-irrelevant Variance (CIV)	Flawed item formats	Flawed cases/checklists/rating scales	Inappropriate rating items
	Biased items (DIF)	DIF for SP cases/rater bias	Rater bias
	Reading level of items inappropriate	SP use of inappropriate jargon	Systematic rater error: Halo, Severity, Leniency, Central tendency
	Items too easy/too hard/non-discriminating	Case difficulty inappropriate (too easy/too hard)	Inadequate sample of student behaviors
	Cheating/Insecure items	Bluffing of SPs	Bluffing of raters
	Indefensible passing score methods	Indefensible passing score methods	Indefensible passing score methods
	Teaching to the test	Poorly trained SPs	Poorly trained raters

Written Examinations

In a written examination, such as an objective test in a basic science course, CU is exemplified in an examination that is too short to adequately sample the domain being tested. Other examples of CU are: test item content that does not match the examination specifications well, so that some content areas are oversampled while others are undersampled; use of many items that test only low level cognitive behavior, such as recall or recognition of facts, while the instructional objectives required higher level cognitive behavior, such as application or problem solving; and, use of items which test trivial content that is unrelated to future learning (Downing, 2002b).

The remedies for the CU threats to validity are straightforward, although not always easily achieved. For any test taker, an achievement test should be a representative sample of items from the domain. That is, the domain may have subdomains, and these subdomains must be adequately sampled on any test. The length of the test should be adequate for the use of the test. For example, for a high-stakes pass–fail test, several hundred items are desired. For a test where assessment of learning is made, approximately 40 items might be minimally sufficient. One dimension of all achievement testing is the cognitive demand required. Does the test taker have to remember, understand or apply information? The proportion of items on such tests should be clearly specified and items should be written to test higher cognitive levels, if the instructional objectives require higher-order learning. Items should test important information, not trivia.

CIV may be introduced into written examination scores from many sources (Haladyna & Downing, 2004). CIV represents systematic "noise" in the measurement data, often associated with the scores of some but not all examinees. CIV is a type of nuisance variable and comprises the unintended measurement of some construct that is off-target, not associated with the primary construct of interest, and therefore interferes with the validity evidence for assessment data. For instance, flawed or poorly crafted item formats, which make it more difficult for some students to give a correct answer, introduce CIV into the measurement (Downing, 2002a, 2005), as does the use of many test items that are too difficult or too easy for student achievement levels and items that do not discriminate high-achieving from low-achieving students. CIV is also introduced by including statistically biased items on which some subgroup of students under- or over-performs compared to their expected performance or by including test items which offend some students by their use of culturally insensitive language. If some students have prior access to test items and other students do not have such access, this type of test security breach represents CIV and makes score interpretation difficult or impossible by seriously reducing the validity evidence for the assessment data. Likewise, other types of test irregularities, such as cheating, introduce CIV and compromise the ability to interpret scores meaningfully. A related CIV issue is "teaching to the test," such that the instructor uses actual test items for teaching, thus creating misleading or incorrect inferences about the meaning of scores (if the construct of interest is student achievement and not simply the ability to memorize answers to test items).

If the reading level of achievement test items is inappropriate for students, reading ability becomes a CIV variable which is unrelated or only minimally related to the construct intended to be measured, thereby introducing CIV (Abedi, 2006). Reading level issues may be particularly important for students taking tests written in their non-native language. By using complex sentence structures, challenging vocabulary, and idiosyncratic jargon, we run the risk of underestimating the achievement of any student whose first language is not English. While guessing is generally not a major issue on long tests, composed of well-crafted multiple-choice test items with at least three options (Haladyna & Downing, 1993; Rodriguez, 2005), random guessing of correct answers on multiple-choice items can introduce CIV, because the student's propensity to guess is a personality factor which is not directly related to the achievement construct intended to be measured (Downing, 2003a). Poorly crafted items, which violate one or more of the standard principles of effective item writing, may introduce CIV (Downing, 2005) by providing clues to the correct answer for some students who do not know the correct answer or by leading other students to answer incorrectly in spite of the fact that they actually know the correct answer.

If one accepts the consequential aspects of validity as a major source of validity evidence, then anything that interferes with the accurate determination of pass–fail status for some students on an assessment, may be considered CIV, since it adds non-random error to the measurement outcomes. All passing score determination methods, whether relative or absolute, are arbitrary. However, these methods and their results should not be capricious nor random (Norcini, 2003). If passing scores or grade-levels are determined in a manner such that they lack reproducibility, are statistically biased for some groups or subgroups, or produce cut scores that are so unrealistic that unacceptably high (or low) numbers of students fail, this introduces systematic CIV error into the final outcome of the assessment.

What are the solutions for these types of CIV problems? On written achievement tests, items should be well crafted and follow the basic evidence-based principles of effective item writing (Case & Swanson, 1998; Haladyna, Downing, & Rodriguez, 2002). The item format itself should not be an impediment to student assessment. The reading ability of students should not be a major factor in the assessment of the achievement construct. Most items should be targeted in difficulty to student achievement levels. All items that are empirically shown to be biased or use language that offends some cultural, racial, or ethnic group should be eliminated from the test. Test items must be maintained securely and tests should be administered in proctored, controlled environments so that any potential cheating is minimized or eliminated. Instructors should not teach directly to the content of the test. Instead, teaching should be to the content domain of which the test is a small sample. And, finally, passing scores (or grading standards) should be established in a systematic and defensible manner, which is unbiased and fair to all students.

Performance Examinations

OSCEs or SP examinations increase the fidelity of the assessment and are intended to measure performance, rather than knowledge or skills (Miller, 1990; Yudkowsky, Chapter 9, this volume). Performance assessments are closer in proximity to the actual criterion performance of interest, but these types of assessment also involve constructs, because they sample performance behavior in a standardized or simulated context. Such tests approximate the real world, but are not the real world. The performance of students, rated by trained SPs in a simulated and controlled environment on a finite number of selected cases requiring maximum performance, is not *actual* performance in the real world; rather, inferences must be made from performance ratings to the domain of performance, with a specific interpretation or meaning attributed to the checklist or the rating-scale data. Validity evidence must be documented to support or refute the proposed meanings associated with these performance-type constructs.

There are many potential CU and CIV threats to validity for performance assessments. In Table 2.3, some examples of validity threats are presented. Many threats are the same as noted for written tests. One major CU threat arises from using too few performance cases to adequately sample or generalize to the domain. The case specificity of performance cases is well documented (e.g., Elstein, Shulman, & Sprafka, 1978; Norman, Tugwell, Feightner, Muzzin, & Jacoby, 1985). Approximately 10 to 12 SP encounters, lasting up to 20 or 25 minutes each, may be required to achieve even minimal generalizability in order to support inferences to the domain (van der Vleuten & Swanson, 1990). Lack of sufficient generalizability is a CU threat to validity. If performance cases are unrepresentative of the performance domain of interest, CU threatens validity by misrepresenting or biasing the inferences to the domain. For example, in an SP examination of patient communication skills, if the medical content of the cases is atypical and unrepresentative of the domain, it may be impossible for students to demonstrate their patient communication skills adequately.

Many SP examinations use trained lay simulated patients to portray actual patient medical problems and to rate student performance, after the encounter, using standardized checklists or rating scales. The quality of the SP portrayal is extremely important, as is the quality of the SPs training in the appropriate use of checklists and rating scales. If the SPs are not well trained to consistently portray the patient in a standardized manner, different students effectively encounter different patients and slightly different patient problems. The construct of interest is, therefore, misrepresented, because all students do not encounter the same patient problem or stimulus.

Remedies for CU in SP examinations include the use of large numbers of representative cases, using well-trained SP raters. SP monitoring, during multi-day performance examinations, is critical, such that any slippage in the standard portrayal can be corrected during the time of the examination.

For a performance examination, such as an OSCE or SP

examination, there are many potential CIV threats. CIV on a SP examination concerns issues such as systematic rater error which is uncorrected statistically, such that student scores are systematically higher or lower than they should be. SP cases that are flawed or of inappropriate difficulty for students and checklist or rating scale items that are ambiguous may introduce CIV. Statistical bias for one or more subgroups of students, which is undetected and uncorrected, may systematically raise or lower SP scores, unfairly advantaging some students and penalizing others. Racial or ethnic rater bias on the part of the SP rater creates CIV and makes the score interpretation difficult or impossible. Also, all the classic rater errors, such as severity/leniency, halo, central tendency, restriction of the range and many other idiosyncratic types of rater error add CIV, since this type of error is systematic rather than random (e.g., Engelhard, 2002).

It is possible for students to bluff SPs, particularly on non-medical aspects of SP cases, making ratings higher for some students than they actually should be. Establishing passing scores for SP examinations is challenging; if these cut scores are indefensibly established, the consequential aspect of validity will be reduced and CIV will be introduced to the assessment, making the evaluation of student performance difficult or impossible.

The remedies for CU in performance examinations are obvious, but may be difficult and costly to implement. Low reliability is a major threat to validity (Messick, 1989), thus using sufficient numbers of reliable and representative cases to adequately generalize to the proposed domain is critical. Generalizability must be estimated for most performance-type examinations, using Generalizability Theory (Brennan, 2001). For high-stakes performance examinations, Generalizability coefficients should be at least 0.80; the phi-coefficient is the appropriate estimate of generalizability for criterion-referenced performance examinations, which have absolute, rather than relative passing scores (van der Vlueten & Swanson, 1990). SPs should be well trained in their patient roles and their portrayals monitored throughout the time period of the examination to ensure standardization. To control or eliminate CIV in performance examinations, checklists and rating scales must be well developed, critiqued, edited, and tried-out and must be sufficiently accurate to provide reproducible data, when completed by the SPs who are well trained in their use. Methods to detect statistical bias in performance-examination ratings should be implemented for high-stakes examinations (De Champlain & Floreck, 2002). Performance cases should be pretested with a representative group of students prior to their final use, testing the appropriateness of case difficulty and all other aspects of the case presentation. SP training is critical, in order to eliminate sources of CIV introduced by variables such as SP-rater bias and student success at bluffing the SP. If passing scores or grades are assigned to the performance examination results, these scores must be established in a defensible, systematic, reproducible, and fair manner.

Ratings of Clinical Performance

In health professions education, ratings of student clinical performance in clerkships or preceptorships are often a major assessment modality. This method depends primarily on faculty observations of student clinical performance behavior in a naturalistic setting (McGaghie, Butter, & Kaye, Chapter 8, this volume). Clinical performance ratings are unstandardized, often unsystematic, and are frequently completed by faculty who are not well trained in their use. Thus, there are many threats to validity of clinical performance ratings by the very nature of the manner in which they are typically obtained.

The CU threat is exemplified by too few observations of the target or rated behavior by the faculty raters (Table 2.3). Williams, Klamen, and McGaghie (2003) suggest that 7 to 11 independent ratings of clinical performance are required to produce sufficiently generalizable data to be useful and interpretable. The use of too few independent observations and ratings of clinical performance is a major CU threat to validity.

CIV is introduced into clinical ratings in many ways. The major CIV threat is due to systematic rater error. Raters are the major source of measurement error for these types of observational assessments, but CIV is associated with systematic rater error, such as rater severity or leniency errors, central tendency error (rating in the center of the rating scale) and restriction of range (failure to use all the points on the rating scale). The halo rater effect occurs when the rater ignores the traits to be rated and treats all traits as if they were one. Thus, ratings tend to be repetitive and inflate estimates of reliability.

Although better training may help to reduce some undesirable rater effects, another way to combat rater severity or leniency error is to estimate the extent of severity (or leniency) and adjust the final ratings to eliminate the unfairness that results from harsh or lenient raters. Computer software is available to estimate these rater-error effects and adjust final ratings accordingly. While this is one potentially effective method to reduce or eliminate CIV due to rater severity or leniency, other rater-error effects, such as central tendency errors, restriction in the use of the rating scale, and idiosyncratic rater error remain difficult to detect and correct (Haladyna & Downing, 2004).

Rating scales are frequently used for clinical performance ratings. If the items are inappropriately written, such that raters are confused by the wording or misled to rate a different student characteristic from that which was intended, CIV may be introduced. Unless raters are well trained in the proper use of the observational rating scale and trained to use highly similar standards, CIV may be introduced into the data, making the proposed interpretation of ratings difficult and less meaningful. Students may also attempt to bluff the raters and intentionally try to mislead the observer into one or more of the systematic CIV rater errors noted.

As with other types of assessment, the methods used to establish passing scores or grades may be a source of CIV. Additionally, methods of combining clinical performance observational data with other types of assessment data, such as written test scores and SP performance examination scores may be a CIV source. If the procedures used to combine different types of assessment data into one composite score are inappropriate, CIV may be introduced such that the proposed interpretation of the final score is incorrect or diminished in meaning (Norcini & Guille, 2002).

Remedies for the CU and CIV threats to validity of clinical performance data are suggested by the specific issues noted. For CU, many independent ratings of behavior are needed, by well trained raters who are qualified to make the required evaluative judgments and are motivated to fulfill these responsibilities. The mean rating, over several independent raters, may tend to reduce the CIV due to systematic rater error, but will not entirely eliminate it, as in the case of a student who luckily draws two or more lenient raters or is unlucky in being rated by two or more harsh raters.

Passing score determination may be more difficult for observational clinical performance examinations, but is an essential component of the assessment and a potential source of CIV error. The method and procedures used to establish defensible, reproducible, and fair passing scores or grades for clinical performance examinations are as important as for other assessment methods and similar procedures may be used (Downing, Tekian, & Yudkowsky, 2006; Norcini & Shea, 1997).

What about Face Validity? —VERBOTEN

The term *face validity*, despite its popularity in some health professions educator's usage and vocabulary, has been derided by educational measurement professionals since at least the 1940s. *Face validity* can have many different meanings. The most pernicious meaning, according to Mosier, is: "the validity of the test is best determined by using common sense in discovering that the test measures component abilities which exist both in the test situation and on the job" (Mosier, 1947, p. 194). This type of face validity represents a belief and has no place in the science of validation research (Downing, 2006a). Clearly, this meaning of *face validity* has no place in the literature or vocabulary of health professions educators. Further, reliance on this type of face validity as a major source of validity evidence for assessments is a major threat to validity and a potential source of harm to our students and society.

Face validity, in the meaning above, is not endorsed by any contemporary educational measurement researchers (Downing, 1996). Face validity is not any type of legitimate source of validity evidence and can never substitute for any of the many evidentiary sources of validity discussed in this chapter (Messick, 1989; Kane, 2006b).

Can face validity have any legitimate meaning in health professions education? If by *face validity* one means that the assessment has superficial qualities that make it appear to measure the intended construct (e.g., the SP case looks like it assesses history taking skills or communications skills), this may be an important characteristic of the assessment, but it is not validity. Such an SP characteristic has to do with acceptance of the assessment by students and faculty or is important for administrators and even the public, but it is not validity. But, the avoidance of this type of *face invalidity* was endorsed by Messick (1989). The appearance of validity is not validity; appearance is not scientific evidence, derived from hypothesis and theory, supported or unsupported, more or less, by empirical data and formed into logical arguments.

Alternate terms for *face validity* might be considered. For example, if an objective test looks like it measures the achievement construct of interest, one might consider this some type of value-added and important trait of the assessment that may be required for the overall success of the assessment program, its acceptance and its utility, but this clearly is not sufficient scientific evidence of validity. The appearance of validity may be necessary, but it is not sufficient evidence of validity. The congruence between the superficial look and feel of the assessment and solid validity evidence might be referred to as *congruent* or *social-political meaningfulness*, but it is clearly not a primary type of validity evidence and can not, in any way, substitute for any of the five suggested primary sources of validity evidence (AERA, APA, & NCME, 1999).

Summary

This chapter has reviewed the contemporary meaning of validity, a unitary concept with multiple facets, which considers construct validity as the whole of validity. Validity evidence refers to the data and information collected in order to assign meaningful interpretation to assessment scores or outcomes, which were designed for a specific purpose and at one specific point in time. Validity always refers to score interpretations or the desired meanings associated with score data and never to the assessment itself. The process of validation is closely aligned with the scientific method of theory development, hypothesis generation, data collection for the purpose of hypothesis testing, and forming conclusions concerning the accuracy of the desired score interpretations. Validity refers to the impartial, scientific collection of data, from multiple sources, to provide more or less support for the validity hypothesis and relates to logical arguments, based on theory and data, which are formed to assign meaningful interpretations to assessment data.

The chapter discussed five typical sources of validity evidence— Content, Response process, Internal structure, Relationship to other variables, and Consequences—as described by validity theorists such as Messick and Kane and embodied in the 1999 *Standards*.

This chapter also summarized two broad general threats to validity in the context of the contemporary meaning of validity. These threats are construct underrepresentation (CU) and construct-irrelevant variance (CIV). CU threats relate primarily to undersampling or biased sampling of the content domain or the selection or creation of assessment items or performance prompts that do not match the appropriate construct definition and thus fail to sample the proper domain. CIV adds "noise" to the assessment data and introduces systematic, rather than random, measurement error, which reduces our ability to interpret assessment outcomes in the proposed manner. Face validity was rejected as any type of legitimate source of validity evidence. Sole reliance on this pernicious type of validity is a threat to validity.

References

Abedi, J. (2006). Language issues in item development. In S.M. Downing & T.M. Haladyna (Eds.), *Handbook of test development* (pp. 377–398). Mahwah, NJ: Lawrence Erlbaum Associates.

American Educational Research Association, American Psychological Association, & National Council on Measurement in Education. (1999). *Standards for educational and psychological testing*. Washington, DC: American Educational Research Association.

Angoff, W.H. (1971). Scales, norms, and equivalent scores. In R.L. Thorndike (Ed.), *Educational measurement* (2d ed., pp. 508–600). Washington: American Council on Education.

Auewarakul, C., Downing, S.M., Jaturatumrong, U., & Praditsuwan, R. (2005). Sources of validity evidence for an internal medicine student evaluation system: An evaluative study of assessment methods. *Medical Education*, 39, 276–283.

Baranowski, R. (2006). Item editing and editorial review. In S.M. Downing & T.M. Haladyna (Eds.), *Handbook of test development* (pp. 349–357). Mahwah, NJ: Lawrence Erlbaum Associates.

Beckman, T.J., & Cook, D.A. (2005). What is the validity evidence for assessments of clinical teaching? *Journal of General Internal Medicine*, 20, 1159–1164.

Boulet, J.R., McKinley, D.W., Whelan, G.P., & Hambleton, R.K. (2003). Quality assurance methods for performance-based assessments. *Advances in Health Sciences Education*, 8, 27–47.

Brennan, R.L. (2001). *Generalizability theory*. New York: Springer-Verlag.

Campbell, D.T., & Fiske D.W. (1959). Convergent and discriminant validation by the multitrait-multimethod matrix. *Psychological Bulletin*, 56, 81–105.

Case, S.M., & Swanson, D.B. (1998). *Constructing written test questions for the basic and clinical sciences* (2nd ed.). Philadelphia, PA: National Board of Medical Examiners.

Cizek, G.J. (2006). Standard setting. In S.M. Downing & T.M. Haladyna (Eds.), *Handbook of test development* (pp. 225–258). Mahwah, NJ: Lawrence Erlbaum Associates.

Cook, D.A., & Beckman, T.J. (2006). Current concepts in validity and reliability for psychometric instruments: Theory and application. *American Journal of Medicine*, 119(2), e7–16.

Cronbach, L.J. (1980). Validity on parole: How can we go straight? New directions for testing and measurement: Measuring achievement over a decade. *Proceedings of the 1979 ETS Invitational Conference* (pp. 99–108). San Francisco: Jossey-Bass.

Cronbach, L.J. (1988). Five perspectives on validity argument. In H. Wainer & H. Braun (Eds.), *Test validity* (pp. 3–17). Hillsdale, NJ: Lawrence Erlbaum.

Cronbach, L.J. (1989). Construct validation after thirty years. In R.E. Linn (Ed.), *Intelligence: Measurement, theory, and public policy* (pp. 147–171). Urbana, IL: University of Illinois Press.

Cronbach, L.J., & Meehl, P.E. (1955). Construct validity in psychological tests. *Psychological Bulletin*, 52, 281–302.

Crossley, J., Davies, H., Humphris, G., & Jolly, B. (2002). Generalisability; a key to unlock professional assessment. *Medical Education*, 36, 972–978.

Cureton, E.E. (1951). Validity. In E.F. Lingquist (Ed.), *Educational measurement* (pp. 621–694). Washington: American Council on Education.

De Champlain, A.F., & Floreck, L.M. (2002, April). Assessing potential bias in a large-scale standardized patient examination: An application of common DIF methods for polytomous items. Paper presented at the Annual Meeting of the American Educational Research Association, New Orleans, LA.

Downing S.M. (1996). Test validity evidence: What about face validity? *CLEAR Exam Review*, Sum, 31–33.

Downing S.M. (2002a). Construct-irrelevant variance and flawed test questions: Do multiple-choice item writing principles make any difference? *Academic Medicine*, 77, S103–S104.

Downing, S.M. (2002b). Threats to the validity of locally developed multiple-choice tests in medical education: Construct-irrelevant variance and construct underrepresentation. *Advances in Health Sciences Education*, 7, 235–241.

Downing, S.M. (2003a). Guessing on selected-response examinations. *Medical Education*, 37, 670–671.

Downing, S.M. (2003b). Item response theory: Applications in modern test theory in medical education. *Medical Education*, 37, 1–7.

Downing, S.M. (2005). The effects of violating standard item writing principles on tests and students: The consequences of using flawed test items on achievement examinations in medical education. *Advances in Health Sciences Education*, 10, 133–143.

Downing, S.M. (2006a). Face validity of assessments: Faith-based interpretations or evidence-based science? *Medical Education*, 40, 7–8.

Downing, S.M. (2006b). Twelve steps for effective test development. In S.M. Downing & T.M. Haladyna (Eds.), *Handbook of test development* (pp. 3–25). Mahwah, NJ: Lawrence Erlbaum Associates.

Downing, S.M., Tekian, A., & Yudkowsky, R. (2006). Procedures for establishing defensible absolute passing scores on performance examinations in health professions education. *Teaching & Learning in Medicine*, 18(1), 50–57.

Ebel, R.L. (1972). *Essentials of educational measurement* (2nd ed.). Englewood Cliffs, NJ: Prentice-Hall.

Elstein, A.S, Shulman, L.S, & Sprafka, S.A. (1978). *Medical problem solving: An analysis of clinical reasoning.* Cambridge, MA: Harvard University Press.

Embretson, S.E., & Reise, S.P. (2000). *Item response theory for psychologists.* Mahwah, NJ: Lawrence Erlbaum Associates.

Engelhard, G. Jr. (2002). Monitoring raters in performance assessments. In G. Tindal & T.M. Haladyna (Eds.), *Large-scale assessment programs for all students: Validity, technical adequacy, and implementation* (pp. 261–288). Mahwah, NJ: Lawrence Erlbaum Associates.

Haladyna, T.M. (2006). Roles and importance of validity studies in test development. In S.M. Downing & T.M. Haladyna (Eds.), *Handbook of test development* (pp. 739–755). Mahwah, NJ: Lawrence Erlbaum Associates.

Haladyna, T.M., & Downing, S.M. (1993). How many options is enough for a

54 STEVEN M. DOWNING AND THOMAS M. HALADYNA

multiple-choice test item? *Education and Psychological Measurement*, 53, 999–1010.

Haladyna, T.M, & Downing, S.M. (2004). Construct-irrelevant variance in high-stakes testing. *Educational Measurement: Issues and Practice*, 23(1), 17–27.

Haladyna, T.M., Downing, S.M., & Rodriguez, M.C. (2002). A review of multiple-choice item-writing guidelines for classroom assessment. *Applied Measurement in Education*, 15(3), 309–334.

Holland, P.W., & Wainer, H. (Eds.). (1993). *Differential item functioning*. Mahwah, NJ: Lawrence Erlbaum.

Kane, M.T. (1992). An argument-based approach to validation. *Psychological Bulletin*, 112, 527–535.

Kane, M.T. (1994). Validating interpretive arguments for licensure and certification examinations. *Evaluation and the Health Professions*, 17, 133–159.

Kane, M. (2006a). Content-related validity evidence in test development. In S.M. Downing & T.M. Haladyna (Eds.), *Handbook of test development* (pp. 131–153). Mahwah, NJ: Lawrence Erlbaum Associates.

Kane, M. (2006b) Validation. In R.L. Brennan (Ed.), *Educational measurement* (4th ed., pp. 17–64). New York: American Council on Education and Greenwood.

Linn, R.L. (2002). Validation of the uses and interpretations of results of state assessment and accountability systems. In G. Tindal & T. Haladyna (Eds.), *Large-scale assessment programs for all students: Development, implementation, and analysis* (pp. 27–48). Mahwah, NJ: Lawrence Erlbaum Associates.

Linn, R.L. (2006). The standards for educational and psychological testing: Guidance in test development. In S.M. Downing & T.M. Haladyna (Eds.), *Handbook of test development* (pp. 27–38). Mahwah, NJ: Lawrence Erlbaum Associates.

Messick, S. (1989). Validity. In R.L. Linn (Ed.), *Educational measurement* (3rd ed., pp. 13–104). New York: American Council on Education and Macmillan.

Messick, S. (1995). Validity of psychological assessment: Validation of inferences from persons' responses and performances as scientific inquiry into score meaning. *American Psychologist*, 50, 741–749.

Miller, G.E. (1990). The assessment of clinical skills/competence/performance. *Academic Medicine*, 65, s63–67.

Mosier, C.I. (1947). A critical examination of the concepts of face validity. *Educational and Psychological Measurement*, 7, 191–205.

Newble, D.I., & Jaeger, K. (1983). The effects of assessment and examinations on the learning of medical students. *Medical Education*, 17, 165–171.

Norcini, J.J. (2003). Setting standards on educational tests. *Medical Education*, 37, 464–469.

Norcini, J., & Guille, R. (2002). Combining tests and setting standards. In G.R. Norman, C.P.M. van der Vleuten, & D.I. Newble (Eds.),

International handbook of research in medical education (pp. 811–834). Dordrecht, The Netherlands: Kluwer Academic Publishers.

Norcini, J.J., & Shea, J.A. (1997). The credibility and comparability of standards. *Applied Measurement in Education*, 10, 39–59.

Norman, G.R., Tugwell, P., Feightner, J.W., Muzzin, L.J., & Jacoby, L.L. (1985). Knowledge and problem-solving. *Medical Education*, 19, 344–356.

Penfield, R.D., & Lam, R.C.M. (2000). Assessing differential item functioning in performance assessment: Review and recommendations. *Educational Measurement: Issues and Practice*, 19, 5–15.

Raymond, M., & Neustel, S. (2006). Determining the content of credentialing examinations. In S.M. Downing & T.M. Haladyna (Eds.), *Handbook of test development* (pp. 181–223). Mahwah, NJ: Lawrence Erlbaum Associates.

Rodriguez, M.C. (2005). Three options are optimal for multiple-choice items: A meta-analysis of 80 years of research. *Educational Measurement: Issues and Practice*, Summer, 3–13.

Subkoviak, M.J. (1988). A practitioner's guide to computation and interpretation of reliability indices for mastery tests. *Journal of Educational Measurement*, 25, 47–55.

Van der Linden, W.J., & Hambleton, R.K. (1997). Item response theory: Brief history, common models, and extensions. In W.J. van der Linden & R.K. Hambleton (Eds.), *Handbook of modern item response theory* (pp. 1–28). New York: Springer-Verlag.

van der Vleuten, C.P.M., & Swanson, D.B. (1990). Assessment of clinical skills with standardized patients: State of the art. *Teaching and Learning in Medicine*, 2, 58–76.

Williams, R.G., Klamen, D.A., & McGaghie, W.C. (2003). Cognitive, social and environmental sources of bias in clinical competence ratings. *Teaching and Learning in Medicine*, 15, 270–292.

Zieky, M. (2006). Fairness review in assessment. In S.M. Downing & T.M. Haladyna (Eds.), *Handbook of test development* (pp. 359–376). Mahwah, NJ: Lawrence Erlbaum Associates.

3

RELIABILITY

RICK D. AXELSON AND CLARENCE D. KREITER

Introduction

Reliability plays a central role in educational measurement and social science research. It provides a set of concepts and indices for assessing the proportionate amount of random error contained in data. While all educational measurements contain some level of measurement error, the particular types of assessments used in the social sciences are especially vulnerable to measurement error.

To illustrate the concept of error, consider the following situation. You and a friend are having a conversation over lunch in a busy restaurant. There are also a number of other sounds—conversations at other tables, rattling of dishes, traffic noises from outside, and air whooshing through the heating vent. This makes it difficult to hear the message of interest. The types of sounds that you hear at lunch could be classified either as distracting background noise (random sounds) or your friend's words (meaningful sound or information). The proportion of your friend's remarks that you heard and could interpret could range from 0 (background noise completely drowned out the conversation) to 1.0 (clearly understood every word he said). The closer you are to 1.0 on this scale, the more likely it would be that you could give a trustworthy and reliable account of the conversation. Similarly, one could look at research and assessment data in this same way; it contains two sources of variation—random error or noise and systematic information. The reliability of assessment data increases as it contains less random error.

Reliable data are fundamental to effective assessment practices and comprise an essential element of validity. Reliable data provide the foundation of trustworthy evidence needed to inform and enhance effective practices. Although reliability and validity are often treated as distinct and separate aspects or indicators of data quality, they are in fact inextricably linked. Perhaps the most succinct description of this relationship is conveyed by the observation that reliability is a necessary but not sufficient condition for validity. It is obvious that if a score is totally unreliable it will also be invalid and meaningless for any particular use or interpretation. This is true because measures with reliability of zero are totally composed of random error and hence cannot be measuring any meaningful aspect of an individual. But, on the other hand, it is possible to imagine scores that are perfectly reliable but totally invalid for certain purposes or interpretations. For example, although a measure of adult height would likely produce highly reliable and consistent values, it would not be valid to use these values as a measure of individuals' general intelligence.

In this chapter, we will explore the concept of reliability in greater detail, show how it can be assessed and enhanced in different assessment contexts, and how it can help determine the adequacy and validity of assessment data for particular uses. We begin with a conceptual discussion of reliability and its relationship to variance, and then move toward a more precise formulation of reliability through a discussion of its role in classical test theory (CTT), which is also often referred to as classical measurement theory (CMT). Each concept is also demonstrated with an applied example from within the context of health science education. The goal is to provide the reader with meaningful ways of understanding, assessing, and applying information about reliability.

The Conceptual Foundation of Reliability in Classical Test Theory

The concept and estimation of reliability assumes a central role in educational assessment. While all measurements are prone to some level of error, individual educational assessment measures often contain high levels of error. For example, consider a single global rating of a nursing or medical student's performance within a clinical setting.

Measurement studies have suggested that such ratings are not primarily dependent on a student's clinical ability, but rather a reflection of the particular circumstances (e.g. the medical case, rater, and so forth) in which the rating took place (e.g., Carline, Wenrich, & Ramsey, 1989; Kreiter, Gordon, Elliott, & Callaway, 1998). When considering the high level of error in such ratings, one might be tempted to reject their usefulness as an educational assessment. Fortunately, however, an understanding of reliability theory and the statistical quantification of error allows educators to generate valid and reliable judgments even when the individual measures employed are quite error prone. In this section we will discuss procedures for understanding and quantifying the measurement error affecting reliability. While simply calculating reliability will not improve measurement precision, we will demonstrate how utilizing reliability related concepts can improve the accuracy of the judgments, grades, and other summary scores employed in health science education.

Statistical Definition of Reliability

Test or assessment data are reliable to the degree to which they can be replicated or reproduced. For instance, imagine the repeated measurement of some characteristic of a single person, for example their height. The dispersion, variation, scatter, or variance of these repeated measures around that person's mean score (height) is referred to as *error variance* (σ^2_{error}), and is an indication of the imprecision of measurement. An individual's mean score across an infinite number of repeated measurements will cancel out all of the random error or "noise" in the measurement and is considered that person's "*true score.*" Note that the *observed* score (the score we record from the test or assessment) is comprised of the true score plus error.

Given the true score distribution across a group of persons, commonly summarized as *true score variance* (σ^2_{true}), and the distribution of repeated measures within examinees (σ^2_{error}), it is possible to represent *reliability* as the ratio of true score variance divided by the sum of true score variance plus error score variance.

$$\text{Reliability} = \frac{\text{True score variance}}{\text{True score variance} + \text{error variance}}$$

$$= \frac{\sigma^2_{true}}{\sigma^2_{true} + \sigma^2_{error}} = \frac{\sigma^2_{true}}{\sigma^2_{observed}} \tag{3.1}$$

Using the noisy room metaphor we began with, we can think of reliability as the proportion of data available that is useful information or "signal":

$$\text{Reliability} = \frac{\text{signal}}{\text{signal} + \text{noise}} \tag{3.2}$$

Note that in CTT, systematic variation is solely attributable to variation in true scores. However, in practice, there are other sources of systematic variation, such as rater or measurement bias. For example, a scale that consistently registers 10 pounds heavier than the object's true weight produces a systematic rather than a random source of error. Systematic measurement error will not be detected in reliability analyses, but it will negatively impact the interpretability of the measure and, hence, its validity. Chapter 2 (Downing & Haladyna, this volume) provides a discussion of systematic error, also called Construct-irrelevant Variance, which is a general threat to test score validity. Chapters 7 to 12 provide recommendations for decreasing systematic error in various types of testing formats.

The Theory: Statistical Foundations of Reliability

In thinking about the statistical estimation of reliability, it is important again to remember its close association with the concept of replication. Conceptually and statistically, when considering how closely two separate measurements or replications agree, we usually think in terms of correlation. Indeed, a correlation coefficient can be used to estimate reliability.

Reliability and Randomly Parallel Tests

As an example, let's suppose that test x and test x' are two "randomly parallel" tests. In this case, the term "randomly parallel" implies that each test is generated by randomly sampling items from the same item bank. If each test were composed of 50 unique biochemistry items sampled at random from a large common item bank, the tests would be quite similar except for the slight variations resulting from sampling error. If both of these tests were administered to a single sample of examinees, the correlation between the two randomly parallel tests could serve as an estimate of the reliability of scores generated by test x.

Although this is a valid methodology for estimating reliability, in practice, instructors seldom have the time or resources to generate and administer randomly parallel tests. Nonetheless, the practice of correlating parallel test scores to derive an estimate of reliability underlies the logic for deriving reliability estimates based on the correlated scores from random halves of a single test (such as internal consistency reliability estimates). Because estimating reliability using split-half methods is efficient and generally reflects the overall replicability or internal test consistency, it is by far the most common technique used in health science assessments. A discussion of procedures for estimating reliability from a single administration of a test is provided in the next section.

The Practice: Practical Methods for Estimating Reliability

In considering a practical method for estimating reliability in a real assessment context, such as a multiple-choice (MC) test, how can we separate random score variation (i.e., measurement error) from systematic variation (i.e., true score)?

Test–Retest Reliability

One way would be to have individuals take the same test multiple times. Then, under classical test theory assumptions, a person's true score (systematic score component) is equal to his/her average score over a very large number of tests, and the differences between a person's average score and each of his/her separate test scores would be error. A major difficulty with using such a test–retest approach to estimate reliability is the impracticality of arranging repeated testing sessions for individuals. Additionally, obtaining accurate estimates with this approach rests upon the dubious assumption that examinees do not remember information from earlier testing sessions. The test–retest method of estimating reliability is of only theoretical and conceptual interest now, since far more efficient techniques—such as the internal consistency methods—are now available.

Single Test Reliability: Internal Consistency

Consequently, rather than replicating testing sessions to estimate reliability, practitioners generally opt for an internal-consistency method. Using an internal-consistency method, only one testing session is needed and it is the consistency among the subparts of the test that becomes the basis for estimating reliability. One early way of doing this was to split the test into two random halves and calculate the correlation between respondents' scores on the two sets of items. This correlation provided an estimate of the agreement between test replications.

The difficulty with the split-half method described above occurs when separating the items into two groups. There are multiple ways of splitting the items. Even in a relatively simple case of separating six items into two groups of three, there are ten possible ways to do this. Each of the ten splits will likely yield different estimates of the coefficient of reliability. Since the selection of any one configuration is arbitrary, what estimate of reliability should be used? One way out of this conundrum is to calculate the average correlation across all splits. This is effectively what coefficient alpha does.

Coefficient alpha, often referred to as Cronbach's alpha, is a widely used measure of internal-consistency reliability. Like other measures of reliability, it represents the proportion of systematic or true score variance in the total test score variance. Consider each item in the test as an attempt to measure an underlying ability or construct such as "knowledge of biochemistry." Then coefficient alpha reflects how strongly the responses to the different items on the test all depend on examinee ability in biochemistry. Greater shared variance or correlations among the items results in higher coefficient alpha values; this indicates closer alignment around the common underlying construct "knowledge of biochemistry."

As an example consider the scores obtained on a five-item biochemistry quiz. Ten examinees who took the quiz had the patterns of correct = 1 and incorrect = 0 responses displayed in Table 3.1.

Using commonly available statistical software applications, we find that coefficient alpha for these five items equals 0.538. An alpha of 0.538 indicates that just over half of the observed variation in total scores is due to variation in examinee ability (true score). Or, conversely, just under half of the observed score variation (0.462 = 1 − 0.538) is due to random error rather than examinee ability. The large random error component is due to the fact that any given item is an imperfect measure of the underlying construct of "knowledge of biochemistry."

Reliability coefficients of less than 0.50 are not uncommon for very short tests and quizzes. Whether this alpha indicates a sufficient level of reliability depends upon how the test will be used. Downing (2004) notes that educational measurement professionals generally suggest the following interpretative guidance for alpha:

Table 3.1 Hypothetical Five-Item MC Quiz Results for 10 Students

Student ID	Item 1	Item 2	Item 3	Item 4	Item 5	Students' Total Correct
A	0	0	1	0	0	1
B	0	1	1	0	1	3
C	0	1	1	0	0	2
D	1	0	0	0	0	1
E	0	0	0	1	1	2
F	1	1	1	0	1	4
G	1	0	0	1	1	3
H	0	0	0	0	0	0
I	0	0	0	0	0	0
J	1	1	1	0	1	4

Notes: Mean score for the class = 2   Standard Deviation (SD) = 1.49

- 0.90 or higher is needed for very high stakes tests (e.g., licensure, certification exams)
- 0.80–0.89 is acceptable for moderate stakes tests (e.g., end-of-year summative exams in medical school, end-of-course exams)
- 0.70–0.79 would be acceptable for lower stakes assessments (e.g., formative or summative classroom-type assessments created and administered by local faculty.

Although many in-course or classroom-type educational assessments have reliabilities below 0.70, there may still be a sound rationale for using test score information with relatively low levels of reliability. For example, test scores with a reliability coefficient below 0.70 might be useful as one component of an overall composite score.

As we will discuss later, adding additional items to a test, or adding total scores from multiple tests, often times yields an enhanced total score reliability.

Standard Error of Measurement (SEM)

To gain a clearer sense of the instrument's reliability, one can also calculate the standard error of measurement (SEM) and form confidence intervals for an obtained score (Downing, 2004; Downing, Chapter 5, this volume). For example, an instructor can interpret a 90% confidence interval as the score range around an obtained score that includes an examinee's true score 90% of the time. Equation 3.3 displays a method for deriving the SEM from a reliability coefficient.

$$\text{SEM} = \text{standard deviation} * \sqrt{(1 - \text{Reliability})} \tag{3.3}$$

For our example quiz, the SEM = $1.49 * \sqrt{(1 - 0.538)}$
= 1.49 * 0.6797 = 1.01.

Multiplying the SEM by 1.65 will provide the needed value to construct a 90% confidence interval around an obtained score. The value 1.65 is appropriate for a 90% confidence interval because for any distribution, the scores that fall within 1.65 standard deviations of the mean will include 90% of all the scores in the distribution.

90% CI = predicted value ± (1.65 * 1.01) = predicted value ± 1.67

So, for examinees who score at the test average of 2.0, 90% of them will have true scores in the interval ranging from 0.33 to 3.67 (2.0 ± 1.67). Given that possible test scores range only from 0 to 5, this 90% confidence interval is very large and is a reflection of the low reliability of this five-item test.

If the reliability of this quiz is too low for the given purpose, there are some options for increasing alpha. One approach is to increase the number of test items. The Spearman-Brown formula can be used to estimate the likely impact on reliability of a lengthened test (see also Downing, Chapter 5, this volume). The formula, shown in Equation 3.4 below, assumes that the items added to the test will have internal consistency, difficulty, and discrimination levels similar to those items already on the test.

$$r_{predicted} = f * r_{current} / (1 + (f - 1) * r_{current}), \tag{3.4}$$

where $r_{predicted}$ = the predicted reliability of the lengthened test; f is the factor by which the test will be lengthened; $r_{current}$ = the reliability coefficient for the current test.

For the 5-item quiz with a reliability of 0.538, what would the likely reliability be for a test of 10 items, i.e., increasing the length of the test by a factor of 2? Using the Spearman-Brown formula,

$$r_{predicted} = 2 * 0.538 / (1 + (2 - 1) * 0.538)$$

$$= 2 * 0.538/1.538$$

$$= 0.70$$

Using the Spearman-Brown formula, we find that the reliability of the new lengthened test is likely to be approximately 0.70.

How to Increase Reliability

If this level of reliability is still too low for the given purpose, what else could be done to improve it? Some options are:

a. Adding even more test items;

b. Conducting an item analysis and removing, revising, or replacing items that are not working well (see Downing, Chapter 5, this volume); and

c. Combining the current test with other types of measures to produce a composite score that may be more reliable than some of the tests or measures individually (see composite scores, below).

Assessing and Improving the Reliability of Rater Data

Up to this point, our focus has been on assessment instruments producing data that can be objectively scored as correct (1) or incorrect (0). However, many educational assessments within the health sciences are conducted through structured observation and the rating of performance (see Yudkowsky, Chapter 9, this volume). Methods for assessing and improving the reliability of such data are discussed next.

Rater data are generated, for example, when observers assign scores to examinees' performances or products. Since scoring a performance or test is typically a labor-intensive process, scoring duties are often distributed across multiple judges. For rating data to be reliable, each rater must be scoring performances consistently and in a manner comparable to the other raters. To enhance the replicability of the scores awarded by judges, an explicit set of scoring guidelines, often referred to as a scoring rubric, should be used to guide their work. In addition, after the judges have assigned scores, it is important to check on the extent to which the scoring rules have been consistently applied by examining inter-rater reliability.

In discussing the wide array of statistics to assess inter-rater reliability, Stemler (2004) identifies three ways of conceptualizing and estimating them:

1. **consensus estimates**—based on exact agreement among raters (*statistics: percent agreement, Cohen's kappa*);
2. **consistency estimates**—based on raters' similar ordering of performances (*statistics: Pearson's r, Spearman's rho, Cronbach's alpha*); and
3. **measurement estimates**—based on using all information from

judges' ratings in a model and providing statistics related to the various facets of the ratings (*models: generalizability theory, principal components, many-facets Rasch model*).

Each of these approaches is discussed below.

Consensus Estimates of Inter-rater Reliability

Consensus estimates are perhaps the most straightforward approach to assessing inter-rater reliability. They examine the percentage of items that are scored the same way by the raters. To illustrate, consider the data in Table 3.2 showing two judges' cross-classified ratings of a student's communication skills (0 = unsatisfactory, 1 = satisfactory, 2 = exemplary). The cases where the judges awarded the same score are found in the diagonal cells of the table. The percent-agreement statistic is calculated by adding the diagonal elements (40 + 60 + 35 = 135) and dividing this sum by the total number of cases (200). Percent agreement = 135/200 * 100 = 67.5%.

The interpretation of this statistic, however, is not as clear-cut as it would first appear. Just by chance alone, there will be some cases of apparent agreement even when there is no relationship between the judges' ratings. To disentangle the systematic agreement from those attributable to chance Cohen developed the kappa statistic, calculated by subtracting the expected value of random occurrences of agreement from the total observed instances of agreement. As a guide for interpreting the level of agreement indicated by kappa values, Landis and Koch (1977) note that values above 0.60 are considered substantial

Table 3.2 Hypothetical Communication Skills Ratings for 200 Students by Two Judges

	Judge 2:			
Scores:	0	1	2	Total
0	40	10	20	70
Judge 1: 1	5	60	5	70
2	15	10	35	60
Total	60	80	60	200

levels of agreement and values of 0.41 to 0.60 are considered moderate.

For the data displayed in Table 3.2 kappa can be obtained from statistical programs and is found to be 0.511. The programs will also provide statistics to test the null hypothesis that the judges' ratings are independent; or, in other words, that there is no more agreement among the judges ratings than would be expected by chance.

In reflecting on the information obtained from kappa, note that it is based on dividing data into classes—agreement and disagreement. When there are only two rating categories, kappa's mapping of responses into agreement and disagreement is unproblematic. Raters either picked the same category (agree) or they did not (disagree). But, what happens, as in the preceding example, if there are three or more rating categories? In such cases, one has to decide which ratings should be classified as "agreement" and "disagreement." In our numerical example, cases that received the same score were defined as "agreement" and the two types of non-identical responses were lumped together in the "disagreement" category. Note, that by lumping the two cases of disagreement together we effectively discard information about the types of disagreements. In our example, it is likely that we would want to consider the disagreements where judges' ratings were two levels apart (0, 2) as more serious than those that only differed by one level (e.g., (0,1) or (1,2)). Thus, when judges are rating performance on an ordinal or interval scale with three or more categories, kappa does not take full advantage of the available information about distances between data categories. For such situations, one could either use a weighted kappa statistic that adjusts for different levels of disagreement; or one of the available consistency- or measurement-based estimates of inter-rater reliability discussed below.

Consistency Estimates of Inter-rater Reliability

Consistency estimates focus on the correspondence among raters' ordering of observed performances. In our example the overall clinical performance of ten pharmacy students is rated by preceptors on a

5-point scale with "4" indicating outstanding performance and "0" indicating unsatisfactory performance; see Table 3.3.

To examine the level of agreement in preceptors' ratings of students, a correlation coefficient such as Pearson's r could be calculated among all possible pairs of preceptors. However, Pearson's r assumes that the raters' scores are based on an at least interval scale of measurement, which like integers on a number line, requires equal distances between each of the adjacent scores. This may not be true, if, for example, raters are only giving failing scores of 0 in the most extreme cases. Such a practice could result in the distance between a 0 and 1 score being much larger than the distance between any of the other adjacent categories (e.g., (1,2), (2,3), and (3,4)). When such a situation is of concern, Spearman's rho should be used since it is based on the rank ordering of the data and does not require an interval scale of measurement. Table 3.4 provides the Spearman's rho correlations obtained from a statistical program:

These coefficients are interpreted in the same way as Pearson's correlation coefficients. Possible values range from −1 to +1, with values closer to −1 or +1 indicating stronger linear relationships between the variables. Note that Rater #4's scores for students do not correspond very well (r < .30) with the scores given by Raters #1, #2, and #3. Also, there is a low correspondence between the scores given by Rater #3 and Rater #5 (r = 0.218). To improve inter-rater reliability, the sources

Table 3.3 Hypothetical Clinical Performance Ratings of 10 Students by 5 Judges/Raters

Student ID	Rater #1	Rater #2	Rater #3	Rater #4	Rater #5	Student Totals
A	1	1	4	1	0	7
B	2	4	4	2	4	16
C	3	4	4	2	3	16
D	4	0	2	2	3	11
E	0	0	1	4	4	9
F	4	4	4	2	4	18
G	4	3	2	4	4	17
H	1	0	1	1	3	6
I	0	1	0	0	2	3
J	4	4	4	1	4	17
Rater Totals	23	21	26	19	31	

Table 3.4 Spearman Rho Correlations of Rater Agreement

	RATER 1	RATER 2	RATER 3	RATER 4	RATER 5
RATER 1	1.00				
RATER 2	.475	1.0			
RATER 3	.541	.765	1.0		
RATER 4	.297	.023	.079	1.0	
RATER 5	.436	.399	.218	.639	1.0

of the disagreement among these raters could be investigated, identified, and used to improve rating procedures (see Yudkowsky, Chapter 9,
this volume).

The above correlation coefficients limited our analysis to pairwise
comparisons between raters. To assess the average correlation across
all raters Cronbach's alpha could be calculated. The alpha is 0.744,
indicating that the shared (true score) variance in the judges ratings
accounts for nearly three-quarters of the variance in students' overall
clinical performance rating.

Measurement Estimates of Inter-rater Reliability

Judges' ratings are often utilized to assess performance in more complex context than that described above. For example, several judges
might rate a student's performance on one task and another set of
judges might rate performance on another task. If we wanted to estimate the reliability of a student's obtained score, a comprehensive
measure of score reliability would need to take into account the overall
judges agreement and the number and variability of tasks presented
to the examinee. We might want to ask how replicable a score might
be if a different set of judges and tasks were selected and the entire
measurement process were repeated. In more complex assessment
environments where there are two or more sources of systematic variation simultaneously impacting an assessment score, more sophisticated approaches are needed to estimate reliability. Such instances
require partitioning of error sources according to the different facets
(e.g., judges, tasks). Generalizability theory, discussed by Kreiter,
(Chapter 4, this volume), is more appropriate in these situations.

Reliability of Composites

Health science instructors often need to generate a summary score based on multiple diverse measures. For example, a course grade might be derived by summing written test scores assessing knowledge achievement and ratings of clinical performance. Given that the final grade is usually the most important and consequential score awarded for a course, it may be important to accurately assess its reliability.

Composite score reliability is a special topic, which requires some unique assumptions, formulas, and software to estimate properly. Wainer and Thissen (2001) provide a thorough treatment of composite score reliability. The key points are that in order to accurately estimate the reliability of composite scores, any differential weighting of the input test or assessment scores must be included in the estimation process. And, composite scores are almost always more reliable than the sum of their respective parts, as alluded to earlier in this chapter.

Nominal and Effective Weights: Standard Scores

In calculating a grade or composite score and its reliability, it is important to first transform each component of the summary score to a standard score (see Downing, Chapter 5, this volume). If an instructor simply applies weights to each component score without first standardizing them to a common scale, the nominal weights applied will often be quite different than the effective weights. For example, when simply summing unstandardized score components (i.e. applying nominal weights of 1.0 to each component), those component scores with larger observed standard deviations will contribute more to the composite score. To eliminate the disparity between nominal and effective weights, it is good practice to standardize all component scores to a common mean and standard deviation before weighting and summing. This will allow the applied weights to equal the effective weights.

Depending on the correlation between scores, it is often observed that a composite score can exhibit higher reliability than any of the component scores individually. The composite reliability will depend on the reliability of the components, the weights chosen, and the correlation between component scores (Kreiter, Gordon, Elliott, & Calloway, 2004).

Summary

In a fashion similar to the noisy restaurant example at the beginning of the chapter, assessment scores usually contain error or noise that hampers our ability to accurately measure an examinee's ability or achievement. Reliability analysis allows educators to quantify error and facilitates the correct interpretation and use of scores containing error.

To provide a conceptual framework for reliability analyses, CTT was introduced as a method for partitioning total test score variance into two components: 1) true score; and 2) error. It was emphasized that the notion of replications provides the necessary framework for representing reliability.

Methods for estimating reliability were discussed and illustrated with numerical examples. For MC exams, the internal consistency of item responses can be used to estimate reliability using Cronbach's alpha or KR-20. Guidelines for interpreting alpha were provided and it was suggested that item analysis, lengthening the test, and creating composite scores are possible approaches for improving reliability.

Procedures for estimating the reliability of rater data were discussed next. Such data are produced when two or more judges rate a student product or performance. Cohen's kappa, Pearson's r, and Spearman's rho assess the correspondence of ratings between pairs of judges. These measures can be used to identify instances of poor agreement among particular judges and to monitor the effectiveness of scoring rubrics and rater training. Cronbach's alpha was mentioned as a measure of the overall inter-rater reliability among judges.

Just as lengthening a test can increase its reliability, creating a composite score by combining tests and other measures can also provide increased reliability over the individual measures.

References

Carline, J.D., Wenrich, M.D., & Ramsey, P.G. (1989). Characteristics of ratings of physician competence by professional associates. *Evaluation and the Health Professions*, 12, 409–23.

Cohen, J. (1960). A coefficient for agreement for nominal scales. *Educational and Psychological Measurement*, 20, 37–46.

Downing, S. M. (2004). Reliability: On the reproducibility of assessment data. *Medical Education*, 38, 1006–1012.

Kreiter, C.D., Ferguson, K., Lee, W.C., Brennan, R.L., & Densen, P. (1998). A generalizability study of a new standardized rating form used to evaluate students' clinical clerkship performance. *Academic Medicine*, 73, 1294–1298.

Kreiter, C.D., Gordon, J.A., Elliott, S., & Callaway, M. (2004). Recommendations for assigning weights to derive an overall course grade. *Teaching and Learning in Medicine*, 16(2), 133–138.

Landis, J.R., & Koch, G.G. (1977). The measurement of observer agreement for categorical data. *Biometrics*, 33, 159–174.

Pedhazur, E.J., & Schmelkin, L.P. (1991). *Measurement, design, and analysis: An integrated approach*. Hillsdale, NJ: Lawrence Erlbaum Associates.

Schmitt, N. (1996). Uses and abuses of coefficient alpha. *Psychological Assessment*, 8(4), 350–353.

Stemler, S.E. (2004). A comparison of consensus, consistency, and measurement approaches to estimating inter-rater reliability. *Practical Assessment, Research & Evaluation*, 9(4), available online from http://PAREonline.net/getvn.asp?v=9&n=4

Wainer, H., & Thissen, D. (2001). True score theory: The traditional method. In D. Thissen & H. Wainer (Eds.), *Test scoring*. Mahwah, NJ: Lawrence Erlbaum Associates, Inc.

4

GENERALIZABILITY THEORY
CLARENCE D. KREITER

Introductory Comments

Since this treatment of generalizability theory (G theory) is limited to a single chapter, it necessarily provides only a brief introduction to many important aspects of the theory. Despite the brevity, the reader is provided with an overview of all the basic concepts and procedures used in G theory. The primary objective of the chapter is to provide the learner with the background to comprehend common health science education applications of the theory in practice and in research. To achieve this goal, generalizability concepts are presented within the context of a hypothetical performance assessment measurement problem. Computational methods and equations are presented only when they promote the reader's conceptual understanding of the theory. To assist those interested in delving deeper into the technical aspects of the theory, notation and terminology is largely consistent with Brennan's authoritative text: *Generalizability Theory* (Brennan, 2001). Although some research, validity, and reliability applications become apparent only with a more in-depth treatment, this chapter will allow the reader to apply and interpret most of the commonly encountered generalizability designs.

The two appendices at the end of this chapter provide a brief description of the ANOVA-based statistical methods used in generalizability analyses. Understanding the material covered in this chapter does not require familiarity with ANOVA, hence, the two statistical appendices can be regarded optional reading.

Background and Overview

As discussed in Chapter 2, in classical test theory (CTT) there is an assumption that an observed score is composed of two components, a "true" score and random error. A shorthand way of representing this concept is:

$$Observed\ Score = True\ Score + Error, \tag{4.1}$$

and the CTT expression for reliability as:

$$Reliability = True\ Score\ /\ True\ Score + Error. \tag{4.2}$$

Similar to CTT, G theory also assumes that the variance of an observed score is partitioned between true score variance and error variance. However, G theory differs from CTT in allowing the examination of multiple sources of error, and hence expands on the CTT equation as:

$$Observed\ Score = True\ Score + Error_1 + Error_2 + Error_3 \ldots, \tag{4.3}$$

and the expression for reliability as:

$$Reliability = True\ Score\ /\ True\ Score + Error_1 + Error_2 + Error_3. \ldots \tag{4.4}$$

In conceptualizing score variance to fall into two broad categories (true score and error), G theory shares a common theoretical framework with CTT. However, G theory differs dramatically from CTT in the details related to estimating the variances associated with both the true score and error, and in its use of these variance estimates to calculate multiple reliability-like coefficients that are appropriate to specific applications.[1] In Chapter 3 it was noted that in CTT, when a measurement process has more than one dimension or *facet* over which measures are averaged, different reliability coefficients can characterize the score. For example, if a measurement process uses raters to rate tasks on a multiple-item form, CTT methods could calculate an inter-rater reliability coefficient, an "inter-task" reliability coefficient, or an internal consistency (split-half) alpha statistic. However, it would be difficult to meaningfully integrate these different CTT measures and globally assess reliability. On the other hand,

G theory can characterize how accurately an obtained score estimates a hypothetical score derived by averaging across many replications of a multi-faceted measurement process. In G theory, this average score, or *universe score*, similar to a "true" score in CTT, is carefully defined in relation to all identified *facets* of the measurement process, and provides a more comprehensive assessment of reliability. In G theory, the *facets* of a measurement problem specify the *conditions of measurement*. In explaining the concepts associated with the *facets* and the *conditions of measurement*, it is useful at this point to introduce a hypothetical performance assessment problem that will be used throughout this chapter to demonstrate the concepts and procedures used in G theory. This problem, designed for instructional purposes, employs a small synthetic data set to demonstrate generalizability study (G study) procedures and to allow the reader to confirm reported statistical findings with simple hand calculations.

The Instructional Problem

A medical education researcher is asked to report on the reliability of test scores from a piloted version of an Objective Structured Clinical Examination (OSCE), and to make recommendations for structuring a larger operational version of the test. The researcher has been provided with global ratings of ten examinees' videotaped performances on a 5-station OSCE exam. The hypothetical ratings, displayed in Table 4.1, represent ratings by two expert physician raters independently rating the ten examinees' performances on a 10-point scale. CTT methods could be used to calculate an inter-rater reliability coefficient or an inter-task reliability coefficient, but it would be difficult to simultaneously represent the multiple sources of error and to meaningfully integrate the CTT coefficients. Therefore, the researcher decides to use G theory to address the measurement problem.

Defining the G Study Model

Before analyzing the information presented in Table 4.1, the researcher must first define the G study measurement model. Reflecting on the

Table 4.1 Data for the Example OSCE Measurement Problem: Ratings from a Piloted Version of the OSCE Examination

	STA 1		STA 2		STA 3		STA 4		STA 5	
	R1	R2	R1	R2	R1	R2	R1	R2	R1	R2
Ex1	5	5	5	5	4	5	5	5	4	5
Ex2	4	7	4	4	4	7	8	9	5	4
Ex3	6	6	8	8	8	7	6	6	5	5
Ex4	0	5	5	5	4	5	5	4	1	1
Ex5	4	4	3	5	5	6	6	4	4	4
Ex6	3	6	5	8	6	4	7	7	4	3
Ex7	2	2	6	5	7	5	5	5	1	2
Ex8	4	5	8	7	8	7	6	6	5	4
Ex9	2	2	7	6	6	7	5	5	3	3
Ex10	3	7	4	7	4	6	4	4	2	3

Notes: STA = Station R = Rater Ex = Examinee

conditions of measurement, or how the data was collected, the researcher observes that the same two expert raters rated all examinees on each of the five stations, and that the exam was designed to assess students' clinical skills. With this information, the researcher can define some important aspects of the G study model. First, since the exam was designed as a measure of examinee performance, as opposed to rater or station performance, the researcher can conclude that the examinee is the *object of measurement.* Once the *object of measurement* has been identified, the researcher can further assume that the remaining conditions of measurement, raters and stations, represent *facets* in the G study measurement model. In this example, there are two *facets*, raters and stations. It should be noted that there may be other important measurement *facets* or influences related to the measures obtained in Table 4.1, however, the researcher does not have information characterizing these other influences.

The researcher is now ready to formally specify a G study model that will represent how the measures within the OSCE exam were collected. In doing so, it is important to first provide some formal definitions along with the notational conventions used in model specifications. First, we must define what we mean by an *object of measurement.* The *object of measurement* is defined as the member of the sample or population that the examination is designed to assess. In most testing applications, the *object of measurement* is the examinee, commonly referred to as the person (p). The notational convention in the majority of G studies is to represent persons, the *object of measurement*, with the small letter "p". After identifying the *object of measurement*, the *facets* within a G study are identified by default as the other main sources of variation in the G study model. A *facet* represents a dimension or source of variation across which the researcher wishes to generalize. In our example problem, we have two *facets*, raters (r) and stations (s), with the first letter of their spelled name representing the *facet*. Hence, in this problem "r" and "s" will represent raters and stations respectively.

Again, considering our example problem, every person (p) experiences every station (s) and is rated by the same two raters (r) on each station. The shorthand way of expressing this concept in generalizability terminology is to say all conditions of measurement are completely *crossed*. The notation for the *crossed* concept is the symbol "x". So, with these simple notational conventions, we can write a symbolic expression that summarizes the G study model as: [p x s x r]. Hence, our G study model is a persons *crossed* with stations *crossed* with raters design. Not all G study models are completely *crossed*. For example, it would be possible to conduct an OSCE exam, similar to the one described in the example problem, using a different pair of raters for each station. In generalizability terminology, this is called a *nested* design and is represented by the symbol ":". For instance, had the ratings been collected using two different raters for each station, we would have represented the G study design as: [p x (r : s)]. In G theory terminology, this would be a persons *crossed* with raters *nested* within stations model design. There will be additional discussions of design variations throughout this chapter.

All G study models must define whether the facets are *random* or *fixed*. A facet is considered *random* when observed values of the facet within the G study are regarded as a sample from a larger population. In our example problem, both raters and stations are considered *random* variables. Hence, in G theory terminology, we would define our G study model from the example problem as being a *random model*.

The reason we consider stations as *random* is that our interest is not focused solely on the five stations observed. Rather, the goal of the measurement process is to generalize from performance on the five stations to performance on a universe of similar stations from which the five stations are a sample. In the example problem, the same argument applies to raters. The two expert physician raters employed in the pilot exam are considered a sample from a population of potential expert physician raters we might use or consider acceptable to rate performance. For example, if no special rater training of the physician raters was provided, the population of acceptable raters might reasonably be defined as: academic physicians at U.S. medical schools. However, if the two academic physician raters in the study received special rater training, we would need to modify our definition of the rater universe as academic physicians who received the special rater training. A facet is regarded as *fixed* when all levels of a facet are observed in the G study. An example of a fixed facet will be presented later in the chapter.

Obtaining G Study Results

Now that the basic G study model has been presented, the next step in the G study is to obtain G study results. *Variance components* (VCs) represent the primary output of a G study analysis. VCs are estimates of the magnitude of variability of each effect in the G study model. The model in the example problem has three main effects: the object of measurement, persons (p), and the two facets, stations (s) and raters (r). In addition, as in analysis of variance (ANOVA), there are also interactions. So, in addition to p, s and r, there are four interaction effects; ps, pr, sr and psr. Therefore, in the example problem, the G study will estimate a total of seven VCs (p, s, r, ps, pr, sr, psr). A description of these effects and how to interpret them is presented shortly. The statistical procedures for the estimation of the VCs are presented in Appendix 4.1.

Table 4.2 displays the G study output for the data displayed in Table 4.1. The VCs in Table 4.2 can be calculated using GENOVA® software (Crick & Brennan, 1982), which is specially designed for

Table 4.2 G Study Results for Example Problem [p x s x r]

Effect	DF	Variance Component (VC)	Standard Error (SE)	Percent Variance
p	9	0.5706	0.3745	16
s	4	1.0156	0.7003	29
r	1	0.0361	0.0851	1
ps	36	0.6694	0.2823	19
pr	9	0.1139	0.1355	3
sr	4	0.1528	0.1439	4
psr	36	0.9372	0.2150	27

(handwritten annotations: person, station, rater)

conducting G study and decision study (D study) analyses and automatically outputs VCs and other statistical information important in the G study analysis. These same results can also be derived with SAS's VARCOMP procedure or with BMDP's V8 statistical software.

Interpreting G Study Results

The first column of Table 4.2 lists each of the effects estimated in the G study, the *main* effects (p, s, r) and the *interaction* effects (ps, pr, sr, psr). The second column displays the degrees of freedom. The third column of Table 4.2 displays the VC values for each of the seven effects estimated. The fourth column of Table 4.2 lists the standard error (SE) for each VC estimate. The fifth column provides the percentage of the total variance represented by each VC.

In the first row of Table 4.2 we observe that 16% of the variance is attributable to systematic differences between examinees (p). This is object of measurement variance and is similar to "true" score variance in CTT. The ratio definition of reliability provided in Equation 4.4 suggests that the larger the percentage of variance accounted for by p, the higher will be the obtained reliability. The second row of Table 4.2 displays the systematic variance attributable to station, and it reflects the degree to which the stations have different means. The station effect, accounting for the largest percentage of variance (29%) in the model, implies that there were considerable differences in the level of difficulty between stations in our sample. The third row shows the variance associated with the systematic effects of rater, and it reflects the difference in raters' overall mean scores across stations and persons. In the example problem, the small proportion of variance related to raters (1%) suggests that the mean difference between raters is small, or stated another way, that the two raters were approximately equal in their overall level of stringency.

The fourth row in Table 4.2 displays the person by station (ps) interaction. This indicates the degree to which stations tended to rank-order persons (examinees) differently. The relatively large amount of variance (19%) attributed to this interaction (ps) suggests that examinee rank orders would change considerably depending on which station(s) were sampled. The person by rater (pr) interaction is relatively small at just 3%, and suggests that raters tended to agree on the ratings assigned to an examinee at a given station, or that rank orders would not change dramatically based upon which single rater's ratings were used. The station by rater (sr) interaction was also small (4%), indicating that the level of station difficulty changed little depending on which rater assigned the ratings. The psr VC accounted for 27% of the total variance and is a confounded measure of the triple interaction of person, station, and rater, and influences not modeled in the [p x s x r] design.

The standard errors (SE) in the fourth column of Table 4.2 convey the level of precision with which we were able to estimate the population VCs. The SE can be interpreted as an estimated standard deviation of a VC estimate upon multiple estimations from multiple replications using the same sample sizes. It should be observed that the SE estimates in Table 4.2 are rather large relative to the size of the VC estimates. This can be attributed to the small sample sizes employed within the G study and suggest that the estimates are likely to display large variability between replications employing these sample sizes.

Conducting the D Study

In the description of our example problem, it was noted that the researcher was asked not only to characterize the reliability of the scores from the pilot test, but also to make recommendations for how an operational version of the test might best be structured. A *decision study* (D study) can provide reliability estimates both for the scores collected in the G study and also for tests employing different designs and sample sizes. Hence, a D study can address questions related to how best to optimize test design. The structure of the G study determines what designs a D study can address. Completely crossed designs allow for the maximum number of addressable designs. A D study uses VCs from the G study to calculate estimated reliability coefficients given variations in the conditions of measurement. In this instance, the researcher using a D study could estimate not only the reliability of the test with the observed conditions of measurement (a completely crossed random model with two raters crossed with five stations), but could also estimate the reliability of a test using any number of raters or stations administered using either the same crossed OSCE test design or a different design (e.g., a nested design). Using a series of D studies to examine various test structure options can help the researcher determine how best to structure an operational version of the test.

Before proceeding further, it is useful here to discuss D study notation. In the G study model of the example problem, we employed small letter notation to represent the facets. The small letter notation is a way of indicating that in the G study analysis, estimated effects are for one rating on a single station by one rater. However, in a D study we are interested in representing average ratings across a sample of conditions, and capital letters are used to indicate this. For this reason, our notational system for the D study model employs capital letters to express the D study model design. For instance, a D study model for the design in our example measurement problem is represented as: $[p \times S \times R]$.

The D study can generate two types of reliability-like coefficients: a generalizability coefficient (G or $E\rho^2$) and a measure of dependability (Phi or Φ). The G coefficient is sensitive to relative error and is useful for expressing the reproducibility of examinee rankings. The dependability measure, commonly referred to as Phi, expresses the absolute reproducibility of a score and reflects the degree to which an obtained score is likely to change upon replication of the measurement process.

Hence, if one imagines a complete replication of the OSCE measurement procedure as documented in our example problem (i.e., a sample of five different stations and two different raters), a Phi will reflect how closely a replication is likely to reproduce an examinee's final score. The G coefficient estimates how consistently a replication will rank examinees. Because of this distinction, the Phi coefficient is useful for answering questions related to criterion-referenced testing, while a G coefficient is most informative for norm-referenced testing applications. A tangible impact of the difference between the G and the Phi coefficients in our example problem is that the large variation in station difficulty (29% of the total variance) lowers Phi substantially; however this variability in station difficulty does not impact the G coefficient. This difference is best understood by considering the outcome of a replication of a [p x S x R] design. Within each replication, all examinees will experience the same stations. Hence, variation in station difficulty will not change the rank ordering of examinees across replications, and therefore will not affect the G coefficient. However, variations in station difficulty will obviously produce variation in the magnitude of the obtained mean scores across replications, and hence will lower Phi. Building on the very general definition of reliability provided in Equation 4.4, we can now write the symbolic expression for these two reliability-like coefficients as:

$$G = E\rho^2 = \frac{\sigma^2(p)}{\sigma^2(p) + \sigma^2(\delta)} \tag{4.5}$$

and

$$Phi = \Phi = \frac{\sigma^2(p)}{\sigma^2(p) + \sigma^2(\Delta)} \tag{4.6}$$

where:

$\sigma^2(p)$ = the variance associated with person,
$\sigma^2(\delta)$ = the sum of relative error variances, and
$\sigma^2(\Delta)$ = the sum of absolute error variances.

Absolute error variance (Δ) includes all sources of error. Relative error (δ) includes only those sources of error variance that will impact examinee rank ordering. This implies that for all D study designs, absolute error will always be greater than or equal to relative error. Hence, Phi (Φ) will always be less than or equal to G ($E\rho^2$). Appendix 4.2 provides additional detail regarding what VCs, or sources of error, are included as part of absolute and relative error calculations. Colliver et al. (Colliver, Verhulst, Williams, & Norcini, 1989) provide an excellent in-depth treatment of how various reliability-like measures can be computed and interpreted within a performance assessment context. As part of the D study in our example problem, Phi (Φ) and G ($E\rho^2$) results were calculated, using Equations 4.12 and 4.13 from Appendix 4.2, and displayed in Table 4.3.

Interpreting the D Study

In interpreting a D study, it is often helpful to graphically display the results as shown in Figure 4.1. When the G coefficients from Table 4.3 are graphed across levels of the two facets, several important outcomes become apparent. First, small gains in reliability are observed by using more than one rater, and increasing the number of raters beyond two yields negligible improvements. On the other hand, utilizing multiple stations substantially increases reliability. For example, increasing the number of stations from one to five increases G by as much as 0.35. In addition, this D study also suggests that the addition

Table 4.3 D Study Results for Example Problem [p x S x R]

Number of Raters	Number of Stations	G ($E\rho^2$)	Phi (Φ)
1	1	0.25	0.16
1	5	0.56	0.45
1	10	0.67	0.57
2	1	0.32	0.20
2	5	0.67*	0.52*
2	10	0.77	0.66
3	1	0.36	0.21
3	5	0.71	0.55
3	10	0.81	0.69

Note: * G and Phi for the mean scores obtained in the G study.

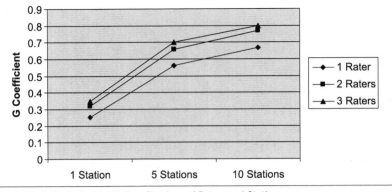

Figure 4.1 G Coefficient for Various Numbers of Raters and Stations.

of stations after the fifth continues to produce appreciable gains in the estimated reliability. To obtain a summary of how the number of raters and stations impacts the dependability of scores, the Phi values in the last column of Table 4.3 could also be plotted in a similar fashion to aid in interpretability. Although the pattern is much the same for Phi and G in our example problem, because stations tended to exhibit considerable variability in difficulty, Phi values are smaller compared to the G coefficients for a given number of stations and raters.

There is a broad G study literature on SP assessments. Van der Vlueten and Swanson (van der Vlueten & Swanson, 1990) provide a useful summary of major findings. For example, they note that in most SP studies the primary source of measurement error is due to variation in examinee performance from station to station (ps variance—sometimes referred to as content specificity variance). This implies that in most instances adding stations is considerably more effective in increasing reliability than adding raters. This finding is particularly true for SP exams employing checklists where inter-rater agreement is generally high.

G and D Study Model Variations

As previously discussed, specialized software is capable of handling many of the technical aspects in G and D study analyses. However, to successfully utilize G study software it is essential that the researcher accurately specify G and D study models. This section briefly discusses two additional measurement examples and considers commonly encountered G and D study model variations.

Our example OSCE problem presented a two-faceted [p x s x r] random model design. However, many commonly encountered G study models use only one facet. For example, a typical standardized multiple-choice test can be modeled as a simple persons (p) crossed (x) with items (i) one-faceted random model design [p x i]. A [p x i] G study design yields estimates for three effects: p, i and pi, and the G coefficient for this design would be:

$$G = E\rho^2 = \frac{\sigma^2\,(p)}{\sigma^2\,(p) + \sigma^2\,(pi)\,/\,n_i} \qquad (4.7)$$

and is equivalent to Cronbach's coefficient alpha. The Phi for the multiple-choice test example is:

$$Phi = \Phi = \frac{\sigma^2\,(p)}{\sigma^2\,(p) + \sigma^2\,(i)\,/\,n_i + \sigma^2\,(pi)\,/\,n_i} \qquad (4.8)$$

To demonstrate a *fixed* facet within a G study, imagine a written test employing two formats (f), multiple-choice (MC) and true–false (TF). Since it is logically impossible for an item to be in both formats, the reader should recognize first that a test employing both formats (MC & TF) implies that items must be nested within format (i : f). Second, since the two formats do not represent a sample from a population of many possible formats, the MC and TF formats are quite likely the only two formats of interest in the study. Given that the two observed levels of format are not a sample from a larger population of formats, and that the two formats represent the only two formats of interest, format (f) is regarded as a *fixed* rather than a random facet. This further implies that the model is *mixed* since it contains both a random facet (items) and a fixed facet (format). Hence, the G study design would be a persons (p) crossed (x) with items (i) nested (:) within format (f) mixed model design [p x (i : f)].

This chapter has briefly discussed modeling concepts of just four G study designs ([p x i], [p x (i : f)], [p x s x r] and [p x (r : s)]).

Even though variants of G study models grow rapidly with the addition of facets, nesting, and mixed model conditions, these four models provide the reader with the building blocks and core concepts to model most commonly encountered designs. As it is beyond the scope of this chapter to provide the reader with an exhaustive list of models, the reader is encouraged to reference texts offering a wider presentation on model detail and design (Brennan, 2001; Shavelson & Webb, 1991; Norman, 2003).

Final Considerations

G theory provides a powerful method for examining a wide array of both simple and complex measures. A thorough consideration of G and D study results can provide a better understanding of the measurement process and how to improve it. Through the facilitation of insights regarding validity and reliability, G theory methods provide social scientists with a powerful research tool. The reader is encouraged to explore more advanced demonstrations of the theory to gain an appreciation of G theory's many applications to health science education.

APPENDIX 4.1: STATISTICAL FOUNDATIONS OF A GENERALIZABILITY STUDY

To understand the derivation of the VC, it is necessary to briefly review methods employed in ANOVA. In ANOVA, *sums of squares* (SS), characterize the distribution of scores around a mean. For example, the total SS in our example problem can be computed as:

$$\Sigma_p \Sigma_s \Sigma_r (X_{psr} - \overline{X})^2 \tag{4.9}$$

where:

Σ is the summation operator,
X_{psr} is a rating for a single person on one station by a single rater,
$\overline{X}$ is the grand mean across all raters, stations and persons.

Hence, the total SS in our example problem is simply the sum of the squared difference of each rating subtracted from the overall mean. The three summation operators (Σ) in Equation 4.9 simply indicate this sum is performed across all persons (p), stations (s) and raters (r). To continue with this example, the SS for stations (s) can be calculated using Equation 4.10. This equation contains just one summation operator, indicating the sum is across just stations. Hence, Equation 4.10 indicates that the SS for stations equals the sum of the squared differences between each stations mean and the grand mean, multiplied by the number of persons (n_p) and raters (n_r). A derivation for the SS for each SS follows similar notation and techniques. It is beyond the scope of this chapter to provide the complete derivation of all SS, however, an in-depth treatment of ANOVA estimation methods is provided in Kirk's *Experimental Design* (Kirk, 1982).

$$SS_{(s)} = n_p \, n_r \, \Sigma_s \, (\overline{X}_s - \overline{X})^2 \tag{4.10}$$

Table 4.4 displays the ANOVA results from the data set in Table 4.1. In the first column is the source of the variance, and the second column displays the degrees of freedom (df) for that source of variance. Dividing the SS (column 3) by the degrees of freedom yields the mean squares (MS) displayed in the fourth column of Table 4.4.

The fifth column of Table 4.4 expresses the expected mean squares (EMS) in terms of variance components (σ^2), and the number of raters (n_r), stations (n_s), and persons (n_p) sampled. The EMSs describes the composition of the MSs, or what elements of variance comprise a MS

Table 4.4 ANOVA Table [p x s x r]

Effect	DF	Sum-of-Squares (SS)	Mean Square (MS)	Expected Mean Square (EMS)
p	9	76.96	8.55	$\sigma^2(psr) + n_s \, \sigma^2(pr) + n_r$ $\sigma^2(ps) + n_s \, n_r \, \sigma^2(p)$
s	4	96.46	24.12	$\sigma^2(psr) + n_p \, \sigma^2(sr) + n_r$ $\sigma^2(ps) + n_p \, n_r \, \sigma^2(s)$
r	1	4.84	4.84	$\sigma^2(psr) + n_p \, \sigma^2(sr) + n_s$ $\sigma^2(pr) + n_p \, n_s \, \sigma^2(r)$
ps	36	81.94	2.28	$\sigma^2(psr) + n_r \, \sigma^2(ps)$
pr	9	13.56	1.51	$\sigma^2(psr) + n_s \, \sigma^2(pr)$
sr	4	9.86	2.47	$\sigma^2(psr) + n_p \, \sigma^2(sr)$
psr	36	33.74	0.94	$\sigma^2(psr)$

obtained from a sample. The MS values in Table 4.4 are for the sample data in Table 4.1. It is important to note that because the MSs are calculated on a sample, only in the case of the psr interaction will the sample MS act as an estimator of the population VC ($\hat{\sigma}^2$) (the "^" symbol over the σ^2 indicates that it is an estimate of the population variance). As shown in the fifth column of Table 4.4, for MS values calculated from a sample, the MS includes both the effect of interest and also other interactions. An estimate of a population VC is derived algebraically, solving in reverse for each VC using observed sample MSs. For example, as indicated in the last row of Table 4.4, for the triple interaction effect (psr) the MS from the sample directly estimates the population VC for the psr effect. Therefore, by using this MS(psr) as an estimated variance component for psr ($\hat{\sigma}^2$(psr)) in the double interaction (ps, pr & sr) EMS equations, simple algebra permits one to isolate the estimated population VCs ($\hat{\sigma}^2$) for each of the double interactions (e.g. $\hat{\sigma}^2$(sr) = (2.47 − 0.94) / 10 = 0.153). Deriving the estimated population VCs ($\hat{\sigma}^2$) for the three main effects (σ^2(p), σ^2(s), σ^2(r)) is only slightly more complicated. For example, the VC for persons can be estimated by inserting the MSs from Table 4.4 into Equation 4.11. Similar equations exist for estimating each population VC with observed sample MS values. Brennan (Brennan, 2001) provides a complete description of the rules and methods used for estimating population VCs from MSs obtained from a sample. Fortunately, specialized statistical software (GENOVA, SAS and BMDP) is capable of computing estimated VCs for the user, and in practice, researchers are not required to manually derive VC estimates.

$$\hat{\sigma}^2_{(p)} = \frac{MS_{(p)} - MS_{(ps)} - MS_{(pr)} + MS_{(psr)}}{n_s\,n_r} \qquad (4.11)$$

APPENDIX 4.2: STATISTICAL FOUNDATIONS OF A DECISION STUDY

This appendix presents the logical and technical background for understanding the ratios used to compute G and Phi coefficients.

Again, employing the design used in the example problem, let us consider what the ratio for the G coefficient would be using various numbers of raters and stations. Equation 4.12 expresses the D study G coefficient as a ratio of VCs. Equation 4.13 expresses the D study Phi as a ratio of VCs. Estimated VCs can be used in Equation 4.12 and 4.13 to provide D study reliability estimates. The reader is encouraged to verify the results reported in Table 4.3 by using Equations 4.12 and 4.13 with the appropriate sample sizes and the VC estimates from Table 4.2. It should be noted that the denominator for the Phi (Equation 4.13) contains all sources of error, whereas the denominator for G (Equation 4.12) contains just the error sources impacting examinee rankings. The reader should additionally recognize that equations 4.12 and 4.13 are simply a more detailed version of equations 4.5 and 4.6 respectively.

$$G = E\rho^2 = \frac{\sigma^2(p)}{\sigma^2(p) + \sigma^2(ps) \,/\, n_s + \sigma^2(pr) \,/\, n_r + \sigma^2(psr) \,/\, n_s\, n_r} \quad (4.12)$$

$$Phi = \Phi = \frac{\sigma^2(p)}{\sigma^2(p) + \sigma^2(s) \,/\, n_s + \sigma^2(r) \,/\, n_r + \sigma^2(ps) \,/\, n_s + \sigma^2(pr) \,/\, n_r + \sigma^2(sr) \,/\, n_s\, n_r + \sigma^2(psr) \,/\, n_s\, n_r} \quad (4.13)$$

For each D study design there is an associated pair of G and Phi equations similar to Equations 4.12 and 4.13, but unique to the D study design. By inserting the appropriate values for n_r and n_s, the number of raters and stations, Equations 4.12 and 4.13 are appropriate for all [p x S x R] designs with any number of stations and raters. However, if the researcher would choose to examine other designs, such as a [p x (R : S)] design for example, a different D study equation would apply. A more detailed treatment of these equations can be found in G theory texts (Brennan, 2001; Shavelson & Webb, 1991). One of the primary strengths of G theory relates to the fact that it is easy to use G study results to calculate G and Phi for designs different from that employed in the G study.

Note

1. As the statistical estimation methods used in a G study are derived from analysis of variance, G theory also shares much in common with analysis of variance. However, there are also important differences between analysis of variance and G theory. The most salient difference is G theory's reliance on variance components and the fact that hypothesis and significance testing does not play a role in a G study analysis.

References

Brennan, R.L. (2001). *Generalizability theory*. New York: Springer-Verlag.

Crick, J.E., & Brennan, R.L. (1982) GENOVA®—A generalized analysis of variance software system (Version 3.1) [Computer software]. University of Iowa, Iowa City, IA. Available from http://www.education. uiowa.edu/casma/GenovaPrograms.htm.

Colliver, J.A., Verhulst, S.J., Williams, R.G., & Norcini, J.J. (1989). Reliability of performance on standardized patient cases: A comparison of consistency measures based on generalizability theory. *Teaching and Learning in Medicine*, 1(1), 31–7.

Kirk, R.E. (1982). *Experimental design: Procedures for the behavioral sciences* (2nd ed.) Pacific Grove, CA: Brooks/Cole Publishing.

Norman, G.R. (2003). Generalizability theory. In D.L. Streiner & G.R. Norman, *Health measurement scales: A practical guide to their development and use* (3rd ed., pp. 153–171). New York: Oxford University Press.

Shavelson, R.J., & Webb, N.M. (1991). *Generalizability theory: A primer*. Newbury Park, CA: Sage.

van der Vleuten, C.P.M., & Swanson, D.B. (1990). Assessment of clinical skills with standardized patients: State of the art. *Teaching and Learning in Medicine*, 2(2), 58–76.

5

STATISTICS OF TESTING

STEVEN M. DOWNING

Introduction

This chapter discusses some of the statistics commonly utilized in testing. Since this book focuses primarily on tests and other types of measures which result in quantitative data, some statistics are inevitable. Many of the tools used to evaluate tests and other measures used in health professions education require the application of some basic quantitative methods or statistics applied to testing.

As in other chapters, this treatment of statistics in testing is general and applied, avoiding statistical proofs and theoretical explanations and derivations. The purpose of this chapter is to give the reader an overview of some commonly used statistical techniques, their purpose and rationale, together with examples of their computation and use.

Using Test Scores

Assessments in health professions education generally yield quantitative data. Thus, it is important to consider some basic uses of such data, including various types of scores and score scale properties, and correlation and some of its special applications in assessment. A few basic statistical formulas that are useful in health professions education settings will also be presented.

Basic Score Types

Test or assessment data can be expressed as many different types of scores or on many different types of score scales. Each type of score or score scale has its advantages and disadvantages and each has certain properties that must be understood in order to properly and legitimately interpret the scores. This section notes some basic information about various types of scores and score scales commonly used in health professions education.

Table 5.1 summarizes various types of scores used in assessment and their characteristics.

Number Correct Scores or Raw Scores For all assessments that are scored dichotomously as right or wrong, such as written achievement tests, the most basic score is the *number correct score*. The number correct or raw score is simply the count of the number of test items the examinee answered correctly. The number correct score or raw score is useful for nearly all types of statistical analyses, score reporting to examinees, and research analyses. The raw score is basic and fundamental and it is therefore useful for nearly all testing applications.

Table 5.1 Types of Scores

Score	Definition	Advantages	Limitations
Raw Scores	Count of number correct; raw ratings	Straightforward; simple to compute, understand, interpret	No relative meaning; need to know total number of items, prompts, points
Percent-correct Scores	Percentage of raw number correct	Simple to compute; widely used and understood	Can not be used with all statistical calculations; may be misleading
Standard Scores	Linear transformed score in SD units	Easily computed and explained relative score; linear transformation; useful in all statistics	May not be familiar to all users
Percentiles	Score rank in distribution	Commonly used and reported; easily computed; traditional score	Easily misunderstood, misused; not useful in statistical calculations; non-equal intervals; often misinterpreted
Equated Scores	Score statistically adjusted to maintain constancy of meaning, score scale	Interchangeability of scores on different test forms, from different administrations	Complex statistical calculations; complex assumptions

Percent-correct Scores   Raw scores are frequently converted to or transformed to *percent-correct scores* in health professions education settings. The percent-correct score is a simple linear transformation of the raw or number-correct score to a percentage, using the formula:

Percent-correct score = (Raw Score / number of items) * 100

The percent-correct score is a linear transformation, which means that the raw scores and percent-correct scores correspond one-to-one and the basic shape of the underlying distribution does not change. Generally, if percent or percent-correct scores are reported and used, one should also report the raw score upon which the percent-correct score is based. (Percents can be misused and can be misleading in some applications, especially when they are presented as the only data.) Also, percent-correct scores do not work properly with all statistical formulas commonly used to evaluate tests (such as the Kuder-Richardson formula 21 used to estimate scale reliability), so it is usually best to use raw scores or linear standard scores in most statistical calculations.

Derived Scores or Standard Scores   Several types of derived or linear standard scores are used in assessment applications. The linear standard score scale is expressed in the standard deviation (SD) score units of the original score distribution. The basic linear standard score, the *z-score*, has a mean of 0 and an SD of 1, and is computed by the following formula:

z-score = (X – mean) / SD
    where:
    X = raw score
    Mean = mean of the raw score distribution
    SD = standard deviation of the raw score distribution

Table 5.2 gives an example of ten raw scores and their transformation to z-scores with a further transformation to *T-scores*, which are defined as having a mean of 50, with an SD of 10. Some users prefer T-scores, because T-scores eliminate negative values and a mean score

Table 5.2 Raw Scores, z-Scores, and T-Scores

Raw Score	z-Score	T-Score
41.00	−.30921	46.91
45.00	−.07584	49.24
50.00	.21587	52.16
55.00	.50758	55.08
60.00	.79929	57.99
74.00	1.61608	66.16
18.00	−1.65108	33.49
20.00	−1.53440	34.66
55.00	.50758	55.08
45.00	−.07584	49.24
Mean = 46.3 (SD = 17.1)	Mean = 0; SD = 1	Mean = 50; SD = 10

equal to zero, which the z-score transformation yields. (Some students may be discouraged to receive a negative score, for example.)

The T-score formula is 10 (z-score) + 50. But, you can create a standard score with any mean and SD you wish. Simply multiply the z-score by a desired SD and add the desired mean score to this quantity (SD*(z-score) + desired mean).

The main advantage of these types of derived or standard scores is that they put score data in the metric of the standard deviation of the original raw scores, and maintain the exact shape of the original score distribution. For example, if the original raw scores are skewed to the right (which means that more students score to the high side of the mean than the low side of the mean) the standard score will have exactly the same shape as the original scores. This is a desirable characteristic for most scores that are computed in assessment settings. Other advantages of standard scores such as z- and T-scores is that they can be used in all other statistical calculations such as correlations, t-tests, and ANOVA, plus they can provide easily interpretable absolute and relative score information.

Normalized Standard Scores   It is possible to carry out another type of score transformation which normalizes or forces the transformed distribution of scores to be normally distributed or to follow the normal curve. These normalized standard scores are sometimes used by large testing agencies for research purposes, but are rarely used in health professions education classrooms or reported at the local university level, since there is little benefit to normalizing scores for these ordinary applications. Standard scores, such as z- and T-scores, are not *normalized* scores, since such derived scores maintain the exact shape of the underlying raw score distribution. Simple z- and T-scores should therefore not be referred to as *normalized scores*.

Percentiles Percentiles or percentile ranks are a favorite type of standard score in health professions education. Percentiles have several slightly different definitions, but generally a percentile refers to a score at or below which that percentage of examinees falls on some distribution of scores.

Percentiles are an inherently relative score, with some benefits and many limitations. The advantage of percentiles is that they are commonly reported and easily computed. Most users think they understand the proper interpretation of percentiles or percentile ranks, yet they are frequently misunderstood or misinterpreted.

Percentiles usually have very unequal intervals, so that, for instance, the 5-point interval between the 50th and 55th percentiles is most likely not the same as the 5-point interval between the 90th and 95th percentile. For example, for a student to increase her test score from the 90th to the 95th percentile typically requires answering many more items correct than to move from the 50th to 55th percentile, because of unequal intervals on the percentile scale. Also, if the underlying raw score distribution upon which percentiles are based is normally distributed, then percentile ranks can be used to make familiar standard score-type of interpretations such as "84 percent of scores fall below + 1 SD above the mean score." But, if the underlying score distribution is non-normal or skewed, as most classroom-type test score distributions are, this interpretation may be incorrect.

Also, percentiles have limited usefulness in other statistical calculations. For example, one cannot legitimately compute correlations of percentiles or use percentiles in inferential statistics, such as *t-tests* or *ANOVA*. Percentiles may be used only to report the rank of the examinee with respect to whatever reference group is used for percentile calculation. And, percentiles may be misunderstood by some users as simple percent-correct scores, which is an incorrect interpretation.

Because of all these limitations, caution is urged in the use and reporting of percentiles or percentile ranks. Linear standard scores, such as z- or T-scores or their variants, are preferred, because there are many fewer limitations for these types of scores and there may be less potential for misinterpretation, misuse, or misunderstanding. Standard scores can be used in almost all statistical calculations, including correlations, inferential statistics, and so on. Plus, standard scores also indicate relative standing using the standard deviation units of the underlying distribution. Generally, derived scores such as z- or T-scores are considered to have equal-interval properties, making the absolute (as opposed to relative) interpretation of these scores more straightforward.

Corrections for Guessing: Formula Scores   One of the persistent controversies in educational measurement concerns the use of so-called "corrections for guessing" or "formula scores" (e.g., Downing, 2003; Downing, Chapter 7, this volume.). These formula scores attempt to compensate for random guessing on selected-response test items, such as multiple-choice items, by either rewarding non-guessing behavior on tests or by punishing guessing behavior. Generally, neither approach works very well and may in fact be somewhat harmful. Since the tendency to guess on selected-response items is a psychological characteristic which varies across a group of examinees, any attempt to control or compensate for presumed guessing is likely to create some error in the measurement. In fact, since the tendency to guess is a psychological construct—which certain bold examinees may exhibit even if they are directed not to guess and threatened with loss of fractional score points—the so-called "corrections for guessing" may add construct-irrelevant variance (CIV) to the scores. CIV, as noted in Chapter 2, is the reliable measurement of some construct other than that which is intended to be measured by the assessment.

Generally, formula scoring or corrections for guessing are not recommended. Simple raw scores or derived or standard scores, in addition to percent-correct scores, are typically sufficient. The best defense against random guessing in selected-response test items is to present well written items in sufficient numbers to reduce any ill effect of random guessing on the part of some examinees.

Equated Scores   Most high-stakes large scale testing programs use and report an *equated standard score*. This score may look similar to standard scores such as z-scores or some variant of the z-score. But, these equated scores can be interpreted differently than linear standard scores and are considerably more complex than simple linear standard scores. Equated scores statistically adjust the average difficulty of test scores up or down slightly in order to hold constant the exact meaning of the measuring scale over time and over various administrations of the test. If this statistical adjustment is carried out properly, equated scores maintain the same meaning over time and test forms and can be legitimately compared and interpreted across different test administrations and different time periods of test administration. In statistical jargon, if the test scores are successfully equated, it is a matter of indifference which test form (at which test administration) the examinee takes because the resulting scores are on the same scale (Kolen & Brennan, 2004).

Test score equating is beyond the scope of this chapter. The major consideration to note here is that equated scores, such as those reported by large-scale testing agencies like the National Board of Medical Examiners (NBME), the Medical Council of Canada (MCC), and the Educational Testing Service (ETS) permit more complex interpretations of scores than the simple z- and T-scores discussed here. Conversely, simple z- or T-scores can be interpreted as invariant with respect to mean difficulty, as are equated scores, only when the groups tested have approximately equal levels of ability, which rarely occurs in practice.

Composite Scores   The term *composite score* refers to a summary score that reflects multiple component scores. Commonly, a composite score is a total score (or grade) which is formed by adding scores from multiple scores generated during a course. For instance, a total composite score may be formed by adding together (and possibly differentially weighting) various individual component test or assessment scores for a class or a clerkship. A simple example of a composite score is a total score which is formed by averaging differentially weighted individual test scores collected during a semester-long class in which several different tests are administered to students. Instructors decide how much to weight each individual test score (and inform students of these weights), then apply these policy weights to test scores prior to summing in order to form an overall composite score, upon which the final grade is determined.

In order to ensure that the weights for each individual component score is exact, it is best to transform each component score to a linear standard score, using the mean and standard deviation of that score distribution, prior to multiplying by the assigned policy weight. If scores are not standardized, the effective weighting may be quite different from the weight applied to the raw scores, since the test score distribution with the larger standard deviation will contribute more weight to the final composite score than component scores with a lower SD (Stagnaro-Green, Deng, Downing & Crosson, 2004).

For composite scores in more complex settings, such as clerkships or other performance settings in health professions education, scores often display widely different scales, with widely different variances, so it is especially important to standardize component scores prior to weighting and summing to a composite. Each individual component score should first be transformed to a standard score, then multiplied by the desired weight (as determined by some rational, judgmental, or empirical process) and then summed or averaged to a final composite (which might be transformed to some other metric for convenience).

The determination of the reliability of the composite score is a special topic in reliability. In order to estimate the reliability of the composite score accurately, it is necessary to take into account the reliability of each individual component score and the weight assigned to that component. Several methods—such as the stratified alpha coefficient—are available to properly estimate the reliability of the composite score (Feldt & Brennan, 1989; Thissen & Wainer, 2001). If the differential policy weights are not considered, the reliability of the composite score will be underestimated.

Correlation and Disattenuated Correlation

Correlation coefficients are central to many statistical analyses used in assessment research. For example, correlation is a primary statistical method used in validity and reliability analyses and also for test item analysis. Various specialized types of correlation coefficients are used in test analysis and research, but all have the Pearson Product Moment Correlation as their basis. All correlations track the co-relationship between two variables, showing both the strength and the direction of any relationship. Correlation coefficients range from −1.0 to +1.0, with ±1.0 indicating a perfect relationship between the variables. A perfect negative correlation is just as strong a predictor as a perfect positive correlation. With a negative correlation, of course, the variables move in exactly opposite directions, such that as one variable increases the other variable decreases. In some test analyses which use correlation coefficients, such as the item discrimination index used in item analysis, it would be rare if the correlation of the item score (0,1) and the total test score were to reach ±1.0.

Correlation coefficients are attenuated or decreased by measurement error. For example, the correlation between test scores on two different tests, administered to the same examinees, is often used as one source of validity evidence for the test scores. But, we know that the observed correlation is lower than the "true" correlation, because unreliable measures reduce or disguise the underlying relationship between the variables. If we could know the perfectly reliable scores (the true scores) from one or both tests, we could correlate these so-called "true scores" and understand the true relationship between the underlying traits that the two tests measure.

Classical measurement theory allows us to estimate this true score correlation or, as it is often called, the disattenuated correlation coefficient. The disattenuated correlation formula is presented in more detail in the appendix of this chapter. This simple formula shows that the observed correlation is divided by the square root of the product of the reliability of each test. If the reliability of only one of the two tests is known, typically 1.0 is used for the value of the unknown reliability, since this will be the most parsimonious or conservative assumption. Obviously, the lower the reliabilities of the measures, the more correction will be observed in the disattenuated correlation coefficient.

The disattenuated correlation is a useful theoretical tool which is often reported in research studies because it helps to elucidate the underlying or true relationship between test or assessment scores and a criterion scores. But, it is important to emphasize that in actual practice, the errors of measurement—for example, the unreliability of the predictor test scores and/or the unreliability of some criterion measure—should be included in the validity coefficients, since this represents the state of nature and the actual or observed correlation of the two variables in the real world setting. Disattenuated correlation coefficients should be clearly labeled as such and always reported together with the observed correlations upon which they are based.

Item Analysis

Item analysis is a quality control tool for tests, providing quantitative data at the item-level, as well as some important summary statistics about the total test. Item analysis should be used extensively for selected-response tests such as multiple-choice tests, but can (and should) also be utilized for observational rating scale data, ratings used in performance assessment simulations, and so on. Careful review of item analysis data can help to improve the reliability and consequently the validity of scores generated by instruments. Item analysis can assist in the improvement of the quality and clarity of test items and other types of rating scale prompts. Item analysis data, which represents the history of past performance of an item, should be stored in an item bank or other secure file for development of future tests. Item analysis data is also frequently used to complete a final key validation step prior to final scoring (Downing, 2006).

In its most basic form, item analysis represents counts (and percentages) of examinee responses to the options that make up a selected-response item. In order to evaluate the performance of the item or rating scale prompt (e.g., Livingston, 2006), these counts are usually further evaluated in terms of groups of high-scoring examinees and low-scoring examinees with various statistics computed to summarize the item difficulty and item discrimination (how well the test item differentiates between high- and low-scoring students).

Item Analysis Report for Each Test Item

Table 5.3 presents a detailed annotated example of typical item analysis data for a single test item. The top portion of the table gives the text of the multiple-choice item. The middle portion of the table presents the item analysis data, followed by a description of each entry of the item analysis data. Software used to calculate item analyses differ in style, format and some of the specific statistics computed, but all are similar to the one displayed in Table 5.3. Common data entries for most item analyses are: test item number or other identifier, index of item difficulty and item discrimination, option performance usually grouped by examinee ability and a discrimination index for each option of the test item.

Looking at the detail in Table 5.3, under the heading of "Option Statistics," note a breakdown of how examinees responded to each MCQ option. The MCQ options are listed as A to E and *Other* refers to those who omitted or failed to answer this item. The column labeled "Total" is the total proportion marking each option. The keyed correct option or answer is indicated and its total is used to calculate the "Prop. Correct" for this test item. The "low" and "high" groups refer to the lowest scoring 27% and the highest scoring 27% of examinees on the total test, with the numbers in the columns indicating the proportion of examinees in each group who responded to each option. (Using the lowest and highest 27% of examinees is the minimum group size needed in order to maximize the reliable difference between these two extreme score groups, because we can be fairly

Table 5.3 Item Analysis Example

Where it is an absolute question of the welfare of our country, we must admit of no considerations of justice or injustice, or mercy or cruelty, or praise or ignominy, but putting all else aside must adopt whatever course will save its existence and preserve its liberty.

This quote is most likely from which of the following?

    A. Niccolo Machiavelli
    B. Attila the Hun
    C. King Henry VIII
    D. Vlad the Impailer
    E. Napoleon Bonaparte

Item Statistics

Option Statistics

Prop.[1] Correct	Disc.[2] Index	Point[3] Biser.	Option[4]	Total[5]	Low[6]	High[7]	Point[8] Biser.
0.70	**0.30**	**0.27**	A*[9]	0.70	0.55	0.85	0.27
			B	0.05	0.08	0.01	−0.14
			C	0.02	0.03	0.02	−0.01
			D	0.13	0.18	0.07	−0.13
			E	0.10	0.16	0.04	−0.15
			Other	0.00	0.00	0.00	0.00

Guide to Item Analysis Statistics

1. Proportion Correct (p-value): The total proportion (percentage) of examinees who marked the item correct. In this example, the p-value or item difficulty is 0.70, indicating that 70% of all examinees who attempted this question marked it correct.
2. Discrimination Index (D): This discrimination index is the simple difference between the percentage of a high and low group of examinees who mark the item correct. In this example, $D = (0.85 - 0.55) = 0.30$.
3. Point Biserial Correlation/Discrimination Index (r_{pbis}): Correlation between the item score (0,1) and the total score on the test.
4. Option: The item options (1–5 or A–E). Other refers to missing data or blanks.
5. Total: Total proportion (percent) marking each option or alternative answer.
6. Low (Group): Proportion marking each option or alternative answer in the lowest scoring group of examinees on the total test. In this case, the group of examinees scoring in the lowest 27% of the total score distribution.
7. High (Group): Proportion marking each option or alternative answer in the highest scoring group of examinees on the total test. In this case, the group of examinees scoring in the highest 27% of the total score distribution.
8. Point Biserial Discrimination Index: This is the r_{pbis} for each option of the item, including the correct option. Note that, for the keyed correct option, the r_{pbis} is the same as noted in #3.
9. * Answer Key: The keyed correct answer.

certain that there is no overlap in group membership between the upper and lower 27% proficiency groupings.)

Item Difficulty

Item difficulty refers to the proportion of examinees who answer an item correctly. This index is usually expressed as a proportion or percent, such as *0.60* which means that 60% of the group of test takers answered the item correctly. (This index might more accurately be called an item easiness index, since it reflects proportion correct but it is usually referred to as an item difficulty index.)

The item difficulty index is the most basic essential information to evaluate about the performance of the test item.

Item Discrimination

Effective test items differentiate high-ability examinees from low-ability examinees. (Ability means achievement proficiency in this context.) This is a fundamental principle of all educational measurement and a basic validity principle. For example, an achievement test in head and neck anatomy purports to measure this achievement construct in a unified manner. Theory posits that those students who are most proficient in the content should score higher than students who are less proficient or who have learned less of the content tested. For this particular construct, the best criterion variable available is probably the total score on this particular test of head and neck anatomy. It follows that highly proficient students should score better on individual test items than less proficient or accomplished students. This logic describes the basic conceptual framework for item discrimination.

Item discrimination is the most important information to evaluate about the performance of the test item, because the level of discrimination reflects the degree to which an item contributes to the measurement objective of the test.

Discrimination Indices   *Item & Group*

Several different statistics are used as discrimination indices for tests. The most basic discrimination index is given by the simple difference in proportions of examinees in a high-scoring group who get the item correct and those in a low-scoring group who get the item correct. This index (*D*) is easily computed and can be interpreted like all other discrimination indices, such that high positive values are best and very low, 0, or negative values are always undesirable. See note 2 in Table 5.3 for the example of *D*.

As an example, if 77% of a high-scoring examinee group gets an item correct, but only 34% of a low-scoring group of examinees gets the item correct, the simple discrimination index, *D*, is equal to $77 - 34 = 43$. This $D = 43$ (usually expressed as $D = 0.43$) indicates strong positive discrimination for this test item and shows that this particular item sharply differentiates between high- and low-achievers on this test. The *D* index should be interpreted like all other item discrimination indices such that a minimum acceptable value is about +0.20 or so.

NU uses, 3

Point Biserial Correlation as Discrimination Index   *Item & Test*

Special types of correlation coefficients are also used as item discrimination indices for test item analyses. The point biserial (r_{pbis}) index of discrimination is the correlation between student performance on the item (that is, getting the item correct or incorrect, where 1 = correct and 0 = incorrect) and performance on the entire test. As in all correlation, the (theoretical) values of the point biserial index of discrimination can range from -1.0 to $+1.0$, indicating the strength of statistical relationships. (Because one variable in the correlation is dichotomous, the upper and lower bound of this type of correlation is usually not actually ±1.0.) Practically, point biserial correlations of about 0.45 to 0.65 or so are considered very high. See note 3 in Table 5.3 for an example.

A simple quantitative illustration of item discrimination calculation for a single test item is given in Table 5.4. This example shows how

Table 5.4 Correlation of One Test Item Score with Score on the Total Test

Student	Item Score (Right-Wrong)	Score on Total Test
1	1	41
2	0	45
3	0	50
4	1	55
5	0	60
6	1	74
7	1	18
8	0	20
9	1	55
10	0	45

Note: Correlation between item score (1, 0)—right or wrong—is $r_{iT} = +0.14$. This low correlation of the item and total scores indicates a low (but positive) item discrimination for this single test item.

10 students score on one test item. The middle column describes how each of these 10 students scored on this particular test item, with a *1* indicating that the student got the item correct and a *0* indicating that the student got the item incorrect. The third column gives the total score on this test. So, in this example, student 1 answered this item correctly and scored 41 on the total test. The discrimination index (r_{iT}) for this item equals +0.14; this shows the correlation between the item scores (1, 0) and the total score on the test for this group of examinees and indicates that this item differentiates high and low scoring examinees positively.

Biserial Correlation as Discrimination Index

Another type of correlation coefficient is sometimes used as an item discrimination index: the biserial correlation. This is similar to the point biserial, but uses slightly different assumptions. It is a matter of some personal preference whether to use the point biserial or biserial. Often, item analysis software computes both of these indices. The main practical difference is that the biserial index is always slightly higher than the point biserial, so the interpretation of this index must be adjusted upward somewhat relative to the interpretation of the point biserial. Either or both correlations are perfectly reasonable to use and both indices provide exactly the same information; the only difference is in the magnitude of the scale.

What is Good Item Discrimination?

High positive discrimination is always better than low or negative discrimination. But, how high is high? Typically, large-scale standardized test developers expect effective items to have point biserial discrimination indices of at least +0.30 or higher, but for locally developed classroom-type tests, one may be reasonably happy with a discrimination index in the mid to high 0.20s. At minimum, all discrimination indices should be a positive number, especially if there are any stakes involved in the assessment. (Negatively discriminating test items add nothing to the measurement and may detract from some of the important psychometric characteristics of the overall test and reduce the validity of the test scores.)

General Recommendations for Item Difficulty and Item Discrimination

Table 5.5 presents an overview of some general recommendations for ideal item difficulty and discrimination for most classroom-type achievement tests. All of these recommended values should be interpreted in terms of the purpose of the examinations, the types of instructional settings, the stakes associated with the tests and so on.

Table 5.5 Item Classification Guide by Difficulty and Discrimination[1]

Item Class	Item Difficulty	Item Discrimination (Point Biserial)	Description
Level I	0.45 to 0.75	+0.20 or higher	Best item statistics; use most items in this range if possible
Level II	0.76 to 0.91	+0.15 or higher	Easy; use sparingly
Level III	0.25 to 0.44	+0.10 or higher	Difficult; use very sparingly and only if content is essential – rewrite if possible
Level IV	<0.24 or >0.91	Any Discrim.	Extremely difficult or easy; do not use unless content is essential

Source: 1. Adapted from Haladyna (2004).

These recommended values for item difficulty and discrimination represent ideals. For most classroom type testing settings, especially those with a more "mastery" instructional philosophy, these recommendations will be too stringent and may have to be realistically adjusted downward somewhat.

These recommendations are based on theory which suggests that the most informative test items are those of middle difficulty which discriminate highly. For most achievement tests, we would like most items to be in this middle range of average item difficulty, with high discrimination. These are the Level I items noted in Table 5.5. The next best item statistical characteristics are those noted as Level II items: somewhat easier items than Level I, but with fair discrimination. Level III and Level IV items are either very easy, or hard with low item discrimination. These are the least effective items psychometrically, but it is certainly possible that such items measure important content and should therefore be used (if absolutely necessary) to enhance the content-related validity of the test scores.

In interpreting the recommendations in Table 5.5, where possible consider both item difficulty and item discrimination. Both item parameters are important, but item discrimination may be more important than difficulty (if you have to choose between the two parameters). It must be noted that item difficulty and item discrimination are not totally independent. Middle difficulty items have a better chance of discriminating well because of higher expected variance. But, be aware that very easy items and very difficult items sometimes have high discrimination indices as an artifact of their extreme difficulty. Since few examinees fall into the category groups for very hard or very easy items, a change of a few examinees can change the discrimination index greatly, but this may be an artifact of the small numbers of examinees in ability groups.

Item Options

The ideal item is one in which each distractor (incorrect option) is selected by at least some students who do not know the content tested by the question. An incorrect option that fails to attract any examinees is a dysfunctional distracter and adds nothing to the item or the test (psychometrically). The correct or best answer option should have a positive discrimination index—the higher the better; of course, this is the discrimination index for the item. Incorrect options—the wrong answers, should have negative discrimination indices because the less able examinees should be choosing the incorrect answers at higher frequency than the more able examinees.

Number of Examinees Needed for Item Analysis

Treat any item difficulty or item discrimination index cautiously if the statistics are based on a test administration with fewer than 100 examinees or so. (We really need about N = 200 examinees to have stable item analysis statistics.) However, even for small samples (e.g., N ≅ 30) the results may still provide some useful guidance for item improvement. Usually some information is better than no information when one is trying to improve a test, realizing that the statistics based on small ns are unstable and may change at the next administration of the item. (In statistical terms, the smaller the sample size on which an item analysis is based, the greater the sampling error and the larger the standard errors around the sample statistics.)

Note that all item analysis data based on classical measurement theory are sample dependent such that all item difficulty and discrimination statistics are confounded with the ability or proficiency of the particular sample of examinees. If the sample of examinees is large and if the range of student ability is fairly consistent for each administration of the test, item difficulty and discrimination values are likely to be stable over time.

Summary Statistics for a Test

Table 5.6 illustrates an example of summary statistics computed as part of a complete item analysis. These statistics are for a total test, with all terms defined in the column on the right of the table.

These statistics describe the overall performance of the test and provide validity evidence useful for test score interpretation by providing

Table 5.6 Example of Summary Item Statistics for Total Test

		Definition of Terms
N of items	35	Number of items
N of examinees	52	Number of examinees
Mean Raw Score	26.56	Mean number-correct raw score
Variance	8.36	Variance, number-correct raw score ($= SD^2$)
S.D.	2.89	Standard Deviation, number-correct raw score
Minimum	21.00	Minimum, number-correct raw score
Maximum	32.00	Maximum, number-correct raw score
Median	27.00	Median, number-correct raw score
Reliability	0.35	Internal consistency reliability: KR 20 or Alpha
SEM	2.34	Standard error of measurement
Mean Difficulty	0.76	Mean proportion/percent correct
Mean r_{pbis} Discrimination—*TEST*	0.08	Mean point biserial item discrimination
Mean Biserial — *GROUP*	0.13	Mean biserial item discrimination

guidance for using scores in making judgments about examinees and also provide useful evaluative information about the performance of the test. This summary (Table 5.6) presents the total number of examinees and the total number of test items, the average raw score (number correct score) with its standard deviation and variance (SD^2). We also see the minimum, maximum, and median raw score. These data give an overview of the shape of the score distribution and describe generally where on the distribution most examinees scored. The mean item difficulty, together with the two mean item discrimination indices, give us additional information about how hard or easy the items were on average and how well they discriminate. The reliability coefficient is the Kuder-Richardson Formula #20 (or Cronbach's Alpha) which is an index of the internal consistency of the measuring scale, indicating the precision of measurement. The standard error of measurement (SEM) is computed from the reliability coefficient, showing the precision of measurement on the raw score scale.

KR-20

Useful Formulas

The appendix presents some useful formulas together with worked examples using synthetic data. These formulas can be found in any basic educational measurement text, such as Mehrens and Lehmann (1991) and also Thissen and Wainer (2001). These four formulas are frequently used in assessment settings and can be hand calculated, using readily available data. If computer software is unavailable, these formulas can provide some useful information about assessments, and assist health professions educators in evaluating assessment data and planning future assessments.

A formula is provided to estimate the internal consistency reliability of a test when only the mean of test scores, the variance (SD^2), and the total number of test items is known. The Kuder-Richardson formula number 21 (KR 21) typically underestimates the more precise Kuder-Richardson formula number 20 (KR 20) slightly, but can be computed by hand, from the limited data available. The KR 20 is usually computed by computer software (within item analysis software), because it is computationally complex, using item-level data to estimate the variances used in the calculation.

The standard error of measurement (SEM) is an important statistic, computed from the reliability coefficient and the standard deviation of scores. Most item analysis software applications compute the SEM, but it is easily computed by hand if software is unavailable. The SEM can be used to build confidence intervals around observed test scores and is a useful application of the reliability coefficient indicating the precision of measurement and the amount of measurement error in scores, expressed in the metric of the standard deviation of the test scores.

The Spearman-Brown Prophecy Formula (S-B) is useful to estimate the expected increase or decrease in test reliability resulting from increasing or decreasing the number of test items in the scale. The S-B formula assumes that items which are added or subtracted from a test are more-or-less identical to the original items with respect to mean item difficulty, mean item discrimination, content, and so on.

The formula for the disattenuated correlation coefficient or the correction for attenuation of a correlation coefficient is also presented in the appendix and was discussed in the text above. With all the cautions for its use noted above, the disattenuated correlation coefficient estimates the correlation of true scores (in classical measurement theory) and answers the theoretical question: "What is the estimated correlation between the two variables—usually test scores or assessment ratings—if the scores or ratings were perfectly reliable?" The disattenuated correlation coefficient should be reported only together with the observed or actual correlation coefficient and should always be clearly labeled as the disattenuated correlation coefficient or the correction for attenuation.

Summary

This chapter has summarized some of the basic statistics used for assessment. Raw scores, the basic number-correct scores which generally serve as the fundamental scoring unit, were discussed. Standard scores, which express assessment scores in the metric of the standard deviation of the raw score scale, were generally recommended as more useful than percentiles. The fundamentals of classical item analysis and summary test score analysis were discussed and item analysis was recommended for all assessments in health professions education as a basic tool to improve assessments. Finally, several statistical formulas which are frequently and usefully used in evaluating assessments were presented, such that the reader can easily compute many of the basic evaluative test statistics.

APPENDIX: SOME USEFUL FORMULAS WITH EXAMPLE CALCULATIONS

Kuder Richardson Formula #21: Reliability Estimate

Use: An estimate of the internal consistency reliability if only the total number of test items, mean score, and standard deviation (SD) are known. Note raw scores, not percent-correct scores, should be used for these calculations.

Note that the KR 21 usually slightly underestimates the more precise KR 20 reliability, but the KR 20 requires computer software for calculation.

$$KR\ 21 = (K\ /\ K - 1)\ (1 - (M^*(K - M)\ /\ (K^*\ Var)))$$

Where:

K = Number of test items (raw number of items)
M = Raw score mean
Var = Raw score variance (SD^2)

Worked Example: A basic science test has 50 test items, with a mean score of 36.5 and a standard deviation of 10. What is the KR 21 reliability estimate for this test?

$$
\begin{aligned}
KR\ 21\ Reliability &= (50\ /\ 49)\ (1 - ((36.5 * (50 - 36.5)\ / \\
&\quad (50 * 100))) \\
&= (1.0204)\ (1 - (36.5 * 13.5)\ /\ 5000) \\
&= (1.0204)\ (1 - (492.75\ /\ 5000) \\
&= (1.0204)\ (1 - (0.09855) \\
&= (1.0204)\ (0.90145) \\
&= 0.92
\end{aligned}
$$

Standard Error of Measurement (SEM)

Use: To form confidence bands (CIs) around the observed score indicating the range of scores within which the "true score" falls, with known probability.

$$SEM = SD * \sqrt{1 - Reliability}$$

Where:

SD = Standard Deviation of the test
Reliability = Reliability estimate for the test

Worked Example: A test of 100 items has a mean of 73 and an SD of 12, with a KR 20 reliability of 0.89. What is the standard error of measurement?

$$SEM = 12 * \sqrt{1 - 0.89}$$

$$= 12 * \sqrt{0.11}$$
$$= 12 * 0.33$$
$$= 3.96$$

X̄ MEAN

If a student has a raw score of 25 on this test, what is the 95% confidence interval for his true score?

$$95\% \ CI = \overline{X} \pm 1.96 \ (SEM)$$
$$= 25 \pm 1.96 \ (3.96)$$
$$= 25 \pm 7.76$$
$$17.24 \geq T \leq 32.76$$

Spearman-Brown Prophecy Formula

Use: To estimate the reliability of a test that is longer (or shorter) than a test with a known reliability

Reliability of longer test = (N * Rel of Org Test) / (1 + Rel of Org Test)

Where:

test # of items +

N = Number of times test is lengthened (or shortened)

Worked Example: A test of 30 items has a reliability of 0.35. What is the expected reliability if the test is lengthened to 90 items?

$$SB \ Reliability, \ 90 \ item \ test = (3 * 0.35) / (1 + 0.35)$$
$$= (1.05) / (1.35)$$
$$= 0.77$$

Disattenuated Correlation: Correction for Attenuation

Use: To estimate the "true score" correlation between two variables; to estimate the (theoretical) correlation between two variables if one or both variables were perfectly reliable. The disattenuated correlation coefficient (theoretically) removes the attenuating effect on the correlation coefficient due to random errors of measurement or unreliability.

Disattenuated Correlation $= R_{tt} = R_{xy} / \sqrt{(R_{xx} * R_{yy})}$

Where:

R_{tt} = Estimated Disattenuated Correlation Coefficient
R_{xy} = The observed correlation coefficient between variables x
and y
R_{xx} = The reliability of variable (test) X
R_{yy} = The reliability of variable (test) Y

Worked Example: Tests A and B correlated 0.48. The reliability of Test A is 0.70 and the reliability of Test B is 0.51. What is the disattenuated correlation between Test A and Test B?

$R_{tt} = 0.48 / \sqrt{(0.70 * 0.51)}$

$= 0.48 / \sqrt{0.357}$

$= 0.48 / 0.597$

$= 0.80$

If both Tests A and B were perfectly reliable, the expected true score correlation is 0.80. The disattenuated correlation should be reported only in conjunction with the observed correlation and the estimate of reliability for both measures.

Note that if the reliability for only one of the two measures is known, set the unknown reliability to 1.0 for this calculation.

References

Downing, S.M. (2003). Guessing on selected-response examinations. *Medical Education*, 37, 670–671.

Downing, S.M. (2006). Twelve steps for effective test development. In S.M. Downing & T.M. Haladyna (Eds.), *Handbook of test development* (pp. 3–25). Mahwah, NJ: Lawrence Erlbaum Associates.

Feldt, L.S., & Brennan, R.L. (1989). Reliability. In R.L. Linn (Ed.), *Educational measurement* (3rd ed., pp. 105–146). New York: American Council on Education and Macmillan.

Haladyna, T.M. (2004). *Developing and validating multiple-choice test items* (3rd ed.). Mahwah, NJ: Lawrence Erlbaum Associates.

Kolen, M.J., & Brennan, R.L. (2004). *Test equating, scaling, and linking: Methods and practices* (2nd ed.). New York: Springer-Verlag.

Livingston, S.A. (2006). Item analysis. In S.M. Downing & T.M. Haladyna (Eds.), *Handbook of test development* (pp. 421–441). Mahwah, NJ: Lawrence Erlbaum Associates.

Mehrens, W.A., & Lehmann, I.J. (1991). *Measurement and evaluation in education and psychology* (4th ed.). New York: Harcourt Brace College Publishers.

Stagnaro-Green, A., Deng, W., Downing, S.M., & Crosson, J. (2004, November). Theoretical model evaluating the impact of weighted percent versus standard scores in determining third year clerkship grades. Paper presentation at the Annual Meeting of the Association of American Medical Colleges, RIME, Boston, MA.

Thissen, D., & Wainer, H. (Eds.). (2001). *Test scoring.* Mahwah, NJ: Lawrence Erlbaum.

6

STANDARD SETTING

RACHEL YUDKOWSKY,
STEVEN M. DOWNING, AND ARA TEKIAN

Introduction

A standard determines whether a given score or performance is good enough for a particular purpose (Norcini & Guille, 2002). The term "standard setting" refers to a process used to create boundaries between categories such as pass | fail, or honors | proficient | needs remediation. Standard setting is "central to the task of giving meaning to test results and thus lies at the heart of validity argument" (Dylan, 1996). Establishing credible, defensible, and acceptable passing or cut-off scores for examinations in health professions education can be challenging (Friedman, 2000; Norcini & Shea, 1997; Norcini & Guille, 2002). There is a large literature of standard setting, much of which is devoted to empirical passing score studies and comparisons of various standard-setting methods which are appropriate for selected-response tests or performance tests used in K-12 educational settings (Cizek, 2001, 2006; Cizek, Bunch, & Koons, 2004; Livingston, 1982; Norcini, 2003). This chapter will discuss key issues and decisions regarding standard setting, identify ways to assess the quality and consequences of resulting standards, and address special situations such as combining standards across subtests, setting standards for performance tests, and multiple-category cut scores. At the end of the chapter we provide detailed instructions for conducting six standard setting methods commonly used in health professions settings: Angoff, Ebel, Hofstee, Borderline Group, Contrasting Groups, and Body of Work.

A cut score is an operational statement of policy. All standard setting methods require judgment; the object of a standard setting exercise is to capture the opinions of expert judges in order to inform a policy decision of "how much is enough" for a given purpose. There is no single correct or best method to set standards for an examination; nor is there a single correct or "true" cut score that must be discovered. All standards are, to some extent, arbitrary. Thus standard setting can best be viewed as "due process"—a procedure to be followed to ensure that the cut score is not capricious; that it is reasonable, defensible, and fair.

Standards can be categorized as either relative (norm-based) or absolute (criterion-based). Relative standards identify a group of passing and failing examinees *relative* to the performance of some well defined group; the cut score or standard will depend on the performance of the specific group tested—for example, the bottom 5% of the class, or those who score more than two standard deviations below the mean of first time test takers. Relative standards are most appropriate when a rank ordering of students is needed in order to distribute limited resources: for example, to give "honors" grades to the top 10% of the students in a surgery clerkship, to select top scoring applicants for entry to dental school, or to identify those pharmacy students most in need of remedial tutoring before progressing to the next stage of training. The placement of the cut score will depend on the resources available.

Absolute or criterion-based standards are based on a predetermined level of competency that does not depend on the performance of the group—for example, a score of 70%. Absolute standards reflect a desired level of mastery; the criterion stays the same whether all students pass or none do. In health professions education the purpose of most examinations is to confirm mastery of a domain of knowledge or skill, so in the past decades most professional schools in the US have moved to the use of absolute standards.

This chapter will focus on ways to obtain defensible and reasonable *absolute* standards. The term "absolute" implies that passing score judgments are made such that judges are blind to actual performance data, looking only at the content of the test or the performance prompts. This is the purist view, but the reality is that totally pure absolute standards rarely turn out to be realistic, acceptable, or useful in the real world of health professions education. Expert judges tend to expect even borderline examinees to know more and be able to do more than is realistic. Studies have demonstrated that judges, absent all performance data, tend to set unrealistically high passing scores, which will fail an unreasonably high proportion of students (Cizek, 2001; Kane, Crooks & Cohen, 1999). Experts almost always expect too much of novice learners.

The point of view adopted in this book is that judges must be "calibrated" to have a realistic expectation of actual student performance. Such calibration requires presenting some performance data to judges so that standard setting panels have a reasonable expectation concerning actual student performance on the assessment. Some experts in education disagree with this point of view and may label such methods biased. We prefer the efficiency of judge calibration to the inefficiency of repeating the standard setting exercise a second or third time if the first rounds result in unacceptably high standards.

Eight Steps for Standard Setting

Hambleton and Pitoniak (2006) divide the process of setting absolute or criterion-based standards into six critical steps: selecting a method, preparing performance category descriptions, forming a standard-setting panel, training panelists, providing feedback to panelists and evaluating and documenting the validity of the process. In this chapter we will use a modification of their scheme, slightly elaborated to include eight steps (see Figure 6.1). We will discuss the key issues involved in each of these steps in turn.

Step 1: Select a Standard Setting Method

There is no "gold standard" for a passing score. There is no perfect passing score "out there" waiting to be discovered. Rather, the passing score is whatever a group of content expert judges determine it is, having followed a systematic, reproducible, absolute, and unbiased process. The key to defensible and acceptable standards is the

Step 1: Select a standard setting method

Step 2: Select judges

Step 3: Prepare descriptions of performance categories

Step 4: Train judges

Step 5: Collect ratings or judgments

Step 6: Provide feedback and facilitate discussion

Step 7: Evaluate the standard setting process

Step 8: Provide results, consequences and validity evidence to final decision makers

Figure 6.1 Eight Steps for Standard Setting.*

Source: * Modified from Hambleton and Pitoniak (2006)

implementation of a careful, systematic method to collect expert judgments, preferably a method that is based on research evidence. Different standard setting methods will produce different passing scores, and different groups of judges, following exactly the same procedures, may also produce different passing scores for the same assessment. Such facts are troubling only if one expects to discover the perfect or "gold standard" passing score. Process is the key concept, remembering that *all passing scores are ultimately policy decisions*, which are inherently subjective (Ebel, 1972).

Methods for setting standards can be described broadly as either test-based or examinee-based. In *test-based methods* such as the Angoff (Angoff, 1971) and Ebel (Ebel, 1972) methods described at the end of this chapter, judges review test items or prompts and estimate the expected level of performance of a borderline examinee (one just at the margin between two categories) on a given task. In *examinee-based methods* (represented here by the Borderline Group (Livingston & Zieky, 1982), Contrasting Groups (Burrows, Bingham, & Brailovsky, 1999; Clauser & Clyman, 1994; Livingston & Zieky, 1982) and Body of Work (Kingston, Kahl, Sweeney, & Bay, 2001) methods) judges categorize the performance of individual examinees, either through direct observation, review of proxies of their behavior such as performance checklists, or review of examinee products such as chart notes written after a standardized patient encounter. In these methods, the scores of examinees in different performance categories are utilized in order to generate the final cut score. Finally, *compromise methods* such as the Hofstee method combine features of absolute and relative standards, asking judges to estimate both acceptable passing scores and acceptable fail rates.

At the end of this chapter we describe these six methods—Angoff, Ebel, Hofstee, Borderline, Contrasting Groups and Body-of-Work—all of which are potentially useful for establishing realistic and acceptable standards for examinations in the health professions (see Table 6.6). Choice of method depends on the type of assessment data, feasibility, resources available, and the preferences of decision makers at a given site.

Step 2: Select Judges

For the absolute methods discussed here, the choice of content expert judges is crucial. The passing scores established are only as credible as the judges and the soundness of the systematic methods used (Norcini & Shea, 1997). Content expertise is the most important characteristic of judges selected for the standard setting exercise. Judges must also know the target population well, understand both their task as judges and the content materials used in the performance assessment, be fair, open-minded, and willing to follow directions, be as unbiased as possible, and be willing and able to devote their full attention to the task. In some settings, it may be important to balance the panel of judges with respect to demographic variables, such as ethnicity, gender, geography, and subspecialization. For most methods and settings, five to six independent judges might be considered minimum, with 10 to 12 judges the maximum. Practical considerations must often play a major role in judge selection, the numbers of judges used, the venues for standard setting exercises, and the exact manner in which the procedures are implemented.

Step 3: Prepare Descriptions of Performance Categories

Standard setting results in one or more cut scores that divide the distribution of scores into two or more performance categories or levels such as Pass | Fail, or Basic | Proficient | Advanced. Judges must have a clear idea of the behaviors expected in each of the categories. What behaviors characterize graduating medical students who are ready for supervised practice as residents? How does an "Advanced" level nursing student differ from a "Proficient" student in the context of a pediatric rotation? Performance categories are narrative descriptions of the minimally acceptable behaviors required in order to be included in a given category. The cut points represent the boundaries between these performance categories on the exam score distribution. The performance category descriptions may be generated by the same judges who will set the cut points, or by a different group of persons familiar with the curriculum and the examinees.

Step 4: Train Judges

It is essential that every standard setting judge fully understands the relationship between passing scores and passing rates. The passing *score* is the score needed to pass the performance test, often expressed as a percent-correct score. The passing *rate* is the percentage of students who pass the test at any given passing score (sometimes expressed as the failure rate). The higher the passing score, the lower the passing rate. If standard setting judges confuse these two statistics, their judgments will confuse the passing score and become a threat to the validity of the standard.

Most absolute standard setting methods pivot on the idea of the borderline student or examinee. This concept originated with Angoff's original work on absolute passing scores (Angoff, 1971). The cut score separating those who pass from those who fail corresponds to the point that exactly separates those who know (or can do) just enough to pass from those who do not know enough (or cannot do enough) to pass. The borderline examinee is thus one who has an exactly 50–50 probability of passing or failing the test. The borderline examinee is the marginal student—one who on some days might just pass your assessment, but on other days might fail.

The definition of borderline examinee is straightforward, but operationalizing this definition can be challenging. Asking judges to

describe borderline students they have known imparts a clear understanding of what it means to be "borderline" and facilitates group
consensus prior to beginning the standard setting work.

Step 5: Collect Ratings or Judgments

See the detailed instructions for each of the six methods provided
at the end of this chapter. Quality control and documentation of
collection processes are essential to provide "response process" type
evidence for the validity of the standards obtained. The procedures
described in this paper are examples of only one particular way to
implement each method. Every setting is unique and minor (or
major) modifications to these standard-setting procedures may be
required in some settings.

Step 6: Provide Feedback and Facilitate Discussion

Many of the test-based methods include an iterative procedure in
which outlier ratings are discussed and justified, performance data
may be provided, and consequences (failure rates based on the judgments at that stage) may be revealed. The item rating procedure is
then repeated, and judges may choose to revise their ratings, but are
not required to do so. The cycle may be repeated one or two times.
Iterative procedures tend to create more of a consensus among judges,
but do not necessarily substantively change the resulting cut score
(Stern, et al., 2005). Some educators forgo discussions and iterations
for local low- to medium-stakes examinations.

We noted above that judges, absent data about actual examinee
performance, tend to set unrealistically high passing scores. While
proponents of iterative procedures tend to advocate the provision of
performance data at the second iteration, few judges change their
ratings once the initial mental effort has been expended (Kane, et al.,
1999). To have a moderating impact on ratings performance data
should be provided at the outset, before the first round of judgments
(Clauser, Margolis, & Case, 2006; Kane, et al., 1999; Shea, Reshetar,
Norcini, & Dawson, 1994).

Some judge panels wish to know, from time to time throughout the process, what passing score and/or passing rate they have established thus far in the process. Again, this is a matter for professional judgment and we take the position that, in general, more data is better than less data for all judgments.

Step 7: Evaluate the Standard Setting Procedure

No matter which standard setting method you choose, some evaluation of the resulting standard is appropriate. Is your cut score acceptable to your stakeholders? If not, is it because the test was not appropriately constructed, because your curriculum did not prepare students for the exam, or because your standard setting judges did not have (or use) information about the actual performance of the students?

Judges can provide information about whether they were sufficiently trained for the procedure, their ability to make the requested judgments and their confidence in the resulting cut scores. Positive answers to these questions from judges chosen for their content expertise provide an additional measure of credibility to the standards. Judges could be surveyed at two points—after training and after the entire procedure is complete. A sample survey is shown in Table 6.1.

Formal approaches to assessing the psychometric characteristics of standards can assist in the evaluation of the standard setting results. Generalizability coefficients can provide a measure of the reliability of the judgments and D-studies can suggest the number of judges needed to achieve a reliable standard. The standard error of the mean (SE Mean) passing score is the standard deviation (SD) of the passing score judgments across all judges, divided by the square root of the number of judges (n):

Standard Error of the Mean Cut Score = (SD of cut score) / $\sqrt{n}$

Computing two SEs of the mean in either direction allows us to build a 95% confidence interval around the cut score. Solving for *n* allows an estimate of the number of judges needed to reach a desired standard error of the mean. Jaeger (1991) suggests that the standard

Table 6.1 Standard Setting Feedback Questionnaire for Judges

After Orientation and Training:

1. How clear is the purpose of the test and the nature of the examinees?	Very clear	Clear	Not clear
2. How clear are the characteristics of a borderline examinee?	Very clear	Clear	Not clear
3. How clear is the rating task to be performed?	Very clear	Clear	Not clear

After the Completion of the Standard Setting Exercise:

4. How difficult was it to provide ratings?	Very difficult	Difficult	Not difficult
5. Was sufficient time provided for the rating task?	Too much time	Right amount of time	Not enough time
6. Was sufficient time provided for discussion?	Too much time	Right amount of time	Not enough time
7. How useful was the performance data provided?	Very useful	Useful	Not useful
8. Do you think the final passing scores are appropriate for the examinees?	Too high	Just right	Too low
9. How confident are you in appropriateness of the cut scores?	Very confident	Confident	Not confident

Comments:

error of the mean of the cut score should be no more than one-fourth of the standard error of measurement of the test. Cohen, Kane, & Crooks, (1999), perhaps more realistically, suggests that there is little impact if the SE of the cut score is less than half of the SE of the test. In a similar vein, Meskauskas (1986) suggests that the standard deviation of the judgments be small (no more than one-fourth) compared to the size of the standard deviation of examinee test scores. These recommendations may be difficult to achieve at a local level with typically small numbers of judges (Yudkowsky, Downing, & Wirth 2008).

Kane (1994) suggests three main sources of evidence to support the validity of standards. *Procedural evidence* includes explicitness, practicability, implementation, feedback from the judges, and documentation.

Internal evidence includes the precision of the estimate of the cut scores (such as the SEMean above), intra-panelist and inter-panelist consistency, and decision consistency. *External evidence* includes comparison to other standard setting methods, comparisons to other relevant criteria such as similar tests, and the reasonableness of the cut scores in terms of pass/fail rates.

Step 8: Provide Results, Consequences and Validity Evidence to Decision Makers

In the final analysis, standards are set not by content experts (judges) but by policy decision makers. They must consider the recommended cut scores, the consequences of applying these scores in terms of pass/ fail rates, and evidence as to the credibility of the cut scores before reaching a decision whether to accept the recommendations. The consequences of different types of classification errors must be considered, especially in high stakes situations such as licensing or certification exams. False negative decisions are those in which someone who is qualified is categorized as "fail"; false positive decisions are those in which someone who is not qualified is categorized as "pass." A false positive error, licensing some unqualified practitioners, may pose patient safety risks; a false negative decision will result in a qualified practitioner being denied a license and may result in some patients being denied access to care. One way to minimize such errors is to increase or decrease the cut score by one standard error of measurement of the test, depending on the type of error deemed most salient (Clauser, et al., 2006).

At times, especially if no performance data was provided to the judges, the recommended standards may be unacceptably high; in that case the options are (1) to reconvene the panel of judges and ask them to repeat the exercise with performance data, (2) to convene a different panel of judges, and/or use a different standard setting method; or (3) to otherwise adjust the standards to be more acceptable. Since different standard setting methods are likely to produce different cut scores, some educators recommend using more than one method and taking a mean across the different methods to increase the credibility of the final cut score (Wayne, Barsuk, Cohen, & McGaghie, 2007).

Special Topics in Standard Setting

Combining Standards Across Components of an Examination: Compensatory vs. Non-compensatory Standards

Some assessments include several distinct components or stations— for example a written test that includes separate sections on physiology, pharmacology and pathology, a performance test composed of a series of standardized patient encounters, or a clerkship grade that encompasses a written exam, end-of-rotation faculty evaluations, and an OSCE. Can good performance on one component compensate for poor performance on another? If so, the overall standard can consist of the simple average of standards across encounters or components (compensatory scoring). Component scores (and standards) can be differentially weighted if desired—in the case of the clerkship grade, for example, the written test can comprise 50% of the final grade, with the faculty evaluations and OSCE each contributing another 25%. Component scores should be transformed to linear standard scores before weighting (see Axelson & Kreiter, Chapter 3, this volume and Downing, Chapter 5, this volume). Alternatively, a whole-test method such as Hofstee can be used to set a single cut score for the entire battery (Schindler, Corcoran, & DaRosa, 2007).

In some cases, however, a non-compensatory approach may be more appropriate, to ensure that students reach a minimum level of competence in several crucial but different domains. In this case standards must be set separately for each domain, and examinees must pass each component separately. Each component must include a sufficiently large sample of student behavior in order to be reliable, since very small samples of items—containing large sampling error— may result in incorrect decisions. Setting multiple hurdles to be passed will inevitably increase the failure rate.

In clinical cases, faculty often feel very strongly that a few crucial items must be accomplished for the student to pass, regardless of overall score. These items should be discussed at both the scoring and standard setting stages of exam planning.

Setting Standards for Performance Tests

Performance tests allow for direct observation of a particular competency in a contrived or simulated environment (see Yudkowsky, Chapter 9, this volume). An Objective Structured Clinical Examination or OSCE is a common example of a performance test, in which examinees rotate through a series of stations, each presenting a particular challenge. If content experts such as faculty observe and rate the performance of the examinees, the borderline group or contrasting groups method can be used. These methods are convenient and simple to implement; faculty are very comfortable with making judgments about an individual performance, and all judgments are made in the course of the exam so no additional faculty time is needed. If experts are not scoring the exam (for example when standardized patients provide checklist scores), methods involving judgments about the test items or test content (Angoff, Ebel, Hofstee) can be used.

The use of item-based methods such as Angoff to set standards for standardized patient cases, while very common, has been challenged on the basis that items within a case are not mutually independent (Ross, Clauser, Margolis, Orr, & Klass, 1996). One solution is to have judges work on the case level instead of the item level, estimating the total number of items a borderline examinee would obtain on the case (Stern, et al., 2005).

See Chapter 9 for additional discussion of standard setting in the context of performance tests.

Setting Standards for Clinical Procedures

The checklists used to assess procedural skills such as phlebotomy or lumbar puncture are often unique in that (1) they cover the *entire* set of behaviors needed to accomplish the procedure (rather than a sampling of salient items), and (2) the checklists are public—students are expected to use the checklist to learn and practice the procedure. Certain items on the checklist may be essential for patient safety. While in general pass/fail decisions should never be based on a single item because of the possibility of rater errors, in the interest of patient safety judges may require that an error on even one of these core items will trigger a retest on that procedure.

Setting Standards for Oral Exams and Portfolios

Standards for oral exams, essay papers and portfolios can be set using methods that combine expert global judgments with analytic scoring methods (i.e. Borderline Group or Contrasting Groups), or using whole test (Hofstee) or Body-of-Work methods for collections of items. Clear and explicit performance category descriptors can provide benchmarks for initial scoring purposes as well as for later standard setting efforts.

Multiple Category Cut Scores

Setting cut scores for multiple categories (e.g. honors | pass | fail, or expert | proficient | beginner) can be done using the same methods as for dichotomous pass/fail standards. The performance category descriptions provided to the judges must clearly differentiate the behaviors expected at each level. Other features of the pass/fail standard setting process may have to be modified somewhat to permit multiple outcome categories.

The accuracy of distinguishing cut score categories (e.g., pass | fail; high honors | honors; expert | proficient | needs remediation) is related to the reliability of the assessment scores and other characteristics of the data, such as the shape of the distribution of the scores, the location of the cut score(s), and the true base rates in the population (Clauser, et al., 2006). In general, the higher the reliability of the assessment scores and the lower the standard errors of measurement, the better classification accuracy can be expected. For example, Wainer and Thissen (1996) show that at a reliability of 0.50, we can reasonably expect scores to vary by at least one standard deviation

(SD) unit for about one-third of those tested. Even for relatively high reliabilities of 0.80, about 11 percent of students will have score changes of 1 SD or more.

False positive and false negative classification errors will occur more frequently when multiple cut points are used. In general, as expected, false negatives increase as the passing score increases and false positives decrease as pass scores are raised. The costs of false positives and false negatives must be considered as standard setting policies and procedures are selected and applied.

Setting Standards Across Institutions

Faculty at different schools setting standards for the same exam using the same standard setting method are very likely to come up with different cut scores. For example, faculty at five medical schools in the UK used the Angoff method to set passing scores for the same six OSCE stations and came up with widely varying cut scores; a student with a given level of competency might pass at one school and fail at another (Boursicot, Roberts, & Pell, 2006). If uniform standards are desired across schools, standard setting teams should include members across the participating schools as well as external experts if appropriate. Groups should be encouraged to reach consensus on the characteristics of minimally competent (borderline) students before beginning the exercise. If several (mixed) groups are convened, a single cut score can be obtained by taking the mean across groups. Stern, Friedman Ben-David, Norcini, Wojtczak, & Schwarz (2006) used the Angoff method creatively in a pilot study to set international standards for medical schools in China. In this study the concept of the "borderline school" was used to define school level outcome standards.

Six Methods for Setting Performance Standards

The Angoff Method

The Angoff method (Angoff, 1971) was the first of the absolute methods and thus has the longest history of successful use, even in high-stakes testing situations. In this method, content experts make judgments about every item, so it is fairly easy to defend the resulting passing scores.

Angoff Standard-Setting Procedures   There are five steps in implementing an Angoff standard setting exercise:

1. The standard-setting judges discuss the characteristics of a borderline examinee and note specific examples of borderline students.
2. Judges come to a consensus agreement on the qualities of the borderline examinee, with specific examples in mind.
3. Each judge estimates the performance of the borderline examinee for each performance prompt, item or rating (0 to 100%).
4. These judgments are recorded (usually by a non-judge recorder or secretary).
5. Judgments are then systematically combined (totaled and averaged) to determine a passing score on the performance test.

Some actual performance data may be given to the judges. Summary data such as the mean and standard deviation of exam scores or scores on a standardized patient case will help to calibrate judges as to the difficulty of the test for real students. Alternately, more specific data may also be presented, such as the proportion of the total group of students who get an item correct.

Item Review and Rating   Judgments are carried out at the item level. The item review begins with one of the judges reading the first item. First the reader and then the other judges on the panel give their estimate of how well a borderline candidate will score on that item; judges rotate clockwise for each new item. Each judge's estimate (judgment) is recorded on a recording sheet or a computer spreadsheet. For each item, the judges answer one of the following two equivalent questions:

1. How many individuals in a group of 100 borderline examinees *will accomplish* this item correctly? (0 to 100%),

or

2. What is the probability that one borderline examinee *will accomplish* this item correctly? (0 to 1.0)

Note that the Angoff question asks judges to estimate how well students *will* perform, not how well they *should* perform. The difference between "will" and "should" needs to be emphasized. If the judgments for an item differ by 20% or more, those judges who provided the high and low scores may lead a discussion of their ratings for that item. Throughout the process, judges can modify their ratings or judgments. The review and rating of prompts continues until the entire checklist has been completed.

Table 6.2 shows the Angoff ratings for a ten-item performance examination rated by seven Angoff judges. The case passing score (percent) is the simple average of passing scores for all items.

A variant of the Angoff method (actually Angoff's original method) is to ask judges to make a simple "yes" or "no" judgment about each item/prompt. The question becomes: "Will the borderline examinee respond correctly to this item?" All "yes" answers are coded as "1," with "no" answers coded "0." The simple sum of the 1's

Table 6.2 Sample Angoff Ratings and Calculation of Passing Score

Item	Rater 1	Rater 2	Rater 3	Rater 4	Rater 5	Rater 6	Rater 7	Mean
1	0.80	0.87	0.85	0.90	0.80	0.95	0.85	0.86
2	0.70	0.75	0.80	0.85	0.75	0.85	0.75	0.78
3	0.50	0.63	0.55	0.60	0.65	0.60	0.60	0.59
4	0.70	0.68	0.70	0.70	0.65	0.70	0.70	0.69
5	0.75	0.70	0.80	0.85	0.70	0.85	0.80	0.78
6	0.60	0.65	0.80	0.75	0.65	0.85	0.80	0.73
7	0.50	0.58	0.55	0.60	0.70	0.90	0.60	0.63
8	0.70	0.78	0.75	0.75	0.65	0.80	0.70	0.73
9	0.45	0.50	0.50	0.45	0.43	0.55	0.45	0.48
10	0.60	0.69	0.65	0.65	0.65	0.70	0.70	0.66
							Sum[1]	**6.93**
							Pass Score[2]	**69.30%**

Notes

1. Raw Passing Score = Sum of item means = 6.93
2. Percent Passing Score = 100% * (sum of item means / number of items) = 100% * (6.93/ 10) = 69.30%

becomes the raw passing score when averaged over all judges (see Table 6.3). This simplified Angoff method (Direct or Yes/No method) may be useful for some types of examinations, such as laboratory tests, for which use of the traditional Angoff method would be difficult (Downing, Lieska, & Raible, 2003; Impara & Plake, 1997).

A variant of the Angoff method called the Extended Angoff procedure can be used with a rating scale rather than a dichotomous item (Hambleton & Plake, 1995). Each judge independently estimates the rating that a borderline student will get on each item. For example, if the student is being rated on a 5-point scale, a borderline student might be expected to achieve a rating of "3" on item 1 and of "4" on item 2. Calculate the mean rating for each item across all judges and average over items to obtain the raw passing rating score.

Table 6.3 Sample Simplified/Direct Angoff Ratings and Calculation of Passing Score

Item	Rater 1	Rater 2	Rater 3	Rater 4	Rater 5	Mean
1	1	1	0	1	1	0.8
2	1	1	1	1	1	1
3	1	0	1	0	1	0.6
4	0	0	0	0	0	0
5	0	0	0	1	1	0.4
6	1	1	1	1	1	1
7	0	0	1	0	1	0.4
8	1	1	1	1	1	1
9	1	1	1	1	0	0.8
10	0	0	1	0	0	0.2
					Sum[1]	**6.2**
					Pass Score[2]	**62%**

Notes

1. Raw Passing Score = Sum of item means = 6.2
2. Passing Score Percent = 100% * (sum of item means / number of items) = 100% * (6.2/ 10) = 62%

The Ebel Method

The Ebel method (Ebel, 1972) requires judges to consider both the difficulty of the item and its relevance. This method gives standard setting judges more information about the test and its individual items, but also requires more work and time of the judges than some other methods.

Ebel Standard-Setting Procedures   There are two major tasks required to implement an Ebel standard setting procedure:

1. prepare a matrix of item numbers categorized by relevance and difficulty;
2. estimate the proportion of borderline examinees who will succeed on the type of item in each cell in this matrix.

Item difficulty is determined by calculating the average difficulty (percent correct) for each item, based on actual data from an administration of the exam to a (representative) group of examinees. Difficulty ranges (easy, medium, hard) are arbitrarily determined, but should have some rational basis in the empirical data.

Relevance ratings (essential, important, acceptable) for each item must be obtained from judges (see # 6 below). It is customary for the same judges used to give the final Ebel ratings to carry out the relevance ratings, but this is not essential. Also, since some time is needed to carry out various computations and to create rating forms once the relevance ratings are obtained, it may be necessary to divide the Ebel standard setting exercise into two separate sessions. A different group of judges could carry out relevance ratings, if circumstances warrant.

Here is a summary of steps to accomplish an Ebel standard setting exercise:

1. Familiarize the judges with the content of the test, performance cases and/or the checklists or rating scales.
2. Discuss specific definitions of the relevance categories used: "essential, important, and acceptable." For example, "essential to good patient care—if this item is not accomplished, the patient's health is at risk."
3. Have each judge rate each item as *essential, important, or acceptable.*

4. Compute summary statistics (average across judges) for the relevance ratings of each item.

5. Compute mean item difficulty (proportion correct) for each item or prompt of each case or station, based on actual performance data.

6. For each case, prepare a matrix of items sorted by relevance and difficulty (see Table 6.4).

7. Lead the judges in a discussion of borderline student performance.

8. Reach some common understanding of the characteristics of the borderline examinee.

9. Ask each judge to provide an answer to the following question for each set of items designated by a cell in the matrix: "If a borderline student had to perform a large number of items or prompts like these, what percentage (0 to 100%) would the student perform correctly?"

10. Each judge records the estimated percentage of students who will correctly perform items like those noted in the cell.

11. Average judgments across all judges are computed and recorded, as shown in Table 6.4.

12. A weighted mean is computed for each row of the matrix, defined as the number of items in the cell multiplied by the mean rating for that cell, and then summed.

13. Adding the total for each row of the matrix gives the raw passing score as determined by the Ebel judges.

The Hofstee Method

The Hofstee method is sometimes referred to as the "relative-absolute compromise method," because it combines features of both relative and absolute standard setting (De Gruijter, 1985; Hofstee, 1983). Judges are asked to define minimum and maximum acceptable passing scores and failure rates. The standard is determined by the midpoint of the cumulative frequency curve of the exam scores as it passes through this bracketing rectangle (see Figure 6.2). Since it considers the assessment as a whole, it can be used conveniently for complex

Table 6.4 Sample Ebel Ratings and Calculation of Passing Score

	Matrix of Checklist Item Relevance by Difficulty			
Item Relevance	Easy (0.80–0.99)	Medium (0.45–0.79)	Hard (0–0.44)	Weighted Mean
Essential	Items # 4, 5 93% correct[1]	Item # 1 81% correct	Item # 3 63% correct	2 (0.93) + 0.81 + 0.63 = 3.30
Important	Item # 2 89% correct	Item # 10 76% correct	Item # 9 59% correct	0.89 + 0.76 + 0.59 = 2.24
Acceptable	N/A	Item # 7 62% correct	Items # 6, 8 42% correct	0.62 + (2(0.42)) = 1.46

Notes: Raw Passing Score = Sum of Weighted Means = 3.30 + 2.24 + 1.46 = 7.0 raw points

Percent Passing Score = 100% × (sum of item means / number of items) = 100% × (7.0 / 10) = 70%

1. In this example, for items rated as essential and easy, 93% correct represents the mean judgment of all the Ebel judges.

assessments composed of multiple disparate elements (for example a clerkship grade composed of a written exam, faculty ratings and an OSCE). Like the Ebel method, the Hofstee method requires analyzing and summarizing performance data prior to collecting judgments. Alternatively performance data can be obtained from a sub-group of representative examinees or from a prior administration of the examination. If the judges do not take actual performance data under close consideration, the cumulative frequency distribution curve may not be included within the score boundaries they define. The Graphical Hofstee (see procedure step 6/alternate) avoids this problem and ensures that the standard setting exercise will result in judgments that are applicable to the specific group examined.

Some researchers discourage use of the Hofstee method for high-stakes examinations, perhaps feeling that it is less credible because the judgments are global rather than based on individual items (Norcini, 2003).

Hofstee Standard-Setting Procedures A group of content-expert judges, who are familiar with the students and the performance examinations under consideration, are assembled and trained in the Hofstee method.

Before the Exercise

1. Based on actual performance data, compute the mean and standard deviation of the test and any other statistics (such as mean scores at quartile cutoffs) that would be helpful in describing the overall performance of students on the test.
2. Consider presenting graphical data showing the overall distribution of scores.
3. Optionally, calculate and present other examination data such as any historical data about student performance on the same or similar tests over time.
4. Calculate and graph the cumulative frequency distribution (as a cumulative percent) of the total performance test score for each case. (Statistical software such as SPSS can be used to plot the cumulative frequency percent.) See Figure 6.2 for an example.

During the Exercise

1. Present and discuss the data discussed above with the standard setting judges.
2. Review the cases and the items, the scoring methods, and other relevant details of the exam.

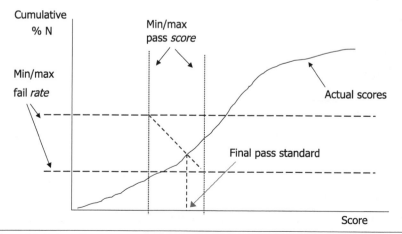

Figure 6.2 Hofstee Method.

3. Discuss the borderline examinee with the group of judges, coming to a consensus agreement on the characteristics of the examinee who just barely passes or just barely fails.

4. Present and discuss the four Hofstee questions, ensuring that each judge fully understands each question (see #6 below) and its implications.

5. Consider doing a practice run to be certain that judges fully understand the Hofstee procedures.

6. Have each judge answer each of the four questions, as noted here:

   a. The *LOWEST acceptable percentage* of students to **FAIL** the examination is: _____ percent (minimum fail rate).

   b. The *HIGHEST acceptable percentage* of students to **FAIL** the examination is: _____ percent (maximum fail rate).

   c. The *LOWEST acceptable percent-correct score* which allows a borderline student to pass the examination is: _____ percent (minimum passing score).

   d. The *HIGHEST acceptable percent-correct score* required for a borderline student to pass the examination is: _____ percent (maximum passing score).

6 (alternate). Alternatively, have judges draw lines designating the highest and lowest acceptable pass scores and fail rates *directly on the cumulative score graph*, with instructions to be sure to include the cumulative score line within the rectangle thus defined (Graphical Hofstee). Have judges specify and record the exact numerical value represented by their lines.

After the Exercise

1. Compute the mean percentage for each of the four questions, across all judges.

2. Plot the mean of the four data points (minimum and maximum acceptable fail percent and pass score) on the cumulative frequency distribution

3. The midpoint of the intersection of the minimum and maximum fail rates and pass scores represents the overall passing score for

the group of judges. See Table 6.5 and Figure 6.3 for a worked example.

If the cumulative frequency distribution curve does not fall within the score boundaries defined by the judges, and the judges cannot be recalled to run the exercise again, the standard can default to the minimum acceptable passing score or the maximum acceptable failure rate determined by the judges. Use of the Graphical Hofstee method (6 (alternate), above) will help prevent this problem since judges can immediately see the results of their judgments and whether the cumulative score line falls within the defined boundaries.

Table 6.5 Sample Hofstee Ratings and Calculation of Passing Score

	Rater 1	Rater 2	Rater 3	Rater 4	Mean
Minimum passing *score*	65	70	60	60	64
Maximum passing *score*	75	75	65	70	71
Minimum fail *rate*	5	0	10	7	6
Maximum fail *rate*	20	25	30	30	26

Note: Use Rater Means to obtain pass score by graphing onto cumulative percent graph, see Figure 6.3.

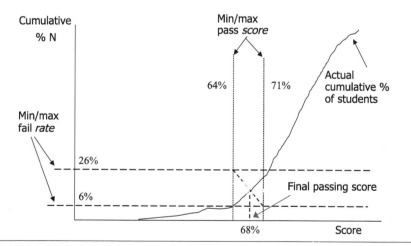

Figure 6.3 Hofstee Example.

Borderline Group Method

The Borderline Group method (Livingston & Zieky, 1982) is an examinee-centered rather than an item-centered method: judgments are made about individual test-takers, not test items or content. The method can be used when content experts who are qualified to serve as standard setters (e.g., faculty) have direct knowledge of the examinees or directly observe a performance test. (Appropriately trained standardized patients may be considered content experts in communication and interpersonal skills.) The judges' global ratings are used to determine the checklist score that will be used as the passing standard. One advantage of the method for performance tests is that it empowers clinician observers, who are familiar with the task of assessing student performance; all the necessary information can be obtained during the course of a performance test, eliminating the need to convene a separate standard setting meeting. A disadvantage of this method is that for small scale examinations there may be few students in the borderline group, possibly skewing the results. The related borderline regression method in which (checklist) scores are regressed on the global ratings uses all of the ratings instead of just those for the borderline group (Kramer, et al., 2003).

Borderline Group Standard Setting Procedures

1. Prepare judges by orienting them to the test, station or case and to the checklist or other rating instruments.
2. Judges may have prior classroom or clinical-setting knowledge of the examinees, or alternatively they may directly observe the test performance of each examinee. Each judge should observe multiple examinees on the same station rather than following an examinee across several stations. The test performance observed may, with appropriate training, consist of performance products such as individual checklist item scores or post encounter notes (in that case this method is similar to the body-of-work method).

3. The judge provides a global rating of [the overall performance of] each examinee on a three-point scale: Fail, Borderline, Pass.
4. The performance is also scored (by the judge or another rater) using a multiple-item checklist or rating scale.
5. The mean or median checklist score of those examinees rated "borderline" becomes the passing score for the test (See Figure 6.4). Alternatively, regress the checklist scores on the global ratings and use the resulting equation to obtain a cut score.

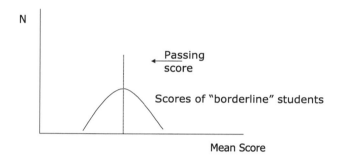

Figure 6.4 Borderline Group Method.

Contrasting Groups Method

The Contrasting Groups method (Burrows, et al., 1999; Clauser & Clyman, 1994; Livingston & Zieky, 1982) is another examinee-centered standard setting method, which requires using an external criterion or other method to divide examinees into two groups: experts vs. novices; passers vs. failers; or competent vs. non-competent. The standard is the score that best discriminates between the two groups. One of the advantages of this method is that the standard can easily be adjusted to minimize errors in either direction. Thus, if the error of greatest concern is mistakenly categorizing an examinee as a "pass" when they should have failed (for example, in certifying examinations), the standard can be moved to the right (see Figures 6.5 and 6.6).

Contrasting Groups Standard Setting Procedures

1. Examinee performance is scored by judges or other raters using a multiple-item checklist or rating scale.
2. Examinees are divided into expert and non-expert groups, based on an external criterion or by having expert observers provide a global Pass/Fail rating of the student's overall performance.
3. Graph the checklist score distributions of the two groups.
4. The passing score is set at the intersection of the two distributions if false-positive and false-negative errors are of equal weight, or moved to the right or the left to minimize the error of greater concern.

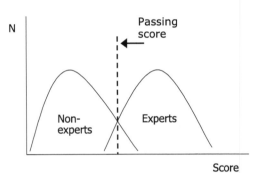

Figure 6.5 Contrasting Groups.

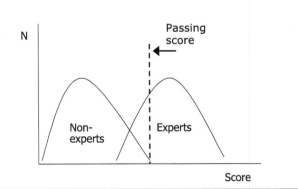

Figure 6.6 Minimizing Passing Errors.

Body of Work Method

PORTFOLIO

Like the Hofstee, the Body of Work method (Kingston, et al., 2001) can be used to set standards for an assessment that is composed of multiple disparate components. The general approach is similar to that of Contrasting Groups, but the judgments are made about samples of examinee's durable work (such as essays, chart notes, or portfolios) rather than about the examinees and their directly observed performance. Work samples are typically scored by judges or other persons before the standard setting exercise takes place.

Body of Work Standard-Setting Procedures

1. Work samples are scored by judges or other raters using a multiple item checklist or rating scale.
2. Prepare judges by orienting them to the test, the examinees, and the definitions of any relevant categories.
3. Present judges with a large number of real, complete examinee work samples, spanning the range of obtained scores.
4. Judges assign each sample into one of the required categories (pass/fail, basic/proficient/advanced etc). This first *range-finding* round defines a "borderline region" where the scores of two categories overlap.
5. Additional work samples with scores from the borderline region only are categorized in a second *pinpointing* round.
6. The final cut score can be derived from the mean or median of scores in the borderline region, the intersection of adjacent distributions, or by use of a logistic regression procedure.

Conclusion

This chapter described the procedures for six different methods of setting standards. Which method should you choose for your examination? Frequently the choice will depend on the practical realities of the test. See Table 6.6 for a comparison of the six methods across several important dimensions.

Table 6.6 Comparison of Six Standard Setting Methods

	Judgment focused on:	Judgments require prior exam data?	Requires expert observers of performance?	Timing of Judgments
Angoff	Test items	No	No	Before exam
Ebel	Test items	Yes	No	After exam
Hofstee	Whole test	Yes	No	After exam
Borderline Group	Examinee performance	No	Yes	During exam
Contrasting Groups	Examinee performance	No	Yes	During exam
Body of Work	Examinee products	No	Yes	After exam

Different standard setting methods will produce different passing scores; there is no "gold standard." The key to defensible standards lies in the choice of credible judges and in the use of a systematic approach to collecting their judgments. Ultimately, all standards are policy decisions, reflecting the collective, subjective opinions of experts in the field.

References

Angoff, W.H. (1971). Scales, norms, and equivalent scores. In R.L. Thorndike (Ed.), *Educational measurement* (2nd ed., pp. 508–600). Washington: American Council on Education.

Boursicot, K.A.M., Roberts, T.E., & Pell, G. (2006). Standard setting for clinical competence at graduation from medical school: A comparison of passing scores across five medical schools. *Advances in Health Sciences Education*, 11, 173–183.

Burrows, P.J., Bingham, L., & Brailovsky, C.A. (1999). A modified contrasting groups method used for setting the passmark in a small scale standard-ized patient examination. *Advances in Health Sciences Education*, 4(2), 145–154.

Cizek, G.J. (2001). *Setting performance standards: Concepts, methods, and perspectives*. Mahwah, NJ: Lawrence Erlbaum.

Cizek, G.J. (2006). Standard setting. In S.M. Downing & T.M. Haladyna, (Eds.), *Handbook of test development* (pp. 225–258). Mahwah, NJ: Lawrence Erlbaum Associates.

Cizek, G.J., Bunch, M.B., & Koons, H. (2004). Setting performance standards: Contemporary methods. *Educational Measurement: Issues and Practice*, Winter, 31–50.

Clauser, B.E., & Clyman, S.G. (1994). A contrasting-groups approach to standard setting for performance assessments of clinical skills. *Academic Medicine*, 69(10), S42–S44.

Clauser, B.E., Margolis, M.J., & Case, S.M. (2006). Testing for licensure and certification in the professions. In R.L. Brennan (Ed.), *Educational measurement* (4th ed.). American Council on Education. Westport, CT: Praeger Publishers.

Cohen, A., Kane, M., & Crooks, T. (1999). A generalized examinee-centered method for setting standards on achievement tests. *Applied Measurement in Education*, 14, 343–366.

De Gruijter, D.N. (1985). Compromise models for establishing examination standards. *Journal of Educational Measurement*, 22, 263–9.

Downing, S.M., Lieska, N.G., & Raible, M.D. (2003). Establishing passing standards for classroom achievement tests in medical education: A comparative study of four methods. *Academic Medicine*, 78 (10, Suppl.), S85–S87.

Downing, S.M., Tekian, A., & Yudkowsky, R. (2006). Procedures for establishing defensible absolute passing scores on performance examinations in health professions education. *Teaching and Learning in Medicine*, 18(1), 50–57.

Dylan, W. (1996). Meaning and consequences in standard setting. *Assessment in Education: Principles, Policy and Practice*, 3(3), 287–308.

Ebel, R.L. (1972). *Essentials of educational measurement* (2nd ed.). Englewood Cliffs, NJ: Prentice-Hall.

Friedman, M. (2000). AMEE Guide No. 18: Standard setting in student assessment. *Medical Teacher*, 22(2), 120–130.

Hambleton, R.M., & Pitoniak, M.J. (2006). Setting performance standards. In R.L. Brennan (Ed.), *Educational measurement* (4th ed.). American Council on Education. Westport, CT: Praeger Publishers.

Hambleton, R.M., & Plake, B.S. (1995). Using an extended Angoff procedure to set standards on complex performance assessments. *Applied Measurement in Education*, 8, 41–56.

Hofstee, W.K.B. (1983). The case for compromise in educational selection and grading. In S.B. Anderson & J.S. Helmick (Eds.), *On educational testing* (pp. 107–127). Washington: Jossey-Bass.

Impara, J.C., & Plake, B.S. (1997). Standard setting: An alternative approach. *Journal of Educational Measurement*, 34(4), 353–66.

Jaeger, R.M. (1991). Selection of judges for standard setting. *Educational Measurement: Issues and Practice*, 10(2), 3–10.

Kane, M. (1994). Validating the performance standards associated with passing scores. *Review of Educational Research*, 64, 425–461.

Kane, M.T., Crooks, T.J., & Cohen, A.S. (1999). Designing and evaluating standard-setting procedures for licensure and certification tests. *Advances in Health Sciences Education*, 4, 195–207.

Kingston, N.M., Kahl, S.R., Sweeney, K., & Bay, L. (2001). Setting performance standards using the body of work method. In G. J. Cizek (Ed.), *Setting performance standards: Concepts, methods and perspectives* (pp. 219–248). Mahwah, NJ: Lawrence Erlbaum Associates.

Kramer, A., Muijtjens, A., Jansen, K., Düsman, H., Tan, L., & Van der Vleuten, C. (2003). Comparison of a rational and an empirical standard setting procedure for an OSCE. *Medical Teacher*, 37, 132–139.

Livingston, S.A., & Zieky, M.J. (1982). *Passing scores: A manual for setting standards of performance on educational and occupational tests.* Princeton, NJ: Educational Testing Service.

Meskauskas, J.A. (1986). Setting Standards. *Evaluation & the Health Professions*, 9, 188–203.

Norcini, J.J. (2003). Setting standards on educational tests. *Medical Education*, 37, 464–469.

Norcini, J., & Guille, R. (2002). Combining tests and setting standards. In G.R. Norman, C.P.M. van der Vleuten, & D.I. Newble (Eds.), *International handbook of research in medical education* (pp. 811–834). Dordrecht, The Netherlands: Kluwer Academic Publishers.

Norcini, J.J., & Shea, J.A. (1997). The credibility and comparability of standards. *Applied Measurement in Education*, 10(1), 39–59.

Ross, L.P., Clauser, B.E., Margolis, M.J., Orr, N.A., & Klass, D.J. (1996). An expert-judgment approach to setting standards for a standardized-patient examination. *Academic Medicine*, 71, S4–S6.

Schindler, N., Corcoran, J., & DaRosa, D. (2007). Description and impact of using a standard-setting method for determining pass/fail scores in a surgery clerkship. *American Journal of Surgery*, 193, 252–257.

Shea, J.A., Reshetar, R., Norcini, J.J., & Dawson, B. (1994). Sensitivity of the modified Angoff standard-setting method to variations in item content. *Teaching and Learning in Medicine*, 6(4), 288–292.

Stern, D.T., Ben-David, M.F., De Champlain, A., Hodges, B., Wojtczak, A., & Schwarz, M.R. (2005). Ensuring global standards for medical graduates: A pilot study of international standard-setting. *Medical Teacher*, 27(3), 207–213.

Stern, D.T., Ben-David, M.F., Norcini, J., Wojtczak, A., & Schwarz, M.R. (2006). Setting school-level outcome standards. *Medical Education*, 40, 166–172.

Wainer, H., & Thissen, D. (1996). How is reliability related to the quality of test scores? What is the effect of local dependence on reliability? *Educational Measurement: Issues and Practice*, 15(1), 22–29.

Wayne, D.B., Barsuk, J.H., Cohen, E., & McGaghie, W.C. (2007). Do baseline data influence standard setting for a clinical skills examination? *Academic Medicine*, 82 (10, Suppl.), S105–S108.

Yudkowsky, R., Downing, S.M., & Wirth, S. (2008). Simpler standards for local performance examinations: The Yes/No Angoff and Whole-test Ebel. *Teaching and Learning in Medicine*, 20(3), 212–217.

7

WRITTEN TESTS

Constructed-Response and Selected-Response Formats

STEVEN M. DOWNING

Introduction

The purpose of this chapter is to provide an overview of the two written testing formats most commonly utilized in health professions education: the constructed-response (CR) and the selected-response (SR) item formats. This chapter highlights some key concepts related to the development and application of these testing modalities and some of the important research evidence concerning their use. This chapter is not intended to be a complete item writing guide or a comprehensive and in-depth critical review of the current theoretical and research literature on written testing or a scholarly defense of written testing in either modality. Rather, the objective of this chapter is to provide a practical summary of information about developing and effectively using CR and SR methods to test cognitive achievement in health professions education, with some suggestions for appropriate use.

Constructed-Response and Selected-Response Formats

The generic terms constructed-response (CR) and selected-response (SR) are accurately descriptive of how these two testing formats work. CR items require the examinee to produce a written response to a stimulus, usually a question or a statement. In this chapter, CR items are discussed as direct or implied open-ended questions or other types of stimuli that require examinees to write (or type) responses or answers, which are then read and scored by content-expert human judges or raters. Essay tests are the most common application of the CR item form in health professions education. Such a narrow definition of CR tests—limited to essay questions alone—would be disputed by many educational measurement professionals who view CR testing as a type of performance testing (e.g., Haladyna, 2004). SR items require examinees to choose a correct or best answer from a fixed listing of possible answers to a question or other stimuli. Examinee answers to SR items may be computer-scored, using answer keys (listing of correct or best answers) developed by content experts. Multiple-choice items (MCQs) are a common example of the SR item form. Table 7.1 summarizes some characteristics of each format discussed in this chapter.

The prototypic CR item type is the essay question. For this chapter two general types of essays are discussed—those requiring long answers and those requiring short answers. A long-answer essay may

Table 7.1 Constructed-Response and Selected-Response Item Formats: Strengths and Limitations

	Constructed-Response	Selected-Response

Strengths	• Non-cued writing
	• Easy to create
	• Logic, reasoning, steps in problem solving
	• Ease of partial credit scoring
	• In-depth assessment
		• Broad representative content
		• Accurate, objective & reproducible scores
		• Defensibility
		• Accurate, timely feedback
		• Secure reuse of banked items
		• Efficient
		  o Time
		  o Cost
		  o Information

Limitations	• Subjective human scoring
	• Limited breath of content
	• Reproducibility issues
	• Inefficient
	  o Scoring time
	  o Testing time
	  o Information
	• Limited psychometrics and quality control
		• Difficult to write well
		• Bad public relations
		  o Guessing
		  o Memorable

require the examinee to write one, two or more pages in response to the question, while short-answer essay questions may require a one- to two-paragraph written response.

The multiple-choice item (MCQ) is the prototypic SR item type. All other examples of fixed-answer test item formats may be considered a variant of the multiple-choice item type. MCQ variants include: the true-false, alternate-choice, multiple-true-false, complex MCQ, matching, and extended matching item types. Table 7.2 lists some examples.

Assessment Using Written Tests

What are written tests good for? Written tests are useful in the measurement of cognitive knowledge or to test learning, achievement, and abilities. Referring to Miller's Pyramid, the "knows" and "knows how" level at the base of the pyramid are best measured by written tests. And, the ACGME toolbox suggests the use of written tests for measuring cognitive knowledge (Downing & Yudkowsky, Chapter 1, this volume). Most cognitive knowledge is mediated verbally, such that humans acquire cognitive knowledge through written or spoken words or by visual, auditory or other stimuli that may be translated or mediated verbally. Thus, written tests are ideally suited to test verbal knowledge. (The nature of "cognitive knowledge" and its acquisition is far beyond the scope of this book.) Many educational measurement texts discuss high-inference and low-inference written item formats, to distinguish the assessment of more abstract verbal knowledge from more concrete verbal knowledge (e.g., Haladyna, 2004; Linn & Miller, 2005).

Written assessments are best suited for the assessment of all the types of learning or cognitive knowledge acquired during courses of study in the health professions—through curricula delivered in classrooms, textbooks, lectures, library and internet research, student discussions in small learning groups, problem-solving group activities, on-line teaching/learning environments, and so on. Written tests are most often and most appropriately used to assess knowledge acquisition—as formative or summative assessments, to provide

Table 7.2 Examples of Constructed-Response and Selected-Response Items

1. **Constructed-Response: Short Answer (Three sentences maximum)**
   Name and describe the function of each of the bones of the human inner ear.

2. **Constructed-Response: Long Answer (Five pages maximum)**
   Discuss the human inner ear, describing in detail how the inner ear structures relate to hearing.

3. **Selected-response: Traditional Multiple-Choice (MCQ)**
   For a stable patient with a ventricular tachycardia of less than 150 beats per minute, which is the most appropriate first measure?

   A. Intravenous lidocaine hydrochloride
   B. Intravenous bretylium tosylate
   C. Synchronized cardioversion

4. **Selected-response: True-False (TF)**
   Random guessing is a major problem with the true-false testing format.

5. **Selected-response: Alternate-Choice (AC)**
   If the number of items on a test is increased from 40 items to 60 items, the reliability of the 60 item test will most likely be:

   A. Higher than the reliability of the 40 item test
   B. Lower than the reliability of the 40 item test

6. **Selected-response: Multiple True-False (MTF)**
   Which of the following increase the content-related validity evidence for an achievement test?   (Mark each option as True or False)

   A. Developing a detailed test blueprint
   B. Training test item writers in item writing principles
   C. Scoring the test using formulas that correct for guessing
   D. Using some test items that are very hard and some items that are very easy
   E. Selecting the most highly discriminating previously used test items

7. Selected-response: Traditional Matching

Match each term on the left (1–3) with a definitions (A–D) on the right.

Each definition can be used once, more than once, or not at all.

1. Hammer
2. Stirrup
3. Pinna

A. Smallest bone in human body
B. Passes sound vibrations from eardrum
C. Passes sound vibrations from malleus
D. Visible part of outer ear
E. Fluid-filled tubes attached to cochlea

8. Selected-Response: Extended Matching (EM)

Match each diagnosis (A–E) with the patient descriptions (1–3).

Each diagnosis can used once, more than once, or not at all.

A. Vasovagal reaction
B. Anaphylaxis
C. Lidocaine toxicity
D. Allergic contact dermatitis
E. Stroke

What is the most likely diagnosis for each patient who is undergoing or has recently undergone pure tumescent liposuction?

1. Immediately post op, a 49 year-old woman says that she "feels sick." Her blood pressure is normal and her pulse is difficult to palpate; her skin is pale, cool and diaphoretic.
2. Six hours post op, a 25 year-old man is agitated and has tingling around his mouth. His speech is rapid.
3. During surgery, a 34 year-old woman says she "feels sick." She has generalized pruritus, her blood pressure begins to decrease and her pulse rate is rapid. Her skin is red and warm.

(Continued Overleaf)

Table 7.2 Continued

9. **Selected-Response: Complex Multiple-Choice (Type-K)**

What is the best treatment for a common cold (URI)?

Mark A if 1, 2, and 3 only are correct
Mark B if 1 & 3 only are correct
Mark C if 2 & 4 only are correct
Mark D if 4 only is correct
Mark E if all are correct

1. Rest
2. Fluids
3. Antihistamines
4. Decongestants

10. **Selected-Response: Testlets or Context-Dependent Item Sets**

One month after returning from Mexico, a 22-year-old college student presents with jaundice and abdominal pain.

1. Which of the following will most likely develop in this patient?

   A. fulminant hepatic failure
   B. carrier state
   C. chronic hepatitis
   D. cirrhosis

2. What is the most likely route of transmission for this disease?

   A. inhalation of contaminated air droplets
   B. ingestion of contaminated food
   C. mucosal exposure to bodily fluids
   D. hematogenous spread

feedback on learning or to measure the sufficiency of learning in order to proceed in the curriculum. Written tests are not at all useful to test performance or "doing," unless that performance happens to be the production of writing (which can be tested only by written tests).

The primary guiding factor in determining the appropriateness of any testing format relates to its purpose, the desired interpretations of scores, the construct hypothesized to be measured, and the ultimate consequences of the test. The characteristics of the testing format should match the needs for validity evidence for some particular assessment setting and there should be a clear rationale for choice of the written format, given the validity needs of the assessment. For example, if the goal is to test student cognitive knowledge about the principles of effective patient communication or the understanding of various principles of effective communication with patients, a written test may match the purpose of the test and the required needs for specific types of validity evidence to support score inferences. But, in order to measure students' use of communication skills with patients requires some type of performance test—a simulation, a standardized oral exam, or a structured observation of student communication with patients in a real setting. A written test would be mismatched to the purpose of this test and the required validity evidence, given the intended purpose of the test.

Both the CR and the SR have some unique strengths and limitations, as noted in Table 7.1. Both testing formats have been researched and written about for nearly a century. Strong beliefs, long-held traditions, and vigorous opinions abound. In this chapter, we review some of the science and research evidence and summarize the best practice that follows from this research.

Constructed-Response Items

Constructed-response (CR) items, in some form, have been used to test students for centuries. In this chapter, CR items are discussed only as essay questions—either short- or long-answer essay questions.

CR formats have many strengths. For instance, the CR format is the only testing format useful for testing writing skills such as the adequacy of sentence and paragraph construction, skill at writing a persuasive argument, ability to organize logical thoughts, and so on. All CR items require non-cued written answers from examinees. The CR item format may permit the essay reader to score specific steps in working through a problem or the logic of each step used in reasoning or problem solving, which may facilitate partial credit scoring (as opposed to "all or nothing" scoring). CR formats may be most time efficient (for the instructor) in testing small groups of students, since less time will be spent writing essay questions or prompts than in creating effective SR items. Small groups of examinees also may make the essay scoring task time efficient. And, essay questions are usually easier to write than MCQs or other SR formats.

However, there are also many issues, challenges, and potential problems associated with essay tests. CR tests are difficult to score accurately and reliably. Scoring is time consuming and costly. Content-related validity evidence is often compromised or limited, especially for large content domains, because of sampling issues related to testing time constraints. And, there are many potential threats to validity for CR items, all related to the more subjective nature of essay scores and various biases associated with human essay readers. There are fewer psychometric quality-control measures, such as item analysis, available for CR items than for SR items.

The purpose of the CR test, the desired interpretation of scores, and hypotheses about the construct measured—validity—should drive the choice of which written format to use in testing cognitive knowledge. For instance, if the goals and objectives of instruction relate to student achievement in writing coherent explanations for some biochemical mechanism and in tracing each particular stage of its development, an essay test may be a good match. "Writing" is the key word, since only CR item forms can adequately test the production of original writing. (SR formats can test many of the components of writing, such as knowledge of vocabulary, sentence structure, syntax and so on.)

Anatomy of a Constructed-Response Prompt

CR items or questions are often referred to generically as prompts, since these stimuli can take many forms in performance testing: written questions, photographs, data tables, graphs, interactive computer stimuli of various types, and so on. These general stimuli serve to prompt a CR response, which can then be scored. In this chapter, we discuss CR items as essay questions only, since these are the most frequently used type of CR format in health professions education worldwide.

An essay question or prompt consists of a direct question on a specific focused topic and provides sufficient information to examinees to answer the question. All relevant instructions concerning answering the question, such as expected length of answer, time limits, specificity of answer, and so on must be clearly stated. See Table 7.2 for some examples.

Basic Principles of Writing Constructed-Response Items

"Writers of performance assessment items must adhere to the same rules of item writing used in the development of multiple-choice test items" (Welch, 2006, p. 312). Table 7.3 presents these item writing principles, as defined by the educational measurement textbooks and the empirical research on these principles (Haladyna, Downing, & Rodriguez, 2002).

CR item writing benefits from attention to these principles and revisions and editing based on independent review by other content experts (Downing, 2006). Clarity of meaning is an essential characteristic for all test items, since such text is highly scrutinized by examinees for subtle meaning. As in all testing, the content to be tested is the most fundamental consideration; the format selected for the test is always of secondary importance.

During the preparation of the essay-type question, a model or ideal answer to the question should also be prepared by the author of the question, just as a correct or best answer key should be designated by a SR item author. The specificity of the model answer must match the

evidence-based
see pp. 168

Table 7.3 A Revised Taxonomy of Multiple-Choice Item Writing Guidelines[1]

Content

1. Every item should reflect specific content and a single specific mental behavior, as called for in the test specifications.
2. Base each item on important content; avoid trivial content.
3. Use novel material to test higher level learning. Don't use exact textbook language in test items, to avoid testing only recall of familiar words and phrases.
4. Keep the content of each item independent.
5. Avoid overspecific and over-general content.
6. Avoid opinion-based items.
7. Avoid trick items.
8. Keep vocabulary simple and appropriate for the examinees tested.

Formatting Concerns

9. Use the question, completion, and best answer versions of conventional MC, the alternate choice, true-false, multiple true-false, matching, and the context-dependent item and item set formats, but avoid the complex MC format.
10. Format the item vertically, not horizontally.

Style Concerns

11. Edit and proof items.
12. Use correct grammar, punctuation, capitalization, and spelling.
13. Minimize the amount of reading in each item.

Stem

14. Ensure that the directions in the stem are very clear.
15. Include the central idea in the stem, not in the options.
16. Avoid window dressing (excessive verbiage).
17. Word the stem positively, avoid negatives such as NOT or EXCEPT. If negative words are used, use the word cautiously and always ensure that the word appears capitalized and in bold type.

The Options

18. Develop as many effective choices as you can, but research suggests three is adequate.
19. Make sure that only one of these choices is the right answer.
20. Vary the location of the right answer according to the number of choices.
    Balance the answer key, insofar as possible, so that the correct answer appears an equal number of times in each answer position.
21. Place the choices in logical or numerical order.
22. Keep choices independent; choices should not be overlapping in meaning.
23. Keep choices homogeneous in content and grammatical structure.
24. Keep the length of choices about equal.
25. *None-of-the above* should be used carefully.
26. Avoid *All-of-the-above*.
27. Phrase choices positively; avoid negatives such as NOT.
28. Avoid giving clues to the right answer, such as:
    a. Specific determiners including *always, never, completely, and absolutely*.
    b. Clang associations, choices identical to or resembling words in the stem.
    c. Grammatical inconsistencies that cue the test-taker to the correct choice.
    d. Conspicuous correct choice.

  e. Pairs or triplets of options that clue the test-taker to the correct choice.
  f. Blatantly absurd, ridiculous options.
29. Make all distractors plausible.
30. Use typical errors of students to write your distractors.
31. Use humor if it is compatible with the teacher and the learning environment.

Source: 1. Quoted from and adapted from Haladyna, Downing, & Rodriquez, 2002, p. 312.

directions to examinees. This model or ideal answer will form the basis of a scoring rubric (the scoring key for CR items) used in the actual scoring of the response to the essay question (see Table 7.4 for example).

The CR item, including its specific directions for examinees, the ideal answer, and the actual scoring rubric should be prepared well in advance of the test administration, so that time for review, revision and editing is available.

Short-Answer versus Long-Answer Constructed-Response

Short-answer CR items require answers of a few words, a few sentences, or a few paragraphs, whereas long-answer CR items require written responses of several pages in length. The purpose of the assessment and the content-related validity requirements for broad sampling versus depth of sampling should drive decisions about CR length. In achievement assessment for most classroom settings, breath of sampling is important because the purpose of the test is to generalize to an examinee's knowledge of some large domain of knowledge from a limited sample. If CR tests are used, short-answer essays permit broader sampling of content than long-answer essays, because more questions can be asked and answered per hour of testing time.

If the purpose of the test is to sample a narrow domain of knowledge in great depth, long-answer essays may be the most appropriate format. Long-answer essays permit asking an examinee to produce answers of great detail, probing the limits and depths of knowledge about a single topic or content area. In some cases, long-answer essays may be appropriate, but generally these longer essays are poor samples of large domains and therefore lack generalizability and validity evidence.

Scoring Constructed-Response Items

Scoring is a major validity challenge for CR items. CR scoring is inherently subjective and therefore requires attention to a number of issues in order to reduce the negative effect of subjectivity on scoring validity. In this context, we discuss scoring methods and rater characteristics together with some basic recommendations to increase scoring accuracy.

Constructed-Response Scoring Methods

There are two different approaches to essay scoring: analytic or holistic ratings. In analytic methods, essays are rated in several different categories or for several different characteristics. For example, analytic scoring might require ratings of the accuracy of the answer to the question and the specificity of the answer, the organization of the written answer, the writing quality, and so on. Analytic methods require the rater to concentrate on several different aspects of the essay, all of which are presumably related to the quality of the essay answer and the construct intended to be measured by the essay question. Score points are assigned to each analytic segment or aspect of the essay, based on some rationale. Holistic or global ratings require the essay reader to make only one single rating of the overall quality of the written answer.

Which is the best method, analytic or holistic? The answer depends on the purpose of the CR test. Analytic scoring methods may permit feedback to examinees on more specific aspects of performance than do global methods. However, many of the separate characteristics rated in the analytic method may correlate highly with each other, thus reducing the presumed benefit of analytic scoring methods. Global or holistic ratings are generally more reliable than individual ratings, but the intended use of the CR rating data should be the major factor in deciding on analytic or holistic methods (see

McGaghie et al., Chapter 8, this volume). Analytic methods usually require more scoring time than global methods, so feasibility and practicality will also be a factor in the choice of method.

Analytic methods may permit the weighting or differential allocation of partial credit scores somewhat more easily or more logically than global methods. For an essay item in which several different essay traits are rated, it is possible to allocate the total score for the essay differentially across the rating categories. For example, the content and structure of the essay answer may be weighted more highly than the writing quality and the organization of the answer; score points for the answer would be allocated accordingly. Analytic methods may assist the essay reader in staying focused on the essential features of the answer.

Model Answers

Whichever scoring method is used, an ideal or model answer should be prepared for each essay question rated. This model answer should list all of the required components to the answer. Model answers are analogous to the scoring key for a SR test, so they should be reviewed by content experts for accuracy and completeness. Model answers strive to reduce the subjectivity due to human raters, by introducing some objectivity and standardization to the scoring process.

Essay Raters

Human readers or raters of essay answers are essential. The subjectivity of human raters creates a potential major scoring problem. Human raters bring biases and many other potential sources of rater error to the task, so counterbalancing efforts must be taken to try to reduce problems due to rater subjectivity.

It is recommended that two independent raters read every essay answer and that their separate ratings be averaged—especially for essays that have higher stakes or consequences for examinees. The expectation is that averaging the ratings from two independent readers will reduce bias. For example, if one rater tends to be a "hawk" or severe and the other rater tends to be a "dove" or lenient, their mean rating will offset both the severity and the leniency bias. On the other hand, if both raters are severe or both are lenient, the average rating will do nothing to offset these rating errors or biases and will, in fact, compound the problem.

It is also often suggested that essay raters read all the answers to one essay question for all examinees, rather than reading all answers to all questions for a single examinee. It is thought that essay raters do better if they can focus on one essay answer at a time, but there is little evidence to support this recommendation.

Scoring Rubrics

A scoring rubric is a detailed guide for the essay rater and attempts to reduce some of the inherent subjectivity of human raters by stating pre-specified behavioral anchors for ratings. Scoring rubrics can take many forms in providing anchors and specific detail for the scoring task; the specific forms will differ for analytic or global rating methods. See Table 7.4 for a simple example of an analytic scoring rubric, to be

Table 7.4 Example of Analytic Scoring Rubric for Short-Answer Essay on the Anatomy of the Inner-Ear

Scale	Scale Point Description	Factual Accuracy	Structural Relationships	Writing
5	Excellent	All facts presented completely accurately	All structural relationships accurately described	Writing well organized, clear, grammatical
4	Good	Most facts correct	Most structural relationships correct	Writing fairly well organized, good clarity, mostly grammatical
3	Satisfactory	Many facts correct, some incorrect	Many structural relationships correct	Moderate organization and clarity, some grammatical errors
2	Marginal	Few facts correct	Few structural relationships correct	Little organization or clarity of writing, many grammatical errors
1	Unsatisfactory	No facts correct	No structural relationships correct	No organization or clarity, many serious grammatical errors

used in the scoring of a short essay answer. Note that the use of essay scoring rubrics fits well with the recommendation to use model answers and two independent raters—all suggestions intended to reduce the idiosyncratic subjectivity due to human raters.

Threats to Validity of Constructed-Response Scoring

Both the content underrepresentation (CU) and the construct-irrelevant variance (CIV) validity threats are potential issues for CR tests (Downing & Haladyna, Chapter 2, this volume; Downing & Haladyna, 2004; Messick, 1989). For example, if only long-answer essays are used for classroom-type achievement assessment, content underrepresentation is a potential threat, especially for large achievement domains. Long-answer essays may undersample large domains, since only a few questions can be posed and answered per hour of testing time.

Construct-irrelevant variance (CIV) threats to validity abound in essay-type testing. Rater error or bias due to reader subjectivity is the greatest source of potential CIV for essay testing. Unless great care is taken to reduce or control this type of rater error, collectively known as rater severity error, components of the final score assigned to essay answers can be composed of reliable ratings of irrelevant characteristics. Raters are notoriously poor, even when well trained, at controlling their tendencies to assign biased scores to essays.

The well-known rater errors of halo, leniency, severity, central tendency, and idiosyncratic rating fully apply to essay readers (McGaghie et al., Chapter 8, this volume). Tracking of raters and providing frequent feedback to essay raters on their performance, especially relative to their peers, may help temper some of these CIV errors. And using the average rating of two independent raters, who have different biases, may diminish some of the ill effects of rater bias. Obviously, formal written model answers seek to lessen the subjectivity of ratings, as do the use of written scoring rubrics.

Another source of error concerns examinee bluffing, which is sometimes attempted by examinees who do not know the specific answer to the question posed. Some bluffing methods include: restating the question to use up required space; restating the question in such as way as to answer a different question; writing correct answers to different questions (which were not posed in the prompt); writing answers to appeal to the biases of the essay reader, and so on (e.g., Linn & Miller, 2005). If bluffing attempts are successful for the examinee, CIV is added because the scores are biased by assessment of traits not intended to be measured by the essay.

Other potential CIV issues relate to the quality of handwriting, which can be either a positive or negative bias, writing skill (when writing is not the main construct of interest); skill in the use of grammar, spelling, punctuation (when these issues are not the primary construct); and so on. All such extraneous characteristics of the written response can unduly influence the essay reader, in either a positive or a negative manner, adding CIV to the scores and thereby reducing evidence for validity.

Constructed-Response Format: Recommendations and Summary

The constructed-response (CR) format is good for testing un-cued written responses to specific questions. If the purpose of the assessment is to test student achievement of the relevant content in a written form—where components of writing are critical to the content—CR is the format of choice. The CR format is the only format to use to test the actual production of writing.

CR formats may be preferred if the number of examinees is small, since scoring essay responses may take less time than writing selected-response items. Also, it may be possible to assign partial credit to CR answers in a logical or defensible manner. Short-answer essays are preferred to long-answer essays for most classroom achievement assessment settings, because of the possibility for better content-related validity evidence.

Scoring of essay answers is a challenge, due to the inherent subjectivity of the human essay reader. Using at least two independent and well trained raters, who use model or ideal answers and clear scoring rubrics to anchor their scores, is recommended. The provision of specific and timely feedback to essay raters may help to reduce some rater bias. The choice of analytic or global and holistic methods of scoring depends on the purpose of the test, the content of the essays, the stakes associated with the scores and feasibility issues.

Selected-Response Items

"Any aspect of cognitive educational achievement can be tested by means of either the multiple-choice or the true-false form." (Ebel, 1972, p. 103)

This quote from Robert L. Ebel, a scholar of the SR format, provides an appropriate introduction to this section.

Selected-response (SR) items, typified by multiple-choice questions (MCQ) as the prototypic form, are the most useful written testing format for testing cognitive knowledge in most health professions education settings. Some examples of commonly used SR item forms are presented in Table 7.2.

The SR item format was developed nearly a century ago to provide an efficient means of cognitive testing for large groups of examinees. Ebel (1972) presents a brief history of the early development of the MCQ format and its first major use by the U.S. military for recruit selection testing in the early twentieth century. In discussions of the relative merits of SR and CR testing, it may be instructive to remember that SR formats were introduced to overcome shortcomings of the CR format.

MCQs are useful for testing cognitive knowledge, especially at higher levels. MCQs are most efficient for use with large groups of examinees because the time spent in preparing test items prior to administering the test is generally less than the time required to read and score CR items after the test, because MCQs can be easily and rapidly computer scored. Effective MCQs can be re-used on future tests, if stored securely in a retrievable item bank. Also, MCQs are most efficient for testing large knowledge domains broadly, so that the test is a representative sample of the total content domain, thus increasing the content-related validity evidence, and permitting valid inferences or generalizations to the whole of the content domain. MCQs can be scored accurately, reliably, and rapidly. Meaningful

MCQ score reports—providing feedback to students on specific strengths and weaknesses—can be produced easily by computer and in a timely and cost effective way—thus potentially improving the learning environment for students. Sound psychometric theory, with a large research base and a lengthy history, underpins MCQ testing. Validity and reliability theory, item analysis and other test quality-control methods, plus an emerging theory of MCQ item writing, provide support for the use of well crafted MCQs in the testing of cognitive achievement (Downing, 2002a, 2006; Downing & Haladyna, 1997).

For a complete and in-depth scholarly treatment of the MCQ format and its variants, refer to *Developing and validating multiple-choice test items*, third edition (Haladyna, 2004). This book-length treatment is the best single source of current research on the MCQ form and its application in educational testing.

Anatomy of an MCQ

A multiple-choice item consists of a *stem* or lead-in, which presents a stimulus or all the necessary information required to answer a direct or implied *question*. The stem and question are followed by a listing of possible answers or *options.*

Basic Principles of Writing Effective MCQs

Over many years of development, research and widespread use, principles for creating effective and defensible MCQs have emerged. These evidence-based principles have been summarized by studies, which reviewed the advice to MCQ item writers by authors of the major educational measurement textbooks and the recommendations based on relevant empirical research concerning these item writing principles (Haladyna & Downing, 1989 a, b; Haladyna, Downing, & Rodriguez, 2002). Table 7.3 lists a summary of these 31 principles and is adapted from Haladyna, Downing, and Rodriguez (2002).

There are empirical studies supporting about one-half of these 31 principles of effective item writing and most major educational measurement textbook authors endorse most of these principles. Thus, these 31 principles offer the best evidence in practice for creating effective and defensible MCQs. But, these general principles alone are not sufficient to assist the MCQ item writer in creating effective test items. For an excellent and detailed item writing guide, aimed specifically toward the health professions educator, see Case and Swanson (1998) and the National Board of Medical Examiners (NBME) website (www.nbme.org). This item writing guide presents excellent suggestions and many relevant examples of effective and ineffective SR items.

MCQs which violate one or more of these standard item writing principles have been shown to disadvantage some students. In one study, flawed items were artificially more difficult for medical students and misclassified 14 percent of students as failing the test when they passed the same content when tested by non-flawed MCQs (Downing, 2005).

Overview of Principles for Effective MCQs

The most effective MCQs are well focused on a single essential or important question or issue. The single most important requirement is that the item's content is relevant, important, and appropriate. Most of the information needed to answer the question is contained in the stem of the item, which is worded positively, and concludes with a direct (or indirect) question. Options (the set of possible answers) are generally short, since most of the information is contained in the stem of the item. There is a good match between the cognitive level posed by the question and the instructional objective of the instruction. Generally, many items test higher-order cognitive objectives of instruction (such as understanding, application, evaluation) using novel content; few items test the lower levels of the cognitive domain such as recall and recognition. The set of options are homogeneous such that all possible answers are of the same general class and every option is a plausible correct answer. One and only one of the options is the correct (or best) answer to the question posed in the stem. Experts agree on the correct or best answer. The wording of the MCQ is extremely clear so that there are no ambiguities of language. No attempt is made to deliberately trick knowledgeable examinees into giving an incorrect answer. All clues to the correct answer are eliminated from the item, as are all unnecessary complexities and extraneous difficulty, and all other ambiguities of meaning (Baranowski, 2006). The MCQ is drafted by the item author—an expert in the content of the item—who asks another content expert to review the draft item and its form. Sufficient time is allowed for review comments to be considered and changes to be incorporated into the final item (Downing, 2006).

On the other hand, a poorly crafted or flawed MCQ may test trivial content, at a low level of the cognitive domain (recall or recognition only). The item may have an unfocused stem, so that the question is not clearly stated—so that the examinee must read all of the options in order to begin to understand the question. Such a flawed MCQ may be worded negatively and so ambiguously that examinees are confused about the question being asked. The stem may be a non-focused, open-ended statement that requires the examinee to read all the options first in order to understand what question is being asked. There may be no correct or best answer to the question or more than one correct answer, so that the correctness of the scoring key can not be defended. The flawed MCQ may incorporate inadvertent cues to the correct answer, so that uninformed examinees can get the item correct; or, the item may be so ambiguously written that examinees who actually know the content intended to be tested by the MCQ get the item wrong (Downing, 2002a).

Elimination of five common flaws in MCQs may greatly reduce the ill effects of poorly crafted MCQs. These flaws are: unfocused stems, negative stems, the "all of the above" and the "none of the above" options, and the so-called partial-K type item (Downing, 2005), which is discussed later in this chapter (see Complex Item Forms). This study and others (e.g., Downing, 2002b) suggest that classroom achievement tests in the health professions typically utilize many flawed items—up to about one-half of the items studied had one or more item flaws, defined as a violation of one or more of the 31 evidence-based principles of effective item writing. And, these item flaws negatively impacted student achievement measurement and biased pass-fail decisions made from scores of tests composed of flawed items.

Creative Item Writing

Writing effective MCQs is both art and science. The *science* is provided by the evidence-based principles noted in Table 7.3. The *art* is associated with variables such as effective item writer training, use of effective training materials, practice, feedback, motivation, item review and editing skills, writing ability and so on. Writers of effective MCQ items are trained not born. Content expertise is the single most essential characteristic of an effective item writer. But content expertise alone is not sufficient, since item writing is a specialized skill and, like all skills, must be mastered through guided practice and feedback on performance. There is no reason to suspect, for example, that an internationally recognized expert in some health sciences discipline will necessarily be an expert MCQ item writer, unless that individual also has some specialized training in the science and art of item writing.

The world is awash in poorly written MCQs (Downing, 2002c). Writing effective, creative, challenging MCQs—which test important knowledge at higher levels—is a difficult and time consuming task. Lack of time for already overburdened instructors may be one major reason that there are so many poorly crafted MCQs used in typical classroom tests in the health professions. But the weakness is not with the MCQ format itself; the issues result from the poor execution of the format and the consequent negative impact of such poor execution on students.

Some MCQs Issues

Many criticisms, issues, and questions arise about MCQs and the details of their structure and scoring. Some of these concerns are reviewed here, with recommendations for practice, based on the research literature.

Number of MCQ Options   Traditionally, MCQs have four or five options. The question of the optimal number of options to use for an MCQ item has been researched over many years. So, the recommendation to use a minimum of three options is based on solid research (see Table 7.3, principle #18). A meta-analysis of studies by Rodriquez (2005) on the optimal number of options shows that generally three options is best for most MCQs.

Most four- or five-option MCQs have only about three options that are actually selected by 5 percent or more of the examinees and have statistical characteristics that are desirable (Haladyna & Downing, 1993). Incorrect options that are selected by 5 percent or more of examinees and have negative discrimination indices are called functional distractors. (See Downing, Chapter 5, this volume, for a discussion of item analysis data and its use.)

Since few examinees typically choose dysfunctional options, the recommendation is to "develop as many effective choices as you can, but research suggests three is adequate" (Haladyna, et al., 2002, p. 312). Using more than three options may not do much harm to the test, but will add inefficiencies for item writers and examinees and permit the use of fewer total MCQs per hour. So, the best advice is to develop as many plausible incorrect options as feasible, noting that plausibility will ultimately be determined empirically by reviewing the item analysis data showing the number of examinees who actually chose the incorrect options. The use of three-option MCQs require a sufficient number of total MCQs be used on the test—the usual advice being a minimum of about 35–40 items total. Also, note that items on a test may have a varying number of options, such that some items may have three options while other items naturally have four, five or even more options.

Three-option MCQ critics suggest that using fewer than four to five options increases random guessing and reduces test score reliability. Of course, for a single MCQ, the probability of randomly guessing the correct answer is 0.33 for a three-option item and 0.20 for a five-option item. But, this random guessing issue is not usually a problem, for well written MCQs, targeted in difficulty appropriately, and used in sufficient numbers to overcome any meaningful gain from an occasional lucky guess. On the issue of reliability, it is true that three-option items will be slightly less reliable than four to five option items, but this slight decrease in scale reliability is rarely meaningful (Rodriguez, 2005).

Random Guessing   Random guessing on SR items is usually over-estimated and concerns about guessing may be overstated. If SR items are well written, targeted at appropriate difficulty levels, reviewed and edited to eliminate all cues to the correct answer, random guessing is usually not a major problem. Examinees may be able to get an occasional item correct using only a lucky random guess so it is important to use sufficient numbers of total SR items on the test. If items are too difficult, examinees may have no choice but to blindly guess, so using appropriate item difficulty levels is important.

Random or blind guessing differs from informed elimination of incorrect answers, in which examinees use partial knowledge to eliminate some options and narrow their selection to the correct answer. In real life, partial knowledge is frequently used to solve problems and answer questions. We rarely have complete knowledge for decision making, especially in the health professions. We do gain information about student ability or achievement even when students use partial knowledge to answer SR items.

Random guessing is not a good strategy to achieve a high or even a satisfactory score on an SR test. For example, consider a 30-item MCQ test in which each item has three options. The probability of getting one item correct is 0.33—a good chance of randomly guessing a correct answer on that single item. But, to get two items correct using chance alone, the probability falls to 0.11; and, to get three items correct using random guesses only, the chance falls to 0.04. Even for a fairly short test of 30 items, using three-option MCQs, the probability of getting a score of 70 percent correct is only 0.000036. When a more typical test length of 50 items, each with three options, is used, the probability of getting a good score of 75 percent correct falls to 0.00000000070. The odds of achieving a high score on a test using random guessing alone are not good and most students understand that random guessing is not a good strategy to optimize their test scores.

The best defense against random guessing on MCQs is to create well crafted items and to present those items in sufficient numbers to reduce any major impact resulting from some random guessing.

Correction-for-Guessing Scoring   Methods or formulas used to score MCQ tests have been researched and debated for many years. There are two basic methods used to score SR tests: count the number of correct items (number-correct score) or use a formula to try to "correct" the number-correct score for presumed guessing. Test users have disagreed about using such formula scores throughout the history of SR testing.

The simple count of the number of items marked correctly is usually the best score. Raw scores such as these can be converted to any number of other metrics, such as percent-correct scores, derived scores, standard scores, and any other linear transformation of the number-correct score (Downing, Chapter 5, this volume).

All correction-for-guessing formula scores attempt to eliminate or reduce the perceived ill effects of random guessing on SR items. These formulas usually work in one of two ways: they try to reward examinees for resisting the temptation to guess or they actively penalize the test taker for guessing (Downing, 2003). However intuitively appealing these guessing corrections may be, they do not work very well and they do not accomplish their stated goals. Both the corrected and uncorrected scores correlate perfectly (unless there are many omitted answers), indicating that both scoring methods rank order examinees identically, although the absolute values of scores may differ. Further, no matter whether examinees are directed to answer all questions or only those questions they know for certain (i.e., to guess or not to guess), savvy, testwise, or bold examinees know that they will usually maximize their score by attempting to answer every question on the test, no matter what the general directions on the test state or what formulas are used to derive a score. So, corrections for guessing tend to bias scores (e.g., Muijtjens, van Mameren, Hoogenboom,

Evers, & van der Vleuten, 1999) and reduce validity evidence by adding construct-irrelevant variance (CIV) to scores, because boldness is a personality trait, and not the achievement or ability construct intended to be measured by the test.

Testlets: Context-Dependent Item Sets

One special type or special use of MCQs is in the testlet or context-dependent item set (e.g., Haladyna, 1992). See Table 7.2 for an example of a testlet. Testlets consist of stimulus materials which are used for two or more independent items, presented in sets. For example, a testlet could consist of a paragraph or two giving a detailed clinical description of a patient, in sufficient detail to answer several different questions based on the same clinical information. One item in the testlet might ask for a most likely diagnosis, another question for laboratory investigations, another on therapies, another on complications, and final question on expected or most likely outcomes.

Testlets are excellent special applications of SR or MCQ items. Testlets are efficient, in that a single stimulus (stem, lead-in) serves multiple items. Several items can be written for the common stem and, for test security purposes, different items can be used on different administrations of the test. Testlets permit a more in-depth probing of a specific content area.

Some basic principles of testlet use must be noted. All items appearing on the same test with a common stem must be reasonably independent such that getting one of the items incorrect does not necessarily mean getting another item incorrect. Obviously, one item should not cue the answer to another item in the set. Each item in the testlet is scored as an independent MCQ, but the proper unit of analysis is the testlet score and not the item score, especially for reliability analysis (Thissen & Wainer, 2001; Wainer & Thissen, 1996). If all of these conditions are met, testlets can be an excellent way to test some types of cognitive knowledge, but some care must be taken not to oversample areas of the content domain because several items are presented on the same topic. Two to three independent items per testlet set appears to maximize reliability (Norman, Bordage, Page, & Keane, 2006).

Other Selected-Response Formats

Extended-Matching

The extended-matching SR format extends the traditional matching format, making this item form useful to test higher-order knowledge (Case & Swanson, 1993). See Table 7.2 for an example. All matching items may be thought of as MCQs turned upside down, so that a common set of options is associated with a fixed set of items or questions. Each separate item of the EM set is scored as a free-standing item.

Like the traditional matching format, the extended-matching format is organized around a common set of options, all fitting the same general theme, and all providing plausible answers to a set of items designed to match this set of possible answers. See the NBME item writing guide (Case & Swanson, 1998) for good examples and discussion of this item type. As in traditional matching items, there should always be more options than items, so that a one-to-one correspondence is avoided. General directions for this form typically state: "Select each option once, more than once, or not at all."

Whereas traditional matching items generally test lower levels of the cognitive domain, like recall and recognition of facts, extended-matching items are ideal for testing higher-order cognitive knowledge relating to clinical situations such as clinical investigations, history taking, diagnoses, management, complications of therapy, outcomes of therapy, and so on. As a bonus, item writers, once they master the basics, may find EM items somewhat easier to create, since several related items are written around a common theme and at the same time. Also, EM items lend themselves to "mixing and matching" over different administrations of a test, since sometimes more item-option pairs than can be used on a single test are created for use on future tests.

For EM items of the clinical situation type, there must be a single common theme (e.g., diagnosis of related illnesses), with all the options fitting this common theme and all the items or questions relating to this theme, as in the example given in Table 7.2. Most EM items briefly describe a clinical situation, presenting all the essentials facts of a patient problem or issue and a single focused question related to these clinical facts or findings. The items should be relatively short (no more than two to four sentences) and the options should be a short phrase or a single word.

The total number of options to use in EM sets is limited only by the constraints of answer sheet design (if machine-scored answer sheets are used). Many standard answer sheets are designed for a maximum of ten or fewer options, so the number of EM options has to be limited to a maximum number of options available on the answer sheet.

Some cautions are in order about EM items. Overuse of this item type on a single test could lead to an oversampling of some content areas to the detriment of other content areas. Since the EM format demands a common theme, it is likely that each EM item in the set will be classified as sampling content from the same general area. Many EM items on the same test could, therefore, oversample some content areas, while other important areas are overlooked (leading to the CU threat to validity).

True-False Formats

The true-false (TF) item format appears to be a simple SR format, requiring the examinee to answer either true or false to a simple proposition (e.g., Ebel & Frisbie, 1991). See Table 7.2 for an example of a true-false item. The TF item form requires an answer that can be absolutely defended as being more true than false or more false than true.

In health professions education, there are many examples of true-false items used to test very low level cognitive knowledge. In fact, many educators believe that the TF item form can be used to test only low-level cognitive knowledge (facts) and that most TF items test trivial content. While this may be an unfair criticism, there are many examples of TF items to support such a belief.

Measurement error due to random guessing on TF items is also a frequent criticism. If true-false items are well written and used in sufficient numbers on a test form (e.g. 50 or more items), measurement error due to blind guessing will be minimized. If these conditions are not met, random guessing may be a problem on TF tests. Like MCQs, TF items are best scored as "right or wrong," with no formula scoring used to attempt to correct for guessing for most achievement testing settings in the health professions.

In fact, TF items can be used to test very high levels of cognitive knowledge (Ebel & Frisbie, 1991). The TF item has some strengths. For example, content-related validity evidence may be increased for TF items because many more TF items can be presented per hour of testing time compared to some other SR formats. Well written TF items can have sound psychometric properties, but TF items will almost always be less difficult than MCQs and the score reliability for TF items may be lower than for MCQs.

Creation of challenging, defensible TF items which measure higher-order knowledge is a challenging task. Some specialized skills pertain to TF item writing and these skills are rare.

Alternate-Choice Items (AC)

The Alternate-Choice (AC) item format (e.g., Downing, 1992) is a variant of the TF format. The AC form (see Table 7.2 for example) requires less absoluteness of its truth or falsity and may, therefore, be more useful in classroom assessment in the health professions. However, the AC format is not used extensively, probably because it has many of the same limitations of the TF item form or at least is perceived to have these limitations.

Multiple True-False Items (MTF)

The Multiple True-False (MTF) item format looks like an MCQ but is scored like a series of TF items. See Table 7.2 for an example. The MTF item consists of a stem, followed by several options, each of which must be answered true or false. Each item is scored as an independent item, as either correct or incorrect (Frisbie, 1992).

The strength of the MTF item is that it can test a number of propositions around a common theme (the stem) in an efficient manner. Some of the criticisms or perceived problems with TF items may apply to MTF items as well.

If MTF items are used together with other SR formats, such as MCQs or TF or EM item sets, it is important to consider how to fairly weight the MTF item scores relative to scores on other SR formats. The relative difference in time it takes to complete MTF items and MCQs is the issue. For example, if a test is composed of 40 MCQs and four MTF items each with five options (a total of 20 scorable units), what is the appropriate weight to assign these format scores when combining them into a single total test score? This weighting problem can be solved easily, but should be attended to, since—in this example—the 40 MCQs are likely to take at least at least twice as long to answer as the 20 MTF scorable units.

Other Selected-Response Formats: Key Features

The SR formats discussed thus far in this chapter all aim to sample an achievement or ability construct comprehensively and representatively, such that valid inference can be made from item samples to population or domain knowledge. The Key Features (KF) format (Bordage & Page, 1987; Page, Bordage, & Allen, 1995) is a specialized written format which aims to test only the most critical or essential elements of decision-making about clinical cases. Thus, the purpose of key features-type assessment and the construct measured by KF cases differs considerably from typical achievement constructs. Farmer and Page (2005) present a practical overview of the principles associated with creating effective KF cases.

The KF format consists of a clinical vignette (one to three paragraphs) describing a patient and all the clinical information needed to begin solving the patient's problem or problems. One or more CR and/or SR items follows this stimulus information; the examinee's task in these questions is to identify the most important or key elements associated with solving the patient's problem. The unique point of KF cases is that these items focus exclusively on only the most essential elements of problem solving, ignoring all other less essential elements. For example, KF items may ask the examinee to identify only the most critical working diagnoses, which laboratory investigations are most needed, and which one or more therapies is most or least helpful.

In some ways, the KF format is similar to the testlet format—a testlet with a unique purpose and form, that focuses in on the most critical information or data needed (or not needed) to solve a clinical problem. But, there are major differences also. KF items usually allow for more than one correct answer, and they often mix CR with SR item forms. In this context, research suggests that two to three items per KF case maximizes reliability; use of fewer items per KF case reduces testing information and lowers reliability while using more than about three items per KF case provides only redundant information (Norman, et al., 2006). Like MCQ testlets, the case score (the sum of all individual item scores in each KF case) is the proper unit of analysis for KF cases.

Development of KF tests is challenging and labor-intensive with specialized training and experience needed for effective development. When the purpose of the assessment matches the considerable strengths of the KF format, the efforts needed to develop these specialized items is worthwhile.

Selected-Response Formats and Forms to Avoid

Some SR formats fail to perform well, despite the fact that they may have some intuitive appeal. Some SR forms have systematic and consistent problems, well documented in the research literature (e.g. Haladyna, et al., 2002), and should be avoided. See the NBME Item Writing Guide (Case & Swanson, 1998) for a good summary of item forms that are problematic and not recommended. Most of the problematic SR formats have the same psychometric issues: Items are either more difficult or less difficult and have lower item discrimination indices than comparable straightforward item forms. These problematic items also tend to be of lower reliability than comparable SR forms. But, these psychometric reasons may be secondary to the validity problems arising from use of item forms that may confuse or deliberately mislead examinees or provide cues to correct answers.

Complex Item Forms AVOID

One example is the complex MCQ format, sometimes called the K-type item format, following NBME convention (Case & Swanson, 1998). This is a familiar format in which the complex answer set consists of various combinations of single options. See Table 7.2 for an example. It was believed that this complex answer arrangement demanded use of complex or higher-order knowledge, but there is little or no evidence to support this belief.

In fact, this complex item form has some less than desirable psychometric properties and may also provide cues to the testwise examinee (e.g., Albanese, 1993; Haladyna, et al., 2002). For example, once examinees learn how to take these items, they learn to eliminate some combined options readily because they know that one of the elements of the combination is false.

Variations of the complex format include the partial-K item which mixes some straightforward options and some complex options (Downing, 2005). Most testing organizations have eliminated these so-called complex formats from their tests.

Negative Items AVOID

Negation or the use of negative words is to be avoided in both item stems and item options. There are some legitimate uses of negative terms, such as the case of medications or procedures that are contraindicated; this use may be legitimate in that "contraindication" is a straightforward concept in health care domains.

Negative items tend to test trivial content at lower cognitive levels. One particularly bad form is to use a negative term in the stem of the item and also in one or more options—making the item nearly impossible to answer. While finding the negative instance is a time-honored testing task, these items tend to be artificially more difficult than positively worded items testing the identical content and tend to discriminate less well—which lowers scale reliability (Haladyna, et al., 2002).

Some item writers are tempted to take a textbook sentence or some phrase taken directly from a lecture or other instructional material, place a "not" or other negative term in the sentence, and then apply this negation to an item stem. For true-false items, this is a particular temptation, but one that should be avoided for all SR item forms.

Unfocused-Stem Items

AVOID

MCQ stems of the type: "Which of the following statements are true?" are a time-honored tradition, especially in health professions education. Such open-ended, unfocused stems are not really questions at all. Rather, such MCQs tend to be multiple-true false items disguised as MCQs. In order to answer the item correctly, the examinee must first decide what question is actually being posed (if any), and then proceed to attempt to answer the question. Research shows that these types of open-ended, unfocused items do not work well (e.g., Downing, 2005), especially for less proficient examinees.

One helpful hint to item writers is that one should be able to answer the question even with all the options covered. Clearly, this is not possible for stems such as "Which of the following statements are true?"

Selected-Response Items: Summary Recommendations

Selected-response items are typified by multiple-choice items (MCQs) and true-false (TF) items. The best advice, based on a long research history, is to create straightforward positively worded SR items, with each item having a clearly stated testing point or objective; adhere to the standard principles of item writing. Complex or exotic formats should be avoided, since the complex form often interferes with measuring the content of interest. SR items should test at the cognitive level of instruction and be presented to examinees in sufficient numbers to adequately sample the achievement or ability domain. Three options are generally sufficient for MCQs, if the items are well targeted in difficulty and used in sufficient numbers on test forms. Random guessing is not usually a serious problem for well written SR tests. Right-wrong scoring is usually best. Attempts to correct raw scores for guessing with formula scores do not work well and may distort validity or bias scores by adding construct-irrelevant variance (CIV) to test scores, although in some cases formula scoring increases test scale reliability (e.g., Muijtjens, et al., 1999).

Summary and Conclusion

This chapter has overviewed some highlights of written testing in the health professions. Constructed-response and the selected-response item formats are used widely in health professions education for the assessment of cognitive achievement—primarily classroom-type achievement. Each format has strengths and limits, as summarized in this chapter.

Overall, the SR format—particularly its prototypic form, the MCQ—is most appropriate for nearly all achievement testing situations in health professions education. The SR form is extremely versatile in testing higher levels of cognitive knowledge, has a deep research base to support its validity, is efficient, and permits sound quality control measures. Effective MCQs can be securely stored for reuse. The principles used to create effective and defensible SR items are well established and there is a large research base to support validity for SR formats. SR can be administered in either paper-and-pencil formats or by computer.

CR items—particularly the short-answer essay—are appropriate for testing uncued written responses. Scoring for CR items is inherently subjective and procedures must be used to attempt to control essay rater biases. CR formats, such as short essay tests, may be appropriate for small classes of students, but scoring procedures must be carefully planned and executed in order to maximize score validity.

References

Albanese, M. (1993). Type K and other complex multiple-choice items: An analysis of research and item properties. *Educational Measurement: Issues and Practice*, 12(1), 28–33.

Baranowski, R.A. (2006). Item editing and item review. In S.M. Downing & T.M. Haladyna (Eds.), *Handbook of test development* (pp. 349–357). Mahwah, NJ: Lawrence Erlbaum Associates.

Bordage, G., & Page, G. (1987). An alternative approach to PMPs: The key features concept. In I. Hart & R. Harden (Eds.), *Further developments in assessing clinical competence* (pp. 57–75). Montreal, Canada: Heal.

Case, S.M., & Swanson, D.B. (1993). Extended matching items: A practical alternative to free response questions. *Teaching and Learning in Medicine*, 5(2), 107–115.

Case, S., & Swanson, D. (1998). *Constructing written test questions for the basic and clinical sciences*. Philadelphia, PA: National Board of Medical Examiners.

Downing, S.M. (1992). True-False, alternate-choice and multiple-choice items: A research perspective. *Educational Measurement: Issues and Practice*, 11, 27–30.

Downing, S.M. (2002a). Assessment of knowledge with written test forms. In G.R. Norman, C.P.M. van der Vleuten, & D.I. Newble (Eds.), *International handbook for research in medical education* (pp. 647–672). Dordrecht, The Netherlands: Kluwer Academic Publishers.

Downing, S.M. (2002b). Construct-irrelevant variance and flawed test questions: Do multiple-choice item-writing principles make any difference? *Academic Medicine*, 77(10), s103–104.

Downing, S.M. (2002c). Threats to the validity of locally developed multiple-choice tests in medical education: Construct-irrelevant variance and construct underrepresentation. *Advances in Health Sciences Education*, 7, 235–241.

Downing, S.M. (2003). Guessing on selected-response examinations. *Medical Education*, 37, 670–671.

Downing, S.M. (2005). The effects of violating standard item writing principles on tests and students: The consequences of using flawed test items on achievement examinations in medical education. *Advances in Health Sciences Education*, 10, 133–143.

Downing, S.M. (2006). Twelve steps for effective test development. In S.M. Downing & T.M. Haladyna (Eds.), *Handbook of test development* (pp. 3–25). Mahwah, NJ: Lawrence Erlbaum Associates.

Downing, S.M., & Haladyna, T.M. (1997). Test item development: Validity evidence from quality assurance procedures. *Applied Measurement in Education*, 10, 61–82

Downing, S.M., & Haladyna, T.M. (2004). Validity threats: Overcoming interference with proposed interpretations of assessment data. *Medical Education*, 38, 327–333.

Ebel, R.L. (1972). *Essentials of educational measurement*. Englewood Cliffs, NJ: Prentice Hall.

Ebel, R.L, & Frisbie, D.A. (1991). *Essentials of educational measurement*. Englewood Cliffs, NJ: Prentice Hall.

Farmer, E.A., & Page, G. (2005). A practical guide to assessing clinical decision-making skills using the key features approach. *Medical Education*, 39, 1188–1194.

Frisbie, D.A. (1992). The multiple true-false item format: A status review. *Educational Measurement: Issues and Practice*, 5(4), 21–26.

Haladyna, T.M. (1992). Context-dependent item sets. *Educational Measurement: Issues and Practice*, 11, 21–25.

Haladyna, T.M. (2004). *Developing and validating multiple-choice test items* (3rd ed.). Mahwah, NJ: Lawrence Erlbaum Associates.

Haladyna, T.M., & Downing, S.M. (1989a). A taxonomy of multiple-choice item-writing rules. *Applied Measurement in Education*, 1, 37–50.

Haladyna, T.M., & Downing, S.M. (1989b). The validity of a taxonomy of multiple-choice item-writing rules. *Applied Measurement in Education*, 1, 51–78.

Haladyna, T.M., & Downing, S.M. (1993). How many options is enough for a multiple-choice test item. *Educational and Psychological Measurement*, 53, 999–1010.

Haladyna, T.M., & Downing, S.M. (2004). Construct-irrelevant variance: A threat in high-stakes testing. *Educational Measurement: Issues and Practice*, 23(1), 17–27.

Haladyna, T.M., Downing, S.M., & Rodriguez, M.C. (2002). A review of multiple-choice item-writing guidelines for classroom assessment. *Applied Measurement in Education*, 15(3), 309–334.

Linn, R.L., & Miller, M.D. (2005). *Measurement and assessment in teaching* (9th ed.). Upper Saddle River, NJ: Pearson/Merrill Prentice Hall.

Messick, S. (1989). Validity. In R.L. Linn (Ed.), *Educational measurement* (3rd ed., pp. 13–104). New York: American Council on Education and Macmillan.

Muijtjens, A.M.M., van Mameren, H., Hoogenboom, R.J.I., Evers, J.L.H., & van der Vleuten, C.P.M. (1999). The effect of a "don't know" option on test scores: Number-right and formula scoring compared. *Medical Education*, 33, 267–275.

Norman, G., Bordage, G., Page, G., & Keane, D. (2006). How specific is case specificity? *Medical Education*, 40, 618–623.

Page, G., Bordage, G., & Allen, T. (1995). Developing key features problems and examinations to assess clinical decision making skills. *Academic Medicine*, 70, 194–201.

Rodriguez, M.C. (2005). Three options are optimal for multiple-choice items:

A meta-analysis of 80 years of research. *Educational Measurement: Issues and Practice*, 24(2), 3–13.

Thissen, D., & Wainer, H. (Eds.). (2001). *Test scoring*. Mahwah, NJ: Lawrence Erlbaum Associates.

Wainer, H., & Thissen, D. (1996). How is reliability related to the quality of test scores? What is the effect of local dependence on reliability? *Educational Measurement: Issues and Practice*, 15(1), 22–29.

Welch, C. (2006). Item/prompt development in performance testing. In S.M. Downing & T.M. Haladyna (Eds.), *Handbook of test development* (pp. 303–327). Mahwah, NJ: Lawrence Erlbaum Associates.

8

OBSERVATIONAL ASSESSMENT

WILLIAM C. MCGAGHIE, JOHN BUTTER, AND MARSHA KAYE

This chapter has nine sections. *Section one* begins with a brief introduction about the use of observational methods for personnel assessment in the health professions. We point out that assessments based on observational data are used widely in health professions education yet the quality and utility of these assessments is rarely gauged. We also assert that observational assessment is chiefly formative, a type of *dynamic testing* (Grigorenko & Sternberg, 1998) where learner assessment and instruction coalesce. *Section two* addresses the purpose and focus of observational assessments. It answers two questions. "How can we describe the clinical performance of learners?" [and] "Are the behaviors we observe in learners similar to the behaviors needed for patient care?" *Section three* focuses on the social character of observational assessment. Here we assert that health professions education and assessment is an interpersonal enterprise, especially when done in clinical settings. Interpersonal behavior can yield accurate data yet always has room for subjectivity, selective perception, and measurement error. Observational assessments need to reduce these sources of bias. *Section four* presents an observational assessment toolbox as a table. Here we show how assessment goals and tools should be matched and identify advantages and problems of these pairings. *Section five* covers the acquisition of observational assessment tools either "off the shelf," from donation or purchase, or by means of constructing new measures. "Off the shelf" acquisition of measurement tools requires a hefty dose of *caveat emptor* [let the buyer beware]. Constructing new observational measures is hard work, yet yields large and lasting benefits if done correctly. *Section six* offers tips about how to administer an observational assessment, especially about standardization and control. *Section seven* is about data quality, arguing that data are useless for any purpose if their reliability and validity are suspect. *Section eight* talks about how to use observational assessment data toward the formative goal of learner improvement and also addresses mastery learning. *Section nine* reiterates a set of practical recommendations published earlier about how to improve the quality and utility of observational assessments in health professions education. There is a coda.

This chapter is long and ambitious. We believe that detail is important because observational assessments are used widely at all levels of education in the health professions. Our hope is that this chapter will help educators use observational assessments wisely.

Introduction

A century ago physician William Osler expressed the metaphor of the hospital as a college (1906). Osler argued that the hospital is not only a site for patient care but also a setting to educate doctors and other health care professionals. The primary source of medical teaching in the early twentieth century was the senior attending physician who lectured and supervised young house staff doctors. Attending physicians also judged their acolytes, chiefly by observing young doctors take patient histories, perform physical examinations, communicate with patients, formulate treatment plans, and provide clinical care. Observing, assessing, and improving learner performance in patient care settings has been a hallmark of health professions education for many years. Today, observational assessment toward the goal of learner improvement is as much a thread in the health professions education fabric as it was before the dawn of aviation and the internal combustion engine. The hospital (or clinic) as a college and observational assessment as a teaching tool are cornerstones of today's health professions education.

Observational assessment, usually guided by a structured checklist or a rating scale, is the most widely used approach to personnel evaluation in the health professions (Holmboe, 2004). Observational assessment is ubiquitous. It involves all health professions and covers all skills, dispositions, and character traits. The prevalence of observational assessment in professional education demands that clinical teachers understand its utility and strength, flaws and pitfalls. This chapter addresses such goals. The aim is to amplify another discussion about direct observation of students' clinical skills published recently (Holmboe, 2005) and several other general reviews about clinical competence evaluation in such health professions as nursing (Mahara, 1998), respiratory therapy (Cullen, 2005) and medicine (Epstein & Hundert, 2002; Waas, van der Vleuten, Shatzer, & Jones, 2001). We also offer some practical advice about how to improve observational assessments and better interpret their data.

Two key points need to be made plain at the start of this chapter. First, we view observational assessment as a form of *dynamic testing* (Grigorenko & Sternberg, 1998). This means that instruction and assessment are inseparable. The dynamic testing model (a) emphasizes the processes involved in learning and change, (b) features frequent feedback to learners based on observational data, and (c) "the test situation and the type of examiner–examinee relationship are modified from the one-way traditional setting of the conventional psychometric approach . . . to a form of two-way interactive relationship" (p. 75). Dynamic testing cast as observational assessment in the health professions is formative, focused on learner growth and change. It does *not* try to reach summative end points.

Second, we acknowledge the obvious by stating that observational assessment depends on the availability of skillful and motivated faculty educators. However, we disagree with the widespread myth that faculty status, seniority, or clinical experience automatically confers rating expertise. Clinical research (Herbers, Noel, Cooper, et al., 1989; Noel, Herbers, Caplow, et al., 1992) and practical experience show that teaching faculty need much preparation and frequent calibration to perform trustworthy observational assessments that yield reliable data (Williams, Klamen, & McGaghie, 2003). The health professions need to be just as diligent about training faculty evaluators to produce trustworthy assessment data as programs now in place to train judges for the Olympics (International Gymnastics Federation, 1989), the Miss America pageant (Goldman, 1990), and competitive dog shows (American Dog Show Judges, 2006).

Purpose and Focus

Purpose

Observational assessment of clinical learning assumes that earlier judgments have been made about learners' readiness for health professions education including their fund of scientific and clinical knowledge, patient care sentiments, and professional responsibility. Observational assessments are usually done after learners have passed muster at school admission and in basic science and professionalism courses. We assume, for example, that the student nurse in clinical training has survived a criminal background check. We expect that medical students in clinical rotations are free of alcohol and drug problems. Screening evaluations may find rare outliers. Yet nearly all students of the health professions who matriculate to clinical settings are prepared intellectually for work with patients and are personally fit for the challenge.

The principal purpose of observational assessments of learner behavior in the health professions is to *describe* what they are doing (Carnahan & Hemmer, 2005). Learners are evaluated in clinical context, embedded in the patient care environment where educational objectives are blurred by clinical priorities. The first personnel evaluation goal is to paint a portrait of each learner's clinical experience, performance, and the conditions under which they occur. Once the description is complete learners can be judged against developmental milestones that indicate how well educational objectives are reached. These evaluations are qualitative but no less rigorous than long quantitative tests.

The RIME framework, pioneered in the internal medicine clerkship at the Uniformed Services University of the Health Sciences (Pangaro, 1999) and amplified in other medical specialties (e.g., Ogburn & Espey, 2003) allows faculty judges to assess student learning developmentally, from "Reporter" to "Interpreter" to "Manager/Educator" (RIME). Described by Carnahan and Hemmer (2005) the RIME model has these elements.

Reporter

Students must: (1) accurately gather information about their patients, through an independent history and physical examination, chart review, and from other sources such as family or referring physicians; (2) use appropriate terminology to clearly communicate their findings, both orally and in writing; (3) interact professionally with patients and staff; and (4) consistently and reliably carry out their responsibilities. This stage requires that students have an adequate knowledge base, the basic skills to perform fundamental tasks, and core attributes of honesty, reliability, and commitment. Students who are Reporters can answer the "What" questions about their patients.

Interpreter

Students must: (1) demonstrate ability to identify and prioritize problems independently, (2) offer three *reasonable* explanations for new problems, and (3) generate and defend a differential diagnosis. This step requires a greater knowledge base, increased confidence and skill in selecting and applying clinical facts to a specific patient, and the ability to begin to pose clinical questions. Interpreters organize, prioritize, synthesize, and interpret problems. Students who are Interpreters can answer the "Why" questions about their patients.

Manager

Students must be more "proactive," suggesting diagnostic and therapeutic plans that include reasonable diagnostic options and possible therapies. This step takes even greater knowledge, more confidence, and the skill to select interventions for an individual patient. Managers understand their patients' needs and desires and can enter into "relationship-centered care."

Educator

Becoming a Manager is intricately tied to being an Educator.

Students must identify questions related to their patients that cannot be answered from textbooks, cite evidence that new or alternative therapies or tests are worthwhile, and share their acquired knowledge with other members of the health care team. Desire and ability to educate oneself and others is intrinsic to being a "manager" and reflects a desire not only to teach colleagues but also, and most importantly, to help the patient. A Manager/Educator answers the "How" questions, for themselves, and their patients. It is not simply a matter of "bringing in articles to the team."[1]

Practical implementation of the RIME model in clinical education involves frequent, tightly managed observational assessments of individual students by faculty using checklists and rating scales; faculty training in student assessment principles; regularly scheduled formal evaluation sessions by faculty to review and judge student progress data; and rigorous overall management (especially record keeping) by the program director. Descriptive student assessment using the RIME model is labor intensive and time consuming. However, the developmental profile the RIME format provides about each student's clinical skill and maturity is a solid return on investment. Students also value RIME based observational assessments for their professional feedback and opportunities for faculty contact (Carnahan & Hemmer, 2005; Holmboe, Yepes, Williams, & Huot, 2004; Ogburn & Espey, 2003).

Focus

The focus of observational assessment in health professions education is on the developmental increase in students' clinical knowledge, skill, patient care disposition, and professionalism as a result of instruction and experience. The focus is narrowed by thinking about student clinical learning in either or both of two outcome frameworks. The first, cast as a pyramid, was created by George Miller (1990). The second, a simple hierarchy, is Donald Kirkpatrick's (1998) invention. The two outcome frameworks are shown side-by-side in Figure 8.1.

The lowest level (least impressive) form of learner outcome assessment is Kirkpatrick's Level 1. Data in this category address customer satisfaction, e.g., "I attended an educational workshop and had a good time." Intermediate levels of the Miller pyramid and the Kirkpatrick hierarchy involve learner acquisition of increasingly complex clinical outcomes (e.g., knowledge and skill acquisition; ability to apply acquired knowledge and skill in classroom, laboratory, and clinical settings). The highest level of clinical learning outcomes is reached when student learning is linked directly to patient improvement (i.e., reduced mortality, improved activities of daily living) or better organizational life (e.g., lower absenteeism, boost in staff morale).

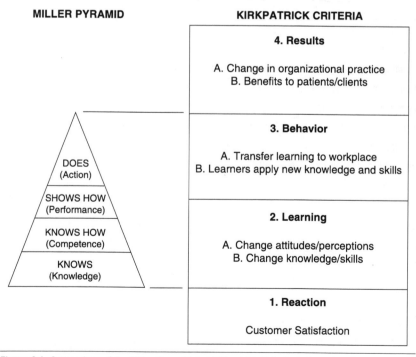

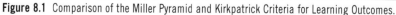

Figure 8.1 Comparison of the Miller Pyramid and Kirkpatrick Criteria for Learning Outcomes.

The levels of learning outcomes shown in the Miller (1990) pyramid and the Kirkpatrick (1998) hierarchy tell faculty evaluators that all descriptive student evaluations are not alike. Low-level expectations for beginning students are gradually raised as students grow in clinical experience, skill, and savvy. Assessments that rely on observations (or other data collection methods) should have a clear sense of the level at which the evaluations are focused using either the Miller (1990) or the Kirkpatrick (1998) scheme.

Social Character of Clinical Evaluation

Observational assessment of students in clinical settings involves watching them learning and delivering patient care, often in a semi-private hospital room or clinic location. Observational assessment by definition is an interpersonal activity and is subject to all of the potential pitfalls of human relations: subjectivity, false impressions, the three "isms" (ageism, racism, sexism), rumor, grudge, and misinterpretation. The goal, of course, is to reduce these potential sources of bias in observational assessments so that student evaluations are uniform, fair, and impartial. This is a big assessment challenge because observational data are always shaped subjectively—they are never fully objective. Informed practice of observational assessment stems from tolerance for error and ambiguity and acknowledgment that even seasoned clinical faculty are wrong sometimes. Decreasing incorrect evaluations is the practical aim because in an interpersonal context they can never be eliminated.

One of the major problems associated with observational assessments of health professions students is that they rarely happen. This is especially the case in medicine where many studies show that medical students and residents are almost never observed performing such basic tasks as taking patient histories and performing physical examinations (Holmboe, 2004). Similar educational research in other health professions including nursing (Darmody, 2005) and respiratory therapy (Cullen, 2005) has been reported less frequently yet shows patterns close to medicine. The practical message is that learner observational assessments must be scheduled regularly and recognized as an important part of faculty work. This work may be either delegated to selected faculty members or done as a shared educational responsibility.

Learners also shape the social character of clinical assessments. Students influence clinical evaluations by preceptors using subtle and overt forms of impression management. These are attempts to "look good," especially in public. To illustrate, qualitative research by Haas and Shaffir (1982, 1987) looked at the development and refinement of medical students' impression management skills over a range of educational experiences. They found that even new students develop a "*pretence* of competence even though one may be privately uncertain" (p. 142). Haas and Shaffir called this the students' "cloak of competence." They summarized their study by stating,

> A significant part of professionalization is an increased ability to perceive and adapt behavior to legitimators' (faculty, staff, and peer) expectations, no matter how variable or ambiguous. . . . In this context of ambiguity, students . . . accommodate themselves, individually and collectively, to convincing others of their developing competence by selective learning and by striving to control the impressions others receive of them. (p. 148)

We expect that students in other health professions are equally adept at managing faculty impressions in classroom and clinical settings. Faculty observational assessments should account for this potential source of bias.

Clinical faculty are not immune to social influences when they observe and record instances of student behavior and when they interpret data representing student learning and professionalism. Most often faculty observations and assessments of students are done one-on-one, usually including feedback and suggestions for improvement. However, several recent studies in clinical medical education present strong evidence that the quality and accuracy of formative decisions about learners is increased when done by faculty *groups* (Carnahan & Hemmer, 2005; Schwind, Williams, Boehler, & Dunnington, 2004). When based on recorded observational data, faculty group decisions about individual students and residents are less likely to be distorted by such sources of bias as students' personal characteristics

(Wigton, 1980), student "likeability" (Kalet, Earp, & Kowlowitz, 1992) or the "Mum Effect" (Tesser & Rosen, 1975), the widespread reluctance to transmit bad news (Carnahan & Hemmer, 2005).

Other research also endorses the importance of faculty observational assessments of students and residents working with real patients in genuine clinical settings (Holmboe, 2004; Holmboe & Hawkins, 1998; Norcini, Blank, Duffy, & Fortna, 2003). These and other investigators argue that evaluations using standardized patients (SPs) (Yudkowsky, Chapter 9, this volume) and other clinical simulations (McGaghie & Issenberg, Chapter 10, this volume) are necessary but not sufficient for completely valid assessment of clinical competence.

Psychologist Elizabeth Loftus, an expert on eyewitness testimony for legal proceedings and studies of judgment accuracy, teaches that even simple observations are done using a cascaded chain of events (Loftus & Schneider, 1987). This is clearly the case for observational assessment of clinical behavior. The chain of events has at least five links.

1. Learner emits the target *response* or *behavior*, e.g., chest percussion;
2. Response is *observed* by faculty;
3. Faculty observation is *interpreted* (e.g., correct–incorrect; superior, excellent, acceptable, marginal, poor);
4. Faculty interpretation is *recorded* as data; and
5. Recorded data are *judged* (e.g., competent–not competent)

The first link (behavioral response) is an objective event. The fifth link is a data-based assessment of the response. Links 2, 3, and 4 are points on the chain where error due to factors like bad eyesight (faculty observation), poor insight (incorrect interpretation) or flawed foresight (incorrect data file structure) can creep into the assessment scheme. The obvious answer is to calibrate the observational assessment mechanism to reduce the introduction of measurement error at links 2, 3, and 4. Since faculty members are the source of error at these locations it makes sense that faculty training and calibration is the best solution to the problem.

Faculty training to improve rating accuracy is rarely done in health professions education despite rigorous empirical demonstrations showing the need for such calibration (Herbers, et al., 1989; Noel, et al., 1992). A recent review on cognitive, social, and environmental sources of bias in clinical competence ratings (Williams, et. al., 2003) identifies four approaches to rater calibration and training that hold promise to improve the quality of observational data: (a) *rater error training*, (b) *performance dimension training*, (c) *frame of reference training*, and (d) *behavioral observation training* (Woehr & Huffcutt, 1994). However, despite published warnings and suggestions for improvement, faculty training and preparation for the work of observational assessment is one of the great unmet educational needs across the health professions.

Observational Assessment Toolbox

Student observational assessment in the classroom or clinic is a practical matter. The faculty evaluator needs to have a clear sense of the assessment goal (the *what* of assessment) and use an assessment tool (the *how* of assessment) for data collection. The proper fit of goals and tools is a key feature of quality observational assessment. A mismatch of goals and tools ("square peg, round hole") will produce measurement error (unreliability) and inaccurate faculty judgments about students.

Table 8.1 identifies ten assessment goals for student learning in the health professions ranging from conducting an interview to performing a physical exam, counseling skills, and professionalism. A set of optional assessment tools is presented beside each goal along with statements about their advantages and disadvantages. At least one citation to the professional literature is also given for each assessment goal for readers who seek more detailed information. The intent is not only to reinforce the idea of the goal–tool match but also to show the variety of ways the match can be made.

Faculty evaluators are urged to study the tabular entries carefully and to make informed choices about student assessment goals and tools.

Table 8.1 Observational Assessment Goals and Tools

Assessment Goal	Assessment Tools	Advantages	Limitations
Interview (History) (Norcini, Blank, Duffy, & Fortna, 2003; Orient, 2005)	Direct observation of clinical behavior	Observes learner over a range of activities; long behavioral record; opportunities for immediate feedback; live observer present	Role conflict; assumes equivalence of faculty; time consuming; impression management/manipulation by learners
	Mini-CEX*	Judgment about single, specific encounter; real patients; high reliability after four assessments	Task and patient specific; assesses only part of the clinical encounter
	SP†	Trained, experienced raters; other observers	Simulation; approximation to realism
	Videotape of clinical encounter	Realistic; capture clinical behavior	Time consuming; need consent; equipment needs; cost
Communication (Norcini, Blank, Duffy, & Fortna, 2003)	Direct observation of clinical behavior	Observes learner over a range of activities; long behavioral record; opportunities for immediate feedback; live observer present	Role conflict; assumes equivalence of faculty; time consuming; impression management/manipulation by learners
	Mini-CEX*	Judgment about single, specific encounter; real patients	Task and patient specific
	SP†	Trained, experienced raters; other observers	Simulation; approximation to realism
	Videotape of clinical encounter	Realistic; capture clinical behavior	Time consuming; need consent; equipment needs; cost
	Patient satisfaction survey	Increased reliability as database grows	Self-selection; positive response bias; no evaluation of patient care quality
	Self-assessment of clinical performance	Encourages learner reflection; convenience	Data usually unreliable; overestimates skill and knowledge levels
	Peer assessment of clinical performance	Practice and value peer review; encourages professionalism	Response bias without anonymity

Skill (references)	Method	Advantages	Limitations
Physical Exam (Norcini, Blank, Duffy, & Fortna, 2003; Orient, 2005)	Direct observation of clinical behavior	Immediate feedback; correct problems quickly	Lack of a "gold standard;" more than one right way
	Mini-CEX*	Structured, focused; more reliable	Encounter specific; physical exam skills needing evaluation may not be present in available patients
	SP†	Standardized, uniform	SP may lack physical findings
	Medical record audit	Readily available; patient centered; written expression of learner's clinical reasoning	Documentation may not be reliable; reflects input from others beside learner
Patient Presentations (Green, Hershman, DeCherie, et al., 2005; Haber & Lingard, 2001)	Direct observation of patient presentations	Immediate feedback; correct problems quickly	Wide variation in evaluation without structured format
Clinical Reasoning (Orient, 2005; Wiese, Varosy, & Tierney, 2002)	Direct observation of episodes	Evaluates reasoning "in vivo"; immediate feedback; opportunities for correction	Wide variation in evaluation without structured format
	One minute preceptor	Structured, probes reasoning	Task and patient specific (narrow focus of evaluation)
Creating a Problem List (Weed, 1968)	Direct observation of events	Patient centered; realistic; promotes immediate feedback	Evaluation and feedback may be cursory due to time constraints
	Retrospective chart review	Patient centered; learner incorporates reading and deliberation to create a more polished product	Learner's skills are supplemented by others; time consuming
Procedures (Wayne, Butter, Siddall, et al., 2005a, 2006)	Direct observation of clinical behavior	Evaluates procedural skill "in vivo"	May involve unsafe practice with real patients
	Simulation-based clinical evaluation	Standardized; safe; forgiving; allows deliberate practice	Varies in realism; may be expensive

(Continued Overleaf)

Table 8.1 Continued

Assessment Goal	Assessment Tools	Advantages	Limitations
	Observational checklists	Structured; convenient	Requires rater training and calibration
	Objective Structured Assessment of Technical Skills (OSAT)	Structured, specific & focused; trained, experienced raters; other observers	Clinical simulation, approximates realism
Counseling Skills (Norcini, Blank, Duffy, & Fortna, 2003)	Direct observation	Realistic; immediate feedback; offers opportunities for patient education and correction	Time consuming for faculty; task specific
	Mini-CEX*	Focused task increases reliability	Time consuming; patient and task specific
	SP†	Trained, experienced raters; other observers	Simulation, approximation to realism
	Videotape of clinical encounter	Realistic; capture clinical behavior	Time consuming; need consent; equipment needs; cost
	Self-assessment of clinical performance	Encourages learner reflection; convenience	Data usually unreliable; overestimates skill and knowledge levels
Treatment Plan	Direct observation of clinical behavior	Patient centered; realistic; promotes immediate feedback	Time consuming for faculty
	Written exams of acquired knowledge	Best assessment of factual recall; large number of items increases reliability	Ability to apply information in clinical context is uncertain
Professionalism (Bracken, Timmreck, & Church, 2001; Norcini, 2006; Smither, London, & Reilly, 2005; Stern, 2006)	Direct observation of clinical behavior	Structured, focused observations yield reliable data; immediate feedback; opportunities for correction	Lack of a "gold standard"; behaviors most conspicuous by their absence; impression management/manipulation by learners

"Physicianship" forms	Involves real patients; identifies behavioral extremes	Only egregious behaviors are reported; depends on faculty motivation to identify problem learners
Videotape of clinical encounter	Realistic; capture clinical behavior	Time consuming; need consent; equipment needs; cost
360° evaluation‡	Comprehensive evaluation surveys that allow data triangulation and multisource feedback	Time and labor intensive; requires much staff training and calibration; evaluations are unique to the organization and culture where they are done
Teamwork (Baker, Beaubien, & Holtzman, 2006; Hamman, 2004; Loughry, Ohland, & Moore, 2007; Thomas, Sexton, & Helmreich, 2004) Direct observation of clinical behavior	Evaluates team functioning "in vivo"; realistic, unconstrained assessment; assess shifts in team leadership	Team functioning may change as problem evolves; lack of a "gold standard"; wide variation in evaluation without structured format
Team surveys	Comprehensive; can cover many facets of teamwork; easy to complete	Usually retrospective; depends on unreliable, selective memory
Checklists	Simple, easy to use; focus and constrain evaluation responses	May oversimplify complex team performances

Notes

* "The mini-CEX was originally designed to evaluate residents [learners] in a setting reflective of day-to-day practice. Faculty observe a resident performing a *focused* history, physical, or counseling session during routine care experiences. . . . The mini-CEX facilitates multiple observations over time by different faculty members. . . . This longitudinal nature of the mini-CEX is its most important strength as an evaluation tool" (Holmboe, 2005).

† "Standardized patients (SPs) are laypersons who are trained and calibrated to present patient health problems uniformly for teaching or evaluation" (McGaghie, 2005).

‡ "360° evaluation is assessment of a learner [or practitioner] using rating data from a variety of sources, e.g., self, peers, supervisors, nursing staff, patients" (McGaghie, 2005).

Acquisition of Observational Assessment Tools

There are two sources of measurement tools that can be used for observational assessment of learners in the health professions. The first is to buy, borrow, or adapt measurement tools "off the shelf" from commercial vendors or colleagues. This is a common practice among educational program directors and faculty evaluators. Since there is no equivalent of *Consumer Reports* for users of professional education measures, "off the shelf" acquisition of these tools must be done with skill and care. We will offer some practical advice about these acquisitions. The second way to acquire observational assessment measures is to construct them yourself. This is hard work. However, evaluators who create assessment measures the right way will gain large and lasting benefits. We will also give practical advice about constructing assessment measures along with examples and references that provide detailed instructions. The bottom line is that trustworthy observational assessment data will only come from solid evaluation tools that are used properly.

General Advice

There are four general rules to follow whether observational assessment tools are selected "off the shelf" or developed locally.

1. Evaluation goals and tools must be matched. This is the clear message of Table 8.1, repeated here for reinforcement.

2. Faculty evaluators must be well-read about student assessment procedures in their profession. Learner assessment is a key professional duty that should be informed by knowledge of the literature.

3. Consult with an educational measurement expert if you have questions or problems. Clinicians in all fields consult with experts routinely about patient care problems. The same approach should be used for educational assessment issues.

4. Consult with a reference librarian for unmet information needs. Reference librarians are highly skilled at working with clinicians to address patient care *and* educational problems.

Selecting Assessment Tools

Educational evaluators who are in the market to buy or borrow observational assessment tools for local use should follow five simple steps before making an acquisition. Above all, they must be careful, smart shoppers.

1. Shop around. There are many commercial and not-for-profit sources of assessment instruments that may suit your needs so careful inspection is essential. A popular not-for-profit source is the *Health and Psychological Instruments* (HAPI) database which is accessible at health sciences libraries. It contains thousands of measurement tools, most reported in the peer-reviewed scientific literature. Instruments that are sold commercially through catalogs and websites rarely undergo rigorous peer review.

2. Critically appraise "off the shelf" assessment tools using textbook principles of clinical decision-making (Fletcher, Fletcher, & Wagner, 1996; Sox, Blatt, Higgins, & Marton, 1988). Potential users need to have a clear idea about the technical qualities of observational measurement tools and especially about the data they yield (i.e., reliability, validity).

3. Study the history of potential assessment tools to find out if they have been used successfully with learners and in settings similar to your own. Historical data should also be recent, not decades old.

4. Conduct pilot studies involving "off the shelf" assessment tools in your local setting. Measurement tools should survive a tryout phase before they are placed in general use.

5. Measure yourself. Place yourself in the role of a student or learner and undergo an observational assessment performed by a colleague. This experience will help you decide if the potential assessment tool truly fits your measurement purpose.

Constructing Assessment Tools

Instruction about how to construct measures that can be used for assessment of learning in the health professions is available from several sources. General advice is found in Wilson (2005). Practical suggestions about creating measures of acquired knowledge are found in Case and Swanson (2002) and Linn and Gronlund (2000). Approaches to creation of attitude measures are described by Robert DeVellis (2003). Development of health status scales is taught by Streiner and Norman (2003). Ronald Stiggins (1987) presents formulae for the design and development of performance assessments that are directly applicable to the health professions. Educational program directors and faculty evaluators are urged to study these sources.

Here are seven thoughts about constructing tools that can contribute to observational assessment of learners in the health care professions. The seven thoughts are grounded in experience and evaluation best practice.

1. Form a team that includes persons having clinical and educational measurement expertise. Clinical and educational skills are complementary. Both skill sets are needed to construct good assessment tools.

2. Planning and blueprinting are the essential first steps in constructing observational assessment tools. This involves clearly stating inclusion and exclusion criteria that structure a checklist, rating scale, or other assessment tool. What are the essential actions, for example, in an ACLS response to a patient with ventricular fibrillation? What actions can be omitted? Thinking through the details of the total assessment, from beginning to end, should be done before items or questions are written. See Chapter 10 (this volume) for an example of a test blueprint in clinical cardiology.

3. What is an item? Test, checklist, or attitude and survey questionnaire items are the building blocks of health professions observational assessments. Items should be discrete and uniform to increase the odds of error free (reliable) educational measurement. More items are usually better, within practical limits.

4. Measurement planning and blueprinting, and item writing and editing (refinement) should be done using a systematic plan.

Construction of assessment tools is a practical yet disciplined exercise, guided by an overall design.

5. Pilot studies should be done after early versions of observational assessments have been crafted. Small scale tryouts will reveal hidden flaws and content coverage failures. Improvements in the measures, informed by pilot test data, can be made before the assessment tools are placed in widespread use.

6. Health professions educators are urged to publish their work on instrument development. Creating assessment tools to serve local needs often has broad utility. A new and better measure of student nurses' proficiency at arterial puncture produced in Peoria will likely receive an eager reception in Portland, Paducah, and Poughkeepsie. Publishing reports about creating learner assessment tools also means the work will undergo rigorous peer review. It also means that the observational assessment tools are available for use by colleagues elsewhere.

7. Constructing assessment tools is hard work. However, there are many long-lasting benefits from these endeavors: Solid evaluations of learner competence, that can lead to educational feedback and improvement, publications, and an important contribution to one's field.

Examples of Constructed Measures

Three concrete examples of published instrument development reports in the health professions illustrate how this work can be done to systematically create assessment tools that measure knowledge, clinical skills, and attitudes.

Issenberg, McGaghie, Brown et al. (2000) used an eight-step development procedure at the University of Miami to create a computer-based measure of clinical skills in bedside cardiology focused on knowledge acquisition and application. This work produced two interchangeable measures for use as a pretest and a posttest that are equivalent in content, difficulty, and data reliability. The measures have been used in several other research studies that produced published reports (Issenberg, McGaghie, Gordon et al., 2002; Issenberg,

Petrusa, McGaghie et al., 1999). The measures have also been adopted by medical teachers at other institutions as part of educational programs in bedside cardiology for students and residents.

A team of medical educators was responsible for teaching students and residents how to recognize and work up patients with musculoskeletal (MSK) disorders. A key part of the educational program involved rigorous evaluations of the learners' clinical skills. Useful measures were not available from outside sources. Thus the team used a systematic, six step process to develop a set of four checklists (knee, shoulder, back, general) needed for observational assessment of the students' and residents' MSK examination skills (McGaghie, Renner, Kowlowitz, et al., 1994). The checklists were practical, useful, and produced reliable data.

The Nutrition Academic Award (NAA) Program was started by the NIH in the late 1990s to boost medical student, resident, and practitioner knowledge, attitudes, and clinical skills about nutrition in patient care. The NAA was a nationwide program with awards granted at scores of sites. Educational outcome measures addressing learner knowledge and clinical skills were available from several sources. However, there was no measure available to probe learners' attitudes about nutrition in patient care. A team of nutritionists, physicians, and behavioral scientists filled the gap by constructing a 45 item attitude measure with five subscales (nutrition in routine care, clinical behavior, physician–patient relationship, patient behavior/motivation, physician efficacy) derived from factor analysis (McGaghie, Van Horn, Fitzgibbon, et al., 2001). The subscales yield reliable data that are useful for learner feedback and research. Because it is published, the nutrition attitude measure is available for use by other educators and investigators at no cost.

Administration of an Assessment

An observational assessment needs to be administered according to a set of simple, practical rules to produce data that are useful for feedback and learner improvement. Such rules are also imposed so that all learners are treated fairly, to underscore the seriousness of health care personnel evaluations, and to convey an expectation of professionalism to students, faculty, and college administrators.

Textbooks on educational measurement and evaluation (e.g., Linn & Gronlund, 2000) devote complete chapters to this topic. Health professions boards and certifying agencies administer examinations and other assessments under draconian conditions. However, health professions teachers and evaluators responsible for delivery of local observational assessments should administer the measures mindful of six simple principles.

1. Use *standardized procedures* throughout the assessment for all trainees. The uniformity gained by using such standardized procedures as the room or setting, time allocation, instruments, and minimum passing levels ensure that all learners are treated equally and fairly.

2. The assessment must be *managed tightly*. This is a part of standardized procedures but is listed separately to underscore the importance of people management: scheduling persons, facilities, and resources; advance preparation; attention to details.

3. Assessment administration needs to be mindful of *personnel control*, especially if multiple faculty members are used for identical observational measures. As measurement devices these faculty members should be calibrated via rater training. Faculty members need preparation (and updating) for this important work.

4. Data collection, entry into files, and storage must be done according to an *orderly plan*. Persons with clerical responsibility need to be competent at using widely available data base management programs (e.g., Microsoft Excel®).

5. Data analyses, summaries, and presentation as reports should be *simple and straightforward*. For individual learners the goal of giving feedback about progress toward professional milestones can be done in the form of a performance profile. The progress of learner groups can be gauged by aggregating individual profiles into a class or program report.

6. Administration of learner assessments should be done according to a *firm schedule* that is posted in advance. This will prevent

expressions of "surprise" that assessments will be done and clarify expectations among learners and their teachers.

Data Quality

The idea of data quality is a basic concept at all phases of health professions education. The quality of data derived from educational measurements is judged by two primary indexes: reliability and validity. *Reliability* refers to the accuracy and consistency of measurement data and is covered in detail earlier in this volume (Axelson & Kreiter, Chapter 3, this volume) and in many other writings (e.g., Downing, 2004). The idea of *validity* addresses the accuracy of permissible decisions or inferences that can be made from test data. Validity is not a property of tests or measurements themselves. Approaches to validity and its threats are also covered in an earlier chapter in this book (Downing & Haladyna, Chapter 2, this volume) and other scholarly writings (e.g., Downing, 2003). Specific validity threats for observational methods are noted in Table 8.2.

The basic point here is that data quality, judged in several ways, is *essential* for all assessment procedures in the health professions. High quality assessment data (high signal, low noise) are needed to ensure that educational feedback to learners is accurate and trustworthy. High quality data are also needed to fulfill research goals. Sound educational research in the health professions simply cannot be done without good outcome measures that yield reliable data that permit valid educational inferences.

Data used for observational assessments in the health professions are never perfect. The data are subject to many different sources of possible bias (Williams, Klamen, & McGaghie, 2003) and usually address a much more limited scope of professional behavior than evaluators intend (Boulet & Swanson, 2004). The aim is for evaluators to acknowledge the limits of observational data, take steps to reduce data flaws, and interpret the results of observational assessments with appropriate caution. While the measurement problems will never be eliminated, they can be addressed thoughtfully.

Table 8.2 Threats to Validity: In vivo Observational Methods

	Problem	Remedy
Construct Under-representation (CU)	Too few observations to sample domain adequately	Use multiple direct observations (e.g. mini-CEX, focused observations)
	Unrepresentative sampling of domain	• Blueprint the activities to be observed to ensure focused observations systematically sample the domain • Blueprint the rating scale to ensure competencies of interest are rated
	Too few independent ratings	• Use multiple raters • Use different raters for different observation events • Use raters from different disciplines with different perspectives (e.g. 360° or multi-source ratings)
Construct-irrelevant Variance (CIV)	Examiner bias	• Provide scoring rubric • Train examiners to use rubric
	Halo and Recency effects	Have examiners complete rating immediately after each direct observation (not at end of rotation)
	Systematic rater errors: Severity, Leniency, Central tendency	• Frame of reference training for examiners • Feedback to examiners showing their ratings compared to all other raters
Reliability Indicators		Generalizability Inter-rater reliability

How to Use Observational Data

The practical matter of educating and evaluating people to fulfill many different high-performance roles in the health professions begs the question of how to best use observational data in these contexts. We have stated several times that best educational practice would use observational assessment data chiefly for formative learner assessment aimed at description, feedback, and improvement. This aim is practical and achievable in most educational settings.

A more visionary goal is to carefully integrate observational data with focused, deliberate practice (Ericsson, 2004) of essential clinical skills; combined with very high standards of expected professional performance (Downing, Tekian, & Yudkowsky, 2006; Wayne, Fudala, Butter, et al., 2005b). This would lead to the ultimate goal of employing the *mastery model* of training and assessment in the health professions where all learners reach identical (and very high) educational outcomes with little or no outcome variation. The only educational feature that would vary among learners is the time needed to reach the high educational goal (McGaghie, Miller, Sajid, & Telder, 1978). This mastery model has been used successfully to educate internal medicine residents to achieve very high and uniform performance levels in advanced cardiac life support (ACLS) skills (Wayne, Butter, Siddall, et al., 2006) and to master thoracentesis (Wayne, Barsuk, O'Leary, et. al., 2008). A detailed description of the features and uses of the mastery model of education and assessment in the health professions has been published recently (McGaghie, Siddall, Mazmanian, & Myers, 2009).

The mastery model is the best available expression of *dynamic testing* (Grigorenko & Sternberg, 1998). This is an environment where learners and evaluators understand that educational activities and assessments coalesce—where assessment data are used as a tool, not as a weapon.

Practical Recommendations About Observational Assessment

We close this chapter by repeating a set of 16 practical recommendations for improving observational assessment practices in the health professions. The recommendations were first stated in a recent journal article (Williams, et al., 2003).

1. Assessments should cover a *broad range of clinical situations and procedures* to draw reasonable conclusions about learners' overall clinical competence.
2. Observational assessments should be done by *multiple raters* to balance the effects of rater differences.
3. Assessment instruments should be *short* and *focused*.

4. Formative assessments for teaching, learning, and feedback should be *separate* from assessments done for learner promotion or advancement.

5. Observational data must be *recorded promptly* to prevent distortion from memory loss or misplaced information.

6. Supplement formal observational assessments with *unobtrusive observations* to obtain a better estimate of trainees' normal clinical behavior.

7. Consider making promotion and grading decisions via a faculty *group review* rather than being the responsibility of a single evaluator.

8. Supplement traditional clinical performance assessments with *standardized clinical encounters* (e.g., standardized patients) and skills training and assessment protocols.

9. *Educate raters* to ensure familiarity with instruments and calibrated assessments.

10. Provide *sufficient time* for assessments so that ratings are thoughtful and candid, not rushed.

11. Be certain that evaluators observe and rate *specific learner performances.*

12. Use *no more than seven* quality rating categories (i.e., 1 = poor to 7 = excellent) on observational assessment instruments.

13. *Establish the meaning of ratings* through constant use and infrequent revision of rating instruments.

14. Give faculty raters *feedback* about their stringency and leniency to prevent formation of diverse groups of faculty "hawks" and "doves."

15. Learn about observational performance assessment from *other professions* (e.g., astronaut corps, business and industry, military) for ideas about how they address personnel evaluation.

16. Acknowledge the *limits of observational assessment* while working toward the goal of continuous quality improvement.

Coda

This chapter began by asserting that observational assessment is the most widely used approach to personnel evaluation in the health professions. We also cited several research studies that reached the uncomfortable conclusion that observational assessment is frequently done poorly, meaning that educational feedback is diluted and opportunities for improvement are lost. The ideas and suggestions given in this chapter are intended to improve the *status quo*. The goal is to help health science educators use observational assessments with wisdom and skill.

Note

1. Reprinted from Section 3, Descriptive Evaluation (authored by D. Carnahan & P.A. Hemmer); in Chapter 6, Evaluation and Grading of Students, L.N. Pangaro & W.C. McGaghie (Eds.). (2005) In R.E. Fincher et al. (Eds.), *The Guidebook for Clerkship Directors* (3rd ed., p. 156). Omaha, NE: Alliance for Clinical Education. Copyright © with permission from the Alliance for Clinical Education.

References

American Dog Show Judges, Inc. (2006). Advanced Institute. Retrieved January 2, 2008 from http://www.adsj.org/

Baker, D.P., Beaubien, J.M., & Holtzman, A.K. (2006). *DoD medical team training programs: An independent case study analysis.* AHRQ Publication No. 06–0001. Rockville, MD: Agency for Healthcare Research and Quality.

Boulet, J.R., & Swanson, D.B. (2004). Psychometric challenges of using simulations for high-stakes assessment. In W.F. Dunn (Ed.), *Simulators in critical care and beyond* (pp. 119–130). Des Plaines, IL: Society of Critical Care Medicine.

Bracken, D.W., Timmreck, C.W., & Church, A.H. (Eds.). (2001). *The handbook of multisource feedback.* San Francisco: Jossey-Bass.

Carnahan, D., & Hemmer, P.A. (2005). Section 3: Descriptive evaluation; in Chapter 6: Evaluation and grading of students. In R. Fincher et al. (Eds.), *Guidebook for clerkship directors* (3rd ed., pp. 150–162). Omaha, NE: Alliance for Clinical Education.

Case, S.M., & Swanson, D.B. (2002). *Constructing written test questions for basic and clinical sciences* (3rd ed.). Philadelphia: National Board of Medical Examiners.

Cullen, D.L. (2005). Clinical education and clinical evaluation of respiratory therapy students. *Respiratory Care Clinics of North America*, 11, 425–447.

Darmody, J.V. (2005). Observing the work of the clinical nurse specialist. *Clinical Nurse Specialist*, 19 (5), 260–268.

DeVellis, R.F. (2003). *Scale development: Theory and applications* (2nd ed.). Applied Research Methods Series No. 26. Thousand Oaks, CA: Sage Publications.

Downing, S.M. (2003). Validity: On the meaningful interpretation of assessment data. *Medical Education*, 37, 830–837.

Downing, S.M. (2004). Reliability: On the reproducibility of assessment data. *Medical Education*, 38, 1006–1012.

Downing, S.M., Tekian, A., & Yudkowsky, R. (2006). Procedures for establishing defensible absolute passing scores on performance examinations in the health professions. *Teaching and Learning in Medicine*, 18, 50–57.

Epstein, R.M., & Hundert, E.M. (2002). Defining and assessing professional competence. *Journal of the American Medical Association*, 287, 226–235.

Ericsson, K.A. (2004). Deliberate practice and the acquisition and maintenance of expert performance in medicine and related domains. *Academic Medicine*, 79 (10, Suppl.), S70–S81.

Fletcher, R.H., Fletcher, S.W., & Wagner, E.H. (1996). *Clinical epidemiology —The essentials* (3rd ed.). Philadelphia: Lippincott Williams & Wilkins.

Goldman, W. (1990). *Hype and glory*. New York: Villard Books.

Green, E.H., Hershman, W., DeCherrie, L., Greenwald, J., Torres-Finnerty, N., & Wahi-Gururaj, S. (2005). Developing and implementing universal guidelines for oral patient presentation skills. *Teaching and Learning in Medicine*, 17, 263–267.

Grigorenko, E.L., & Sternberg, R.J. (1998). Dynamic testing. *Psychological Bulletin*, 124, 75–111.

Haas, J., & Shaffir, W. (1982). Ritual evaluation of competence. *Work and Occupations*, 9, 131–154.

Haas, J., & Shaffir, W. (1987). *Becoming doctors: The adoption of a cloak of competence*. Greenwich, CT: JAI Press.

Haber, R.J., & Lingard, L.A. (2001). Learning oral presentation skills: A rhetorical analysis with pedagogical and professional implications. *Journal of General Internal Medicine*, 16, 308–314.

Hamman, W.R. (2004). The complexity of team training: What we have learned from aviation and its applications to medicine. *Quality and Safety in Health Care*, 13 (Suppl. 1), i72–i79.

Health and Psychological Instruments (HAPI). Database retrieved January 22, 2008 from: http://www.northwestern.edu/libraries/

Herbers, J.E., Noel, G.L., Cooper, G.S., Harvey, J., Pangaro, L.N., & Weaver, M.J. (1989). How accurate are faculty evaluations of clinical competence? *Journal of General Internal Medicine*, 4, 202–208.

Holmboe, E.S. (2004). Faculty and the observation of trainees' clinical skills. *Academic Medicine*, 79, 16–22.

Holmboe, E.S. (2005). Section 4: Direct observation of students' clinical skills; in Chapter 6: Evaluation and grading of students. In R.E. Fincher et al. (Eds.), *Guidebook for clerkship directors* (3rd ed., pp. 163–170). Omaha, NE: Alliance for Clinical Education.

Holmboe, E.S., & Hawkins, R.E. (1998). Methods for evaluating the clinical competence of residents in internal medicine: A review. *Annals of Internal Medicine*, 129, 42–48.

Holmboe, E.S., Yepes, M., Williams, F., & Huot, S.J. (2004). Feedback and the mini clinical evaluation exercise. *Journal of General Internal Medicine*, 19, 558–561.

International Gymnastics Federation (1989). *Code of points*. Indianapolis, IN: International Gymnastics Federation.

Issenberg, S.B., McGaghie, W.C., Brown, D.D., Mayer, J.D., Gessner, I.H., Hart, I.R., et al. (2000). Development of multimedia computer-based measures of clinical skills in bedside cardiology. In D.E. Melnick (Ed.), *The eighth international Ottawa conference on medical education and assessment proceedings. Evolving assessment: Protecting the human dimension* (pp. 821–829). Philadelphia: National Board of Medical Examiners.

Issenberg, S.B., McGaghie, W.C., Gordon, D.L., Symes, S., Petrusa, E.R., Hart, I.R., et al. (2002). Effectiveness of a cardiology review course for internal medicine residents using simulation technology and deliberate practice. *Teaching and Learning in Medicine*, 14, 223–228.

Issenberg, S.B., Petrusa, E.R., McGaghie, W.C., Felner, J.M., Waugh, R.A., Nash, I.S., et al. (1999). Effectiveness of a computer-based system to teach bedside cardiology. *Academic Medicine*, 74 (10, Suppl.), S93–S95.

Kalet, A., Earp, J.A., & Kowlowitz, V. (1992). How well do faculty evaluate the interviewing skills of medical students? *Journal of General Internal Medicine*, 7, 499–505.

Kirkpatrick, D.L. (1998). *Evaluating training programs* (2nd ed.). San Francisco: Berrett-Koehler.

Linn, R.L., & Gronlund, N.E. (2000). *Measurement and assessment in teaching* (8th ed.). Upper Saddle River, NJ: Prentice-Hall.

Loftus, E.F., & Schneider, N.G. (1987). Behold with strange surprise: Judicial reactions to expert testimony concerning eyewitness reliability. *University of Missouri-Kansas City Law Review*, 56, 1–45.

Loughry, M.L., Ohland, M.W., & Moore, D.D. (2007). Development of a theory-based assessment of team member effectiveness. *Educational and Psychological Measurement*, 67 (3), 505–524.

Mahara, M.S. (1998). A perspective on clinical evaluation in nursing education. *Journal of Advanced Nursing*, 28 (6), 339–346.

McGaghie, W.C. (2005). Section 1: General introduction; in Chapter 6: Evaluation and grading of students. In R.E. Fincher et al. (Eds.), *Guidebook for clerkship directors* (3rd ed., pp. 134–142). Omaha, NE: Alliance for Clinical Education.

McGaghie, W.C., Miller, G.A., Sajid, A., & Telder, T.V. (1978). *Competency-based curriculum development in medical education.* Public Health Paper No. 68. Geneva, Switzerland: World Health Organization.

McGaghie, W.C., Renner, B.R., Kowlowitz, V., Sauter, S.V.H., Hoole, A.J., Schuch, C.P., et al. (1994). Development and evaluation of musculo-skeletal performance measures for an objective structured clinical examination. *Teaching and Learning in Medicine, 6,* 59–63.

McGaghie, W.C., Van Horn, L., Fitzgibbon, M., Telser, A., Thompson, J.A., Kushner, R.F., & Prystowsky, J.B. (2001). Development of a measure of attitude toward nutrition in patient care. *American Journal of Preventive Medicine, 20,* 15–20.

McGaghie, W.C., Siddall, V.J., Mazmanian, P.E., & Myers, J. (n.d.). Lessons for continuing medical education. From simulation research in undergraduate and graduate medical education. *Chest, 135,* in press.

Miller, G.E. (1990). The assessment of clinical skills/competence/performance. *Academic Medicine, 65* (9, Suppl.), S63–S67.

Noel, G.L., Herbers, J.E., Caplow, M.P., Cooper, G.S., Pangaro, L.N., & Harvey, J. (1992). How well do internal medicine faculty members evaluate the clinical skills of residents? *Annals of Internal Medicine, 117,* 757–765.

Norcini, J. (2006). Faculty observations of student professional behavior. In D.T. Stern (Ed.), *Measuring medical professionalism* (pp. 147–157). New York: Oxford University Press.

Norcini, J., Blank, L.L., Duffy, F.D., & Fortna, G.S. (2003). The mini-CEX: A method for assessing clinical skills. *Annals of Internal Medicine, 138,* 476–481.

Ogburn, T., & Espey, E. (2003). The R-I-M-E method for evaluation of medical students on an obstetrics and gynecology clerkship. *American Journal of Obstetrics and Gynecology, 189,* 666–669.

Orient, J.M. (2005). *Sapira's art & science of bedside diagnosis* (3rd ed.). Philadelphia: Lippincott Williams & Wilkins.

Osler, W. (1906). The hospital as a college. In W. Osler (Ed.), *Aequanimitas* (2nd ed., pp. 329–342). Philadelphia: P. Blakiston's Son & Co.

Pangaro, L.N. (1999). Evaluating professional growth: A new vocabulary and other innovations for improving descriptive evaluation of students. *Academic Medicine, 74,* 1203–1207.

Schwind, C.J., Williams, R.G., Boehler, M.L., & Dunnington, G.L. (2004). Do individual attendings' post rotation performance ratings detect residents' clinical performance deficiencies? *Academic Medicine, 79,* 453–457.

Smither, J.W., London, M., & Reilly, R.R. (2005). Does performance improve following multisource feedback? A theoretical model, meta-analysis, and review of empirical findings. *Personnel Psychology*, 58, 33–66.

Sox, H.C., Blatt, M.A., Higgins, M.C., & Marton, K.I. (1988). *Medical decision making*. Boston: Butterworth-Heinemann.

Stern, D.T. (Ed.). (2006). *Measuring medical professionalism*. New York: Oxford University Press.

Stiggins, R.J. (1987). Design and development of performance assessments. *Educational Measurement: Issues and Practice*, 6 (3), 33–42.

Streiner, D.L., & Norman, G.R. (2003). *Health measurement scales: A practical guide to their development and use* (3rd ed.). New York: Oxford University Press.

Tesser, A., & Rosen, S. (1975). The reluctance to transmit bad news. In L. Berkowitz (Ed.), *Advances in experimental social psychology* (Vol. 8., pp. 193–232). New York: Academic Press.

Thomas, E.J., Sexton, J.B., & Helmreich, R.L. (2004). Translating teamwork behaviors from aviation to healthcare: Development of behavioral markers for neonatal resuscitation. *Quality and Safety in Health Care*, 13 (Suppl. 1), i57–i64.

Waas, V., van der Vleuten, C., Shatzer, J., & Jones, R. (2001). Assessment of clinical competence. *The Lancet*, 357, 945–949.

Wayne, D.B., Butter, J., Siddall, V.J., Fudala, M.J., Lindquist, L., Feinglass, J., et al. (2005a). Simulation-based training of internal medicine residents in advanced cardiac life support protocols: A randomized trial. *Teaching and Learning in Medicine*, 17, 210–216.

Wayne, D.B., Fudala, M.J., Butter, J., Siddall, V.J., Feinglass, J., Wade, L.D., et al. (2005b). Comparison of two standard setting methods for advanced cardiac life support training. *Academic Medicine*, 80 (10, Suppl.), S63–S66.

Wayne, D.B., Butter, J., Siddall, V.J., Fudala, M.J., Wade, L.D., Feinglass, J., et al. (2006). Mastery learning of advanced cardiac life support skills by internal medicine residents using simulation technology and deliberate practice. *Journal of General Internal Medicine*, 21, 251–256.

Wayne, D.B., Barsuk, J., O'Leary, K., Fudala, M.J., & McGaghie, W.C. (2008). Mastery learning of thoracentesis skills by internal medicine residents using simulation technology and deliberate practice. *Journal of Hospital Medicine*, 3, 48–54.

Weed, L.L. (1968). Medical records that guide and teach. *New England Journal of Medicine*, 278, 593–600; 652–657.

Wiese, J., Varosy, P., & Tierney, L. (2002). Improving oral presentation skills with a clinical reasoning curriculum: A prospective controlled study. *American Journal of Medicine*, 112, 212–218.

Wigton, R.S. (1980). The effects of student personal characteristics on the evaluation of clinical performance. *Journal of Medical Education*, 55, 423–427.

Williams, R.G., Klamen, D.A., & McGaghie, W.C. (2003). Cognitive, social, and environmental sources of bias in clinical competence ratings. *Teaching and Learning in Medicine*, 15, 270–292.

Wilson, M. (2005). *Constructing measures*. Mahwah, NJ: Lawrence Erlbaum Associates.

Woehr, D.J., & Huffcutt, A.I. (1994). Rater training for performance appraisal: A quantitative review. *Journal of Occupational and Organizational Psychology*, 67, 189–205.

9
PERFORMANCE TESTS
RACHEL YUDKOWSKY

A performance test is an examination designed to elicit performance on an actual or simulated real-life task. In contrast to observation of naturally occurring behavior "in vivo" (McGaghie, Butter, & Kaye, Chapter 8, this volume), the task is contrived for the purpose of the examination, and explicitly invites the examinee to demonstrate the behavior to be assessed. Thus a performance test is an "in vitro" assessment, at Miller's "shows how" level (Miller, 1990); see Figure 9.1. Since the examinees know they are being assessed, their performance likely represents their personal best or maximum performance, rather than a typical performance. Examples of performance tests include a road test to obtain a driver's license, an undersea diving test, and the Unites States Medical Licensing Exam (USMLE) Step 2 Clinical Skills Assessment. In this chapter we'll review some of the purposes, advantages and limitations of performance tests, and provide practical guidelines for the use of standardized patients (SPs), a simulation modality commonly used in health professions education. Focusing on the use of SPs for assessment rather than instruction, we'll discuss scoring options, multiple-station Objective Structured Clinical Exams (OSCEs), standard setting, and threats to validity in the context of SP exams; the same principles apply to performance tests using other modalities. There are several other types of simulations currently in use, such as bench models, virtual (computer-based) models, and mannequins. Many of the assessment issues addressed here also apply to these forms of simulation, which are discussed in greater detail in Chapter 10.

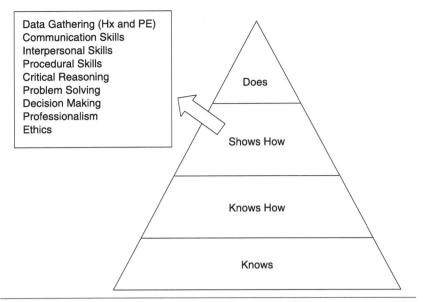

Data Gathering (Hx and PE)
Communication Skills
Interpersonal Skills
Procedural Skills
Critical Reasoning
Problem Solving
Decision Making
Professionalism
Ethics

Does

Shows How

Knows How

Knows

Figure 9.1 Miller's Pyramid (Miller, 1990): Competencies to Assess with Performance Tests.

Strengths of Performance Tests

Performance tests provide the opportunity to observe students in action as they respond to complex challenges, while controlling when, where, how and what will be tested. Performance tests are not limited to patients and problems that chance to present in clinical settings in a specific span of time. The simulation option provides a high degree of control over the examination setting, allowing standardization across examinees, advance training of examiners, and a systematic sampling of the domain to be assessed. When used formatively performance tests provide unique opportunities for feedback, coaching and debriefing, thus facilitating deliberate practice (Ericsson, 1993, 2004) and the development of skills and expertise. From a patient safety perspective, performance tests allow educators to ensure that learners have reached a minimal level of competency and skill before they are allowed to work with real patients. Disadvantages of performance tests are related to the complex logistics and difficulty of realistically modeling clinical tasks; simulations can be expensive, and the need for multiple stations or cases (see below) increases the resource cost in terms of both money and time.

Defining the Purpose of the Test

As with all assessments, faculty must be clear about the purpose of the test. What are the underlying constructs (competencies or skills) to be assessed?

Since performance tests are time consuming and expensive, they are best reserved for the assessment of skills that cannot be observed or assessed effectively elsewhere or by other means. Skills that involve interactions with patients are particularly amenable to performance tests. Communication and interpersonal skills with patients, family, staff and colleagues; data gathering by means of a history and physical exam (H&P); clinical reasoning and decision making; documentation in the patient chart; ethical and professional behavior and procedural skills all can be elicited and assessed effectively in simulated settings.

The choice of whether to assess individual skills or a complete clinical encounter depends in part on the level of the learner (Petrusa, 2002). Students early in training often learn discrete skills such as "examining the shoulder" or "taking a sexual history." These skills can be assessed by means of brief, five to seven minute stations in which they are instructed to demonstrate the particular skill: "please examine the shoulder of this patient." Intermediate learners must select salient history and physical exam items on their own when encountering a patient, and must construct a differential diagnosis and management plan. These learners are more appropriately tested in a longer, integrated patient encounter that elicits these competencies in the context of a given complaint. For more advanced learners, the ability to handle complex critical situations can be tested in an "error prone" environment that features staff blunders, non-functioning equipment, and distracting family members.

An observation of an actual (not simulated) clinical encounter can be part of a performance test if the encounter is taking place for the purpose of the exam: for example a mini-CEX (McGaghie, Butter, & Kaye, Chapter 8, this volume), the live interview in the

U.S. Psychiatry Board exam, or the first part of a traditional "viva," in which a preceptor rates the performance of a history and physical exam on an unknown patient. Note that a performance test does not require the subsequent oral examination or discussion of the patient—the encounter itself is the object of the rating. All of the principles discussed in this chapter, such as blueprinting, scoring the encounter, and standard setting, apply equally to performance tests based on real patients and to simulations.

Standardized Patients

Standardized patients (SPs) are persons who are trained to portray a given patient presentation in a consistent and believable manner, allowing the realistic simulation of patient encounters (Barrows, 1993; Barrows & Abrahamson, 1964). SPs can come from a range of backgrounds including professional actors, retired teachers, community volunteers, patients with stable physical findings, nurses, medical residents and students. "Hybrid" simulations use SPs in conjunction with bench models and mannequins (Kneebone, Kidd, Nestel, et al., 2005) to encourage a patient-centered approach to procedural skills. Unannounced SPs can be sent incognito into clinician offices and clinics to assess performance in actual practice (Rethans, Drop, Sturmans, & van der Vleuten 1991; Rethans, Gorter, Bokken, & Morrison, 2007). The SP methodology also has been extended to the portrayal of standardized students for faculty development (Gelula & Yudkowsky, 2003), and standardized family members, colleagues and staff.

"Simulated patient" is a generic term that includes portrayals that do not need to be highly consistent across encounters, for example patient simulation for the purpose of small group instruction. In contrast, the "standardized" aspect of the SP is crucial to the use of SPs for assessment. In a high-stakes assessment setting SPs must be able to keep the portrayal consistent across a large number of examinees, each bringing his or her own idiosyncratic questions and behaviors to the encounter. Consistent portrayal requires two elements: a highly specified script, and rigorous training of the SP.

The *SP script* contains the details of the portrayal. The script stipulates the age, gender, and other salient characteristics of the patient, and describes the patient's medical history and physical exam findings, their "backstory" (family, job, and life circumstances), their personality and affect. The script specifies information to be provided in response to open ended questions, information to be provided only if specifically elicited by the examinee, SP prompts for the examinee (e.g. questions such as: "Can I go home now?"), and the desired SP responses to different examinee behaviors. The extent and richness of the script depends in part on the length and nature of the expected interaction. A five-minute encounter in which a student examines the shoulder of the SP without gathering any historical information may require only a description of physical exam findings to be simulated (if any). A 30-minute encounter in which an examinee is asked to develop a differential diagnosis and treatment plan for a depressed elderly woman demands a highly detailed and elaborated script.

SP scripts should be written by teams of experienced clinicians, preferably based on their own experiences with an actual patient, with modifications to maintain patient confidentiality. Basing the script on a real patient provides the foundation for a rich backstory, supporting details such laboratory results, and the assurance that the script "hangs together" to present a plausible and realistic patient. Figure 9.2 lists suggested elements of an effective script and provides a template or scaffold for the needed information. SP scripts can also be found in published casebooks (The Macy Initiative, 2003; Schimpfhouser, Sultz, Zinnerstrom, & Anderson, 2000) and in online resource banks such as MedEd Portal (www.aamc.org/mededportal) and the Association of Standardized Patient Educators (www.aspeducators.org).

SP training: Once the script is available an SP can be trained to portray the patient accurately, consistently, and believably (van der Vleuten & Swanson 1990; Tamblyn, Klass, Schnabl & Kopelow, 1991; Colliver & Williams, 1993; Wallace, 2007). Training includes review, clarification and memorization of the case material, followed by rehearsal of the material in simulated encounters with the trainer and/or simulated examinees. The SP must be able to improvise

General Case Information

☐ Presenting complaint
☐ Diagnosis
☐ Case Author contact information
☐ Learning objectives, competencies addressed in case
☐ Target learner group (e.g. medical students, residents, nursing students, nurse practitioner students, other)
☐ Level of learner (year of training, advanced clinician, etc.)
☐ Duration of patient encounter

Case Summary and SP Training Notes

☐ SP demographics: name, gender, age range, ethnicity
☐ Setting (clinic, ER, etc.)
☐ History of present illness
☐ Past medical history
☐ Family medical history
☐ Social history and backstory
☐ Review of systems
☐ Physical examination findings (if indicated)
☐ Special instructions for the SP:
    ☐ Patient presentation (affect, appearance, position of patient at opening, etc.)
    ☐ Opening statement
    ☐ Embedded communication challenges
    ☐ Responses to open-ended questions
    ☐ Responses to specific interviewing techniques or errors
☐ Special case considerations/props:
    ☐ Specific body type/physical requirements
    ☐ Props (e.g. pregnancy pillow)
    ☐ Make-up (please include application guidelines if available)

Additional Materials

☐ Door chart information
☐ Laboratory results, radiology images (if indicated)
☐ Student instructions
☐ Student pre- or post-encounter challenge
☐ SP checklist or rating scale for scoring the encounter
☐ Observer checklist or rating scale
☐ SP feedback guidelines
☐ Other supporting documents (faculty instructions, etc.)

Figure 9.2 Essential Elements of a Standardized Patient Case.

Source: Adapted with permission from the Association of Standardized Patient Educators (ASPE) (Copyright 2008).

appropriately and in character when confronted with unexpected questions from the examinee. If more than one SP will be portraying the same case, training them together will promote consistency across different SPs. Video recordings of previous SPs portraying the case help provide consistency across different administrations of the test. If the SPs will be providing verbal or written feedback to the examinee, they should be trained to do so effectively (Howley, 2007). If the SPs will be rating the examinees, this requires training as well (see rater training, below). The entire training process can range from 30 minutes to eight hours and more, depending on the complexity of the script and the responsibilities of the SP. Once the SP is performing at the desired level, periodic assessment and feedback can help maintain the quality of the exam (Wind, Van Dalen, Muijtjens, & Rethans, 2004).

Scoring the Performance

Checklists and rating scales are used to convert the examinee's behavior during the SP encounter (or other observed performance) into a number that can be used for scoring. *Checklist* items are statements or questions that can be scored dichotomously as "done" or "not done"—for example, "The examinee auscultated the lungs." *Rating scales* employ a range of response options to indicate the quality of what was done—for example, "How respectful was the examinee?" might be rated on a four-point scale ranging from "extremely respectful" to "not at all respectful."

Case-specific checklists identify actions essential to a given clinical case, and are usually developed by panels of content experts or local faculty (Gorter, Rethans, Scherpbier, et al., 2000). Checklist items can also be derived by observing the actions of experienced clinicians as they encounter the SP (Nendaz, Gut, Perrier, et al., 2004). Ideally, items should be evidence-based and reflect best-practice guidelines. Since checklists are intended simply to record what took place in the encounter, completing the checklist does not necessarily require expert judgment. Nonetheless, to minimize disagreements between raters the checklist items must be very well specified, and raters must be trained to recognize the parameters of examinee behaviors that merit a score of "done" for a particular action. For example, the checklist item cited above "the examinee auscultated the lungs" might be more fully specified as "the examinee auscultated the lungs on skin, posteriorly, bilaterally, at three levels, while asking the patient to breath deeply through the mouth." If any one of these conditions is not met, the item is scored as "not done" or as "done incorrectly." The item could be split into individual items for each of the essential conditions (on skin, bilateral, three levels, etc.) if more detailed feedback is desired. Checklists may be completed by observers during the encounter or by the SP immediately after the encounter. Checklists of 12 to 15 items can be completed quite accurately by well-trained SPs (Vu, Mary, Colliver, et al., 1992). Some extensively trained SPs can complete much longer checklists, such as those required for a full head-to-toe screening physical exam (Yudkowsky, Downing, Klamen, et al., 2004).

While checklists can be used effectively with beginning learners to confirm that they followed all steps of a procedure or elicited a thorough medical history, comprehensive checklists are not always appropriate for more advanced examinees (Hodges, Regehr, McNaughton, et al., 1999). Expert clinicians often receive relatively low scores on history and physical exam (H&P) checklists that reward thoroughness; they tend to reach a diagnosis based on non-analytic processes such as pattern matching and thus perform a highly abbreviated H&P. When assessing more complex performance and/or advanced clinicians, rating scales completed by experts may be a more appropriate tool.

Rating scales provide the opportunity for observers to exercise expert judgment and rate the quality of an action. Global scale items rate the performance as an integrated whole; for example "Overall, this performance was: excellent | very good | good | marginal | unsatisfactory." Analytic scale items allow polytomous (multiple level) rating of specific behaviors: "Student followed up on patient nonverbal cues: frequently | sometimes | rarely | never." Primary trait rating scale items are used to assess a small number of salient features or characteristics of the overall performance; thus when assessing communication skills one might be asked to rate verbal communication, non-verbal communication, and English language skills. While checklists are usually case-specific, rating scales can be used to score behaviors or skills that are demonstrated across different cases, such as data gathering, communication skills, or professionalism. A variety of instruments for rating communication and interpersonal skills have been published (ACGME Outcome Project 2008: Tools from the field, Makoul, 2001a and b; Kurtz, Silverman, Benson, & Draper, 2003; Stillman, Brown, Redfield, & Sabers, 1977; Yudkowsky, Downing & Sandlow, 2006).

Because rating scales require the exercise of judgment, they are inherently more subjective than checklists. Providing anchors for the different rating options can improve agreement between raters (inter-rater reliability), especially if these anchors are behaviorally anchored (Bernardin & Smith, 1981). See Figure 9.3 for examples of different types of rating scale anchors.

Rubrics can be used to rate written products such as chart notes completed after an SP encounter. The rubric is, in effect, a behaviorally anchored rating scale providing detailed information about the performance expected at each score level (see Chapter 7 for more about rubrics in the context of written tests). A sample rubric for scoring a chart note is shown in Figure 9.4.

A. Likert-type Scales:

The student provided a clear explanation of my condition and the treatment plan.

1	2	3	4	
Strongly disagree	Disagree	Agree	Strongly Agree	

How clear were the student's explanations?

1	2	3	4	5
Not at all Clear	Somewhat Clear	Clear	Very Clear	Extremely Clear

B. Behaviorally Anchored Rating Scale (BARS)

Did the student provide a clear explanation of your condition?

1	2	3	4
Provided little or no explanation of my condition	Provided brief or unclear explanations of my condition	Provided a full and understandable explanation of my condition, pertinent findings, and important next steps	Provided a full explanation of my condition, his/her thinking about it and recommendation, and probed my understanding by asking me to summarize pertinent information

---

Figure 9.3 Rating Scale Anchors.

Please assess each component of the note	All key items present?		Any incorrect or dangerous items?	
History	Yes	No	Yes	No
Physical exam	Yes	No	Yes	No
Differential diagnosis	Yes	No	Yes	No
Plan for immediate workup	Yes	No	Yes	No

Please rate the overall quality of this patient note:

Rating	Example
1 = Not acceptable	Major deficiencies or disorganization in multiple sections
2 = Borderline acceptable	Major deficiencies or disorganization in one section but most essential points covered
3 = Acceptable	Minor deficiencies or disorganization in one or more sections.
4 = Excellent	Thorough, complete and well organized note. All four sections (History, PE, DDx and Workup) are complete.

Figure 9.4 Sample Rubric for Scoring a Student's Patient Chart Note.

Training Raters

Raters must be trained to use checklists and rating scales accurately and consistently. Training is best done with all raters in one group to facilitate consensus and cross-calibration. After reviewing the purpose of the exam and each of the items, frame of reference training (Bernardin & Buckley, 1981) can help ensure that all raters are calibrated and using the scale in the same way. The raters observe and individually score a live or recorded performance such as an SP encounter or chart note, then together discuss their ratings and reach a consensus on the observed behaviors corresponding to the checklist items and rating anchors. Ideally, raters should observe performances at high, middle, and low levels of proficiency and identify behaviors that are characteristic of each level.

Pilot-Testing the Case

Before deploying the case in an assessment, the station and rating instruments should be piloted with a few representative raters and examinees to ensure that the test will function as intended. Pilot tests frequently result in changes to the examinee instructions, specification of SP responses to previously unanticipated queries, and clarification of checklist items and rating anchors.

Multiple-station Performance Tests: The Objective Structured Clinical Exam (OSCE)

Performance on one clinical case or challenge is not a good predictor of performance on another case; this phenomenon is known as "case specificity" (Elstein, Shuman, & Sprafka, 1978). The ability to manage a patient with an acute appendicitis does not predict the ability to diagnose depression; demonstrating an appropriate history and physical exam (H&P) for a patient with chronic diabetes does not predict the ability to conduct an appropriate H&P for a patient with acute chest pain. Just as one would not assess a student's knowledge based on a single multiple-choice question, one cannot assess competency based on a single observation. One solution is the Objective Structured Clinical Examination or OSCE (Harden, Stevenson, Downie, & Wilson, 1975), an exam format that consists of a series or circuit of performance tests. Within an OSCE each test is called a "station"; students start at different points in the circuit and encounter one station after another until the OSCE is complete. A given OSCE can include stations of different types: SP-based patient encounters, procedures such as IV insertion, written challenges such as writing prescriptions or chart notes, interpretation of lab results, EKGs or radiology images, and oral presentations to an examiner (Figure 9.5). A larger number of stations allows for better sampling of the domain to be assessed, thus improving the reliability and validity of the exam—see the threats to validity discussion below.

The duration of an OSCE station can range from five minutes to 30 minutes or longer, depending on the purpose of the exam (Petrusa, 2002). Shorter stations allow the testing of discrete skills such as eliciting reflexes; longer stations allow the assessment of complex tasks in a realistic context—for example, counseling a patient reluctant to undergo colorectal screening. Ten to twenty minutes are usually

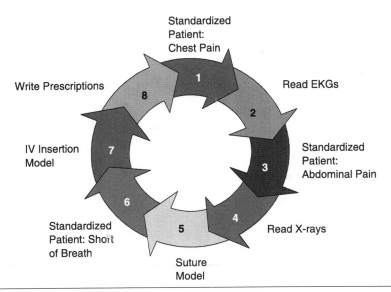

Figure 9.5 An 8-Station OSCE for an Internal Medicine Clerkship.

sufficient for a focused history and physical exam (Petrusa, 2002). For logistic convenience, all stations in a given OSCE should be of equal duration. "Couplet" stations consist of two linked challenges—for example, writing a chart note about the patient just seen in the previous station. The duration of the couplet station—the SP encounter plus note—will be equal to the combined time of two stations.

Scoring an OSCE: Combining Scores Across Stations

The unit of analysis in an OSCE is the station or case, not the checklist item, since items within a case are mutually dependent: whether a resident examines the heart depends on whether she elicited a history of chest pain. Checklist or scale items should be aggregated to create a station score. Subsets of the checklist can give information about performance on different aspects of the task, for example history taking vs physical exam, but these subscales rarely have enough items to stand on their own as reliable measures. However, skills subscales or primary-trait ratings of skills that are common to several cases can be averaged across cases to obtain an exam-level score for that skill. For example, communication and interpersonal skills (CIS) scores show moderate correlations across cases, so it is reasonable to average CIS rating scale scores across cases to obtain an exam-level score.

Compensatory vs non-compensatory or conjunctive scoring issues were discussed in Chapter 6 (Yudkowsky, Downing, & Tekian, this volume). Should good performance on one case or task compensate for poor performance on another? This is a policy-level decision. A skills-based compensatory approach would mean that good communication skills in one case could reasonably compensate for poor communication skills in another. On the other hand, decision-makers may feel that examinees should demonstrate competency in an absolute number of critical clinical situations such as chest pain, abdominal pain or shortness of breath—good performance on one would not compensate for poor performance on another. The ability to perform different clinical procedures is generally conjunctive—good performance inserting an IV does not compensate for poor performance obtaining an EKG.

Standard Setting

Many of the standard-setting methods described in Chapter 6, originally developed for written tests, have been adapted for use with performance tests (Downing, Tekian, & Yudkowsky, 2006). Item-based methods such as Angoff are commonly and easily employed to set cut scores for checklists, however the use of item-based methods for performance tests has been challenged since items on a checklist are not mutually independent (Ross, Clauser, Margolis, et al., 1996). Moreover, not all checklist items have equal clinical valence—the omission of one item may endanger a patient's life, while the omission of another may be of little import to the outcome of the clinical case. Standard setting methods based on the direct observation of examinees' performance, such as borderline-group (BG) and contrasting-group (CG), avoid these problems. Programs that use expert examiners (faculty) to observe and score SP encounters can easily use these examinee-based methods by having the examiners assign a global rating of fail, marginal pass, or pass in addition to completing the checklist for each examinee. The mean or median checklist score of examinees with a marginal pass rating is set as the cut score in the Borderline Group method, while the intersection of the passing and failing groups provides the basis for the cut score in the Contrasting-Group method (see Chapter 6 for details). Programs that use non-clinicians such as SPs to complete the checklists can have faculty experts rate the SP-scored checklists as proxies for examinee performance, use a compromise method such as Hofstee, or opt to fall back on item-based methods such as Angoff or Ebel while acknowledging their limitations. Case-level cut scores can be aggregated across cases to provide a compensatory-type standard for the whole test. Conjunctive standards will require that a specific number of cases be passed, or that two or more subscales be passed (for example, both data gathering and communication skills). Conjunctive standards will always result in a higher failure rate than compensatory standards, since each hurdle adds its own probability of failure.

Procedural skills testing brings a different set of challenges to standard setting. A mastery approach is especially appropriate in situations where the checklist is public and incorrect performance comprises a threat to patient safety or to the successful outcome of the procedure.

Logistics

Conducting an OSCE can be daunting. Some schools have full-time SP trainers, paid professional actors who serve as SPs, and a dedicated facility that includes several clinic-type rooms with audio-visual recording capability, affording remote observation and scoring of SP encounters. Online data-management systems facilitate checklist data capture and reporting, and allow both learners and faculty to view and comment upon digital recordings of encounters from remote locations. On the other hand, OSCEs also can be conducted on a more limited budget by using faculty as trainers and raters, recruiting students, residents, or community volunteers as SPs, and exploiting existing clinic space in the evening or weekend. Video-recording the encounters is helpful but by no means essential.

As an example of a high stakes OSCE, Figure 9.6 provides a summary description of the United States Medical Licensing Exam Step

The United States Medical Licensing Examination (USMLE) Step 2 CS*

Exam purpose	To ensure that new residents have the knowledge and skills needed to provide patient care under supervision.
Content domain	Patients and problems normally encountered during medical practice in the United States
Level of skill assessed (discrete skills vs full encounter)	Full encounter: Ability to obtain a pertinent history, perform a physical examination, and communicate findings to patients and colleagues.
Format	(1) Standardized patient encounters (15 minutes each) (2) Patient note written after each encounter (10 minutes), including pertinent history and physical exam findings, differential diagnoses, and plans for immediate diagnostic work up.
Number of stations (encounters)	Twelve
Skill section scores reported	(1) Integrated clinical encounter (ICE): Data gathering + patient note (2) Communication and Interpersonal Skills (CIS) (3) English language proficiency
Rating instruments	• Checklists for data gathering (Hx and PE) • Global rating scales for patient note and English proficiency • Primary trait rating scale for CIS
Raters	• SPs for Hx and PE checklists, CIS and English • Clinicians for patient note
Combining Scores across cases, cut scores	Compensatory within skill section (ICE, CIS, English) Conjunctive across skills—must pass each section separately

Figure 9.6 OSCE Case Example.

Note: * http://www.usmle.org/Examinations/step2/step2cs_content.html

2 Clinical Skills Assessment (USMLE Step 2 CS). Additional information about this OSCE is available at the USMLE website.

Threats to the Validity of Performance Tests

Threats to the validity of performance tests are summarized in Table 9.1. Our discussion will focus on the two main threats discussed in Chapter 2: under-sampling (construct under-representation) and noise (construct-irrelevant variance).

Construct under-representation, or under-sampling, can be a particular threat to the validity of performance tests since performance varies

RACHEL YUDKOWSKY

Table 9.1 Threats to the Validity: Performance Tests

	Problem	Remedy
Construct Under-representation (CU) "Undersampling"	Not enough cases or stations to sample domain adequately	Use multiple stations (at least 8–10)
	Not enough items to reflect the performance in a given case	Use several checklist or rating scale items to capture the performance in each case
	Unrepresentative sampling of domain	Blueprint to be sure stations systematically sample the domain
Construct-irrelevant Variance (CIV) "Noise"	Unclear or poorly worded items	Pilot stations and rating instruments Train raters on items
	Station or item difficulty inappropriate (too easy/too hard)	Pilot stations and rating instruments with learners of the appropriate level
	Checklist items don't capture expert reasoning (mis-match of items to competencies)	Careful design of checklist and rating scale items to match level of examinee Use content-expert raters who can rate the quality of the response (vs done/not done)
	Rater bias	Provide behaviorally anchored scoring rubric Train raters to use rubric Use multiple raters across stations
	Systematic rater error: Halo, Severity, Leniency, Central tendency	Frame of reference training for raters
	Inconsistent ratings	Remove rater
	Language/cultural bias	Train raters Pilot and revise stations
	Indefensible passing score methods	Formal standard setting exercises
Reliability Indicators	Generalizability Inter-rater reliability Rater consistency Internal reliability of checklist or rating scale	

from station to station ("case specificity") but only a small number of stations or performances can be observed. A multiple-station performance test (OSCE) thus falls between the written test with hundreds of multiple-choice questions and the traditional viva or oral exam which may include only a single observation or questions about a single patient case.

The validity of an OSCE depends on its ability to sufficiently and systematically sample the domain to be assessed (Figure 9.7). Systematic sampling is supported by blueprinting and creating a table of test specifications (see Chapter 2). In the case of an SP-based OSCE, the blueprint should specify three C's: *content* subdomains, *competencies* to be assessed, and patient *characteristics;* the OSCE should include cases that comprise a systematic sampling of these elements. Figure 9.8 provides an example of blueprint elements for an SP-based assessment of psychiatry residents. A conceptual framework can assist in identifying salient elements to be sampled and assessed; examples of such frameworks are the ACGME competencies for residents in the US (ACGME outcome project: competencies), and the Kalamazoo consensus statement on medical communication (Makoul, 2001a and b); see Figure 9.9.

To be valid, OSCE stations must be long enough to allow the observation of the behavior of interest. If the behavior of interest is the ability to conduct a focused history and physical exam and generate a differential diagnosis and treatment plan based on that H&P, the OSCE will need to utilize longer (10–20 minute) stations and extend the testing time to allow for a sufficient number of encounters. Generally about 4–8 hours of testing time are needed to obtain minimally reliable scores (van der Vleuten & Swanson, 1990).

A potential disjunction between the exam and the clinical curriculum comprises an additional challenge to the content validity of the exam. An OSCE blueprint systematically maps the exam stations to the curriculum content and objectives. However, the clinical experiences of trainees are often opportunistic—the particular set of patient problems seen by a given student will depend on the patients who happen to be admitted to the hospital or seen in the clinic during the weeks of their clerkship. Comments from students that they have

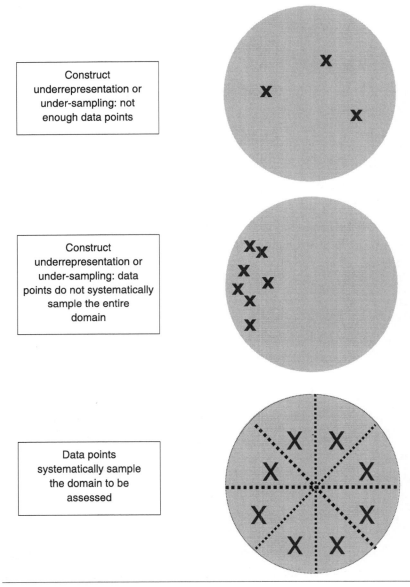

Figure 9.7 Construct Underrepresentation.

not encountered the clinical challenges included in the OSCE, or unusually low mean scores on a specific station, may provide valuable information regarding curricular gaps.

Another type of threat to validity is *construct–irrelevant variance,*

Content: *Identify the content subdomains to be assessed. For a psychiatry OSCE, these might include:*
- Psychotic disorders
- Affective disorders
- Anxiety disorders
- Substance abuse
- Child psychiatry

Competencies: *Identify tasks, competencies and skills to be assessed. For example:*
- History
- Physical exam
- Mental status exam
- Communication skills
- Differential diagnosis
- Writing a prescription
- Documentation in chart

Characteristics: *Identify patient demographics and other salient dimensions to be sampled. For example:*
- Age—child, adult, elderly
- Gender
- Ethnicity
- Chronic vs acute complaint
- Hospital vs outpatient clinic setting

Compile a set of cases or challenges that samples across the listed content, competencies and characteristics.

Sample stations for a psychiatry OSCE
- Interview a 25-year old woman who is in the emergency room complaining of panic attacks; write a chart note including pertinent findings and differential diagnosis.
- Perform and document a mental status exam for a 65-year old man hospitalized with chronic depression.
- Discuss medication changes and write a prescription for a 35-year old man with an exacerbation of hallucinations.
- Counsel a parent with an autistic child; document in the chart.

Figure 9.8 Creating Blueprint Specifications for an OSCE.

in which the spread of scores across students (score variance) reflects something other than differences in student ability. Any source of variance other than that due to actual differences of ability between students is considered error variance ("noise"). In SP-based performance tests the items, cases, SPs, raters, and occasion are all potential sources of measurement error. The Generalizability Coefficient G is a measure of the reliability of the exam as a whole (see Chapter 4); Generalizability analyses can help identify the

---

Accreditation Council for Graduate Medical Education: Six Competencies*
- Patient Care
- Knowledge
- Communication and Interpersonal Skills
- Professionalism
- System-Based Practice
- Practice-Based Learning and Improvement

The Kalamazoo consensus statement: Essential elements of communication in medical encounters**
- Build the doctor-patient relationship
- Open the discussion
- Gather information
- Understand the patient's perspective
- Share information
- Reach agreement on problems and plans
- Provide closure

Figure 9.9 Some Frameworks to Assist in Blueprinting OSCEs.

Source: *ACGME Outcome Project: Competencies. http://www.acgme.org ** Makoul (2001a). Reprinted with permission from Lippincott Williams & Wilkins (Copyright 2001).

major sources of error for a given OSCE. Complementing the Generalizability analysis, Many Faceted Rasch Measurement (MFRM) analyses can identify any individual items, cases and raters that are problematic and the specific types of errors involved (Iramaneerat & Yudkowsky, 2007; Iramaneerat, Yudkowsky, Myford, & Downing, 2007). Case specificity, the variance due to cases and the interaction between cases and persons, is usually the greatest source of variance in performance tests, and is a much greater source of error than differences between raters. Thus it is much more effective to use one rater per station and increase the number of stations than to have two or more raters per station with a smaller number of stations (van der Vleuten, 1990). With proper training SPs contribute little error variance; repeated studies have shown that SPs can be trained to portray cases and complete checklists with a high degree of accuracy and consistency (van der Vleuten & Swanson 1990; Colliver & William, 1993). In general, if there is sufficient sampling of content via a sufficient sampling of cases or stations, and different raters and SPs are used across stations, then sampling across raters and SPs will also be sufficient to provide reproducible results.

Table 9.2 describes the sources of variance in a typical OSCE, along with typical errors and possible remedies.

Table 9.2 Sources of Error in an OSCE

Source of Variance	Reason	Result	Remedy
Person	Persons differ in their ability to do the behavior to be assessed	Differences in scores due to true differences in ability between persons	No remedy needed—this (and only this) is the desired score information
Item	Checklist or rating scale items or anchors not clear	Different raters will have different understandings of the item so will rate the same performance differently	Carefully word items Pilot the items Train raters
	Item-specific variance	Individual students find some items in a case more difficult than others (performance is variable across items within a case)	Use several items per case
Case	Case-specific variance	Individual students find some cases more challenging than others (performance is variable across cases within an exam)	Use many cases per exam
	Case situation or task is unclear or ambiguous	Students respond differently depending on their interpretation of the case	Pilot the case to be sure that it is clear and unambiguous
SP	SP portrays the case incorrectly	Students respond to a different case than authors intended	Train SP, Quality Assurance
	Different SPs vary in how they portray the case	Students respond differently to different SPs	Train SPs together
Raters	Systematic rater error: Halo, Severity, Leniency, Central tendency	Systematically biased ratings—e.g. an individual rater gives consistently high or low ratings	Provide behaviorally anchored scoring rubric. Frame of reference training for raters. Use different raters across stations. Statistical corrections for systematic errors.

(Continued Overleaf)

Table 9.2 Continued

Source of Variance	Reason	Result	Remedy
	Rater bias	Ratings depend on irrelevant characteristics such as gender or race	Rater training Remove rater
	Inconsistent ratings	A given rater gives randomly inconsistent ratings—adds to the random noise in the system	Rater training Remove rater
Occasion	Occasion-specific factors environmental factors such as noise and temperature, individual factors such as illness or lack of sleep	Performance is affected by the occasion-specific factor	Control environmental factors Test on several different occasions

Consequential Validity: Educational Impact

One important aspect of an assessment is its impact on learning (van der Vleuten & Schuwirth, 2005). Adding an SP-based OSCE to the usual battery of MCQ written tests has been found to increase students' attention to clinical experiences and their requests for direct observation and feedback (Newble & Jaeger, 1983; Newble, 1988); testing procedural skills similarly leads students to seek opportunities for practicing these skills, a desirable result. However, the use of checklists in SP-based assessments can sometimes have unintended consequences. For example, if checklists require students to elicit a list of historical items and SPs are trained not to disclose the information unless specifically asked, students will learn to ask closed-ended questions in shotgun fashion instead of taking a patient-centered approach. Training SPs to give more elaborated and informative responses to open-ended questions can reduce this effect. Similarly, assessing the physical exam by means of a head-to-toe screening exam (Yudkowsky, Downing, Klamen, et al., 2004) ensures that students acquire a repertoire of PE maneuvers, but encourages students to learn these maneuvers by rote with no consideration of diagnostic hypotheses or potential physical findings. Using a hypothesis-driven

PE approach to assessment (Yudkowsky, 2007) can promote the development of clinical reasoning instead of rote learning. Educators should be alert to the potential for both positive and negative consequences of any assessment method, and ensure that the assessment experience encourages good habits of learning and practice.

Conclusion

Performance tests provide opportunities for examinees to demonstrate a particular competency or skill under controlled conditions. By utilizing standardized patients and other simulations, performance tests can control or manage many elements that are not predictable in live patient settings. Systematic sampling across cases, items and raters in performance tests is essential to minimizing sources of error and maximizing the Generalizability and validity of the score. The combination of systematic sampling, control and standardization afforded by performance tests allows for a valid, fair and defensible assessment of clinical skills.

Recommended Readings and Resources:

- For additional reading on standardized patients, see the excellent review papers by van der Vleuten & Swanson, 1990; Colliver & Williams, 1993; van der Vleuten, 1996; and Petrusa, 2002.
- For a look at the future of standardized patients see Adamo, 2003 and Petrusa, 2004.
- For a fascinating narrative of the history of standardized patients, see Wallace, 1997.
- To network with health professions educators working with standardized patients and simulations around the world, go to the websites of the Association of Standardized Patient Educators http://www.aspeducators.org/ and the Society for Simulation in Healthcare http://www.ssih.org/.

References

Accreditation Council for Graduate Medical Education: Outcome Project. Retrieved June 19, 2008 from: http://www.acgme.org

Adamo, G. (2003). Simulated and standardized patients in OSCEs: Achievements and challenges 1992–2003. *Medical Teacher*, 25(3), 262–270.

Barrows, H.S. (1993). An overview of the uses of standardized patients for teaching and evaluating clinical skills. *Academic Medicine*, 68, 443–451.

Barrows, H.S., & Abrahamson, S. (1964). The programmed patient: A technique for appraising student performance in clinical neurology. *Journal of Medical Education*, 39, 802–805.

Bernardin, H.J., & Buckley, M.R. (1981). Strategies in rater training. *The Academy of Management Review*, 6(2), 205–212.

Bernardin, H.J., & Smith, P.C. (1981). A clarification of some issues regarding the development and use of behaviorally anchored rating scales (BARS). *Journal of Applied Psychology*, 66, 458–463.

Colliver, J.A., & Williams, R.G. (1993). Technical issues: Test application. *Academic Medicine*, 68, 454–460.

Downing, S., Tekian, A., & Yudkowsky, R. (2006). Procedures for establishing defensible absolute passing scores on performance examinations in health professions education. *Teaching and Learning in Medicine*, 18(1), 50–57.

Elstein, A.S., Shuman, L.S., & Sprafka, S.A. (1978). *Medical problem solving: An analysis of clinical reasoning*. Cambridge, Massachusetts: Harvard University Press.

Ericsson, K.A. (2004). Deliberate practice and the acquisition and maintenance of expert performance in medicine and related domains. *Academic Medicine*, 79 (10, Suppl.), S70–S81.

Ericsson, K.A., Krampe, R.T., & Tesch-Römer, C. (1993). The role of deliberate practice in the acquisition of expert performance. *Psychological Review*, 100, 363–406.

Eva, K.W., Rosenfeld, J., Reiter, H.I., & Norman, G.R. (2004). An admissions OSCE: The multiple mini-interview. *Medical Education*, 38, 314–326.

Gelula, M., & Yudkowsky, R. (2003). Using standardized students in faculty development workshops to improve clinical teaching skills. *Medical Education*, 37, 621–629.

Gorter, S., Rethans, J.J., Scherpbier, A., van der Heijde, D., van der Vleuten, C., & van der Linden, S. (2000). Developing case-specific checklists for standardized-patient-based assessments internal medicine: A review of the literature. *Academic Medicine*, 75(11), 1130–1137.

Harden, R., Stevenson, M., Downie, W., & Wilson, M. (1975). Assessment of clinical competence using objective structured examinations. *British Medical Journal*, 1, 447–451.

Hodges, B., Regehr, G., McNaughton, N., Tiberius, R., & Hanson, M. (1999). OSCE checklists do not capture increasing levels of expertise. *Academic Medicine*, 74, 1129–1134.

Howley, L. (2007). Focusing feedback on interpersonal skills: A workshop for standardized patients. MedEdPORTAL: http://services.aamc.org/jsp/mededportal/retrieveSubmissionDetailById.do?subId=339.

Iramaneerat, C., & Yudkowsky, R. (2007). Rater errors in a clinical skills assessment of medical students. *Evaluation & the Health Professions 2007*, 30(3), 266–283.

Iramaneerat, C., Yudkowsky, R., Myford, C.M., & Downing, S. (2007). Quality control of an OSCE using generalizability theory and many-faceted rasch measurement. *Advances in Health Sciences Education*, published online, February 20, 2007.

Issenberg, S.B. (2006). The scope of simulation-based healthcare education. *Simulation in Healthcare*, 1, 203–208.

Kneebone, R.L., Kidd, J., Nestel, D., Barnet, A., Lo, B., King, R., et al. (2005). Blurring the boundaries: Scenario-based simulation in a clinical setting. *Medical Education*, 39, 580–587.

Kurtz, S.M., Silverman, J.D., Benson, J. & Draper, J. (2003). Marrying content and process in clinical method teaching: Enhancing the Calgary-Cambridge guides. *Academic Medicine*, 78(8), 802–809.

Makoul, G. (2001a). Essential elements of communication in medical encounters: The Kalamazoo consensus statement. *Academic Medicine*, 76(4), 390–393.

Makoul, G. (2001b). The SEGUE Framework for teaching and assessing communication skills. *Patient Education and Counseling*, 45, 23–34.

Miller, G. (1990). The assessment of clinical skills/competence/performance. *Academic Medicine*, 65 (Suppl.), S63–S67.

Nendaz, M.R., Gut, A.M., Perrier, A., Reuille, O., Louis-Simonet, M., Junod, A.F., et al. (2004). Degree of concurrency among experts in data collection and diagnostic hypothesis generation during clinical encounters. *Medical Education*, 38(1), 25–31.

Newble, D.I. (1988). Eight years' experience with a structured clinical examination. *Medical Education*, 22, 200–204.

Newble, D., & Jaeger, K. (1983). The effects of assessments and examinations on the learning of medical students. *Medical Education*, 17, 165–171.

Petrusa, E. (2002). Clinical performance assessments. In G.R. Norman, C.P.M. van der Vleuten, & D.I. Newble (Eds.), *International handbook of research in medical education* (pp. 647–672). Dordrecht, The Netherlands: Kluwer Academic Publishers.

Petrusa, E.R. (2004). Taking standardized-patient based examinations to the next level. *Teaching and Learning in Medicine*, 16, 98–110.

Rethans, J.J., Drop, R., Sturmans, F., & van der Vleuten, C. (1991). A method for introducing standardized (simulated) patients into general practice consultations. *British Journal of General Practice*, 41, 94–96.

Rethans, J.J., Gorter, S., Bokken, L., & Morrison, L. (2007). Unannounced standardized patients in real practice: A systematic literature review. *Medical Education*, 41(6), 537–549.

Ross, L.P., Clauser, B.E., Margolis, M.J., Orr, N.A., & Klass, D.J. (1996). An expert-judgment approach to setting standards for a standardized-patient examination. *Academic Medicine*, 71, S4–S6.

Schimpfhauser, F.T., Sultz, H., Zinnerstrom, K.H., & Anderson, D.R. (2000). *Communication cases involving standardized patients for medical student and resident training.* Buffalo, NY: The State University of New York at Buffalo School of Medicine and Biomedical Sciences.

Stillman, P., Brown, D., Redfield, D., & Sabers, D. (1977). Construct validation of the Arizona clinical interview rating scale. *Educational and Psychological Measurement*, 77, 1031–1038.

Stillman, P.L., Sabers, D.L., & Redfield, D.L. (1976). The use of paraprofessionals to teach interviewing skills. *Pediatrics*, 57, 769–774.

Stillman, P.L., Swanson, D.B., Smee, S., Stillman, A.E., Ebert, T.H., Emmel, V. S., et al. (1986). Assessing clinical skills of residents with standardized patients. *Annals of Internal Medicine*, 105, 762–771.

Tamblyn, R.M., Klass, D.J., Schnabl, G.K., & Kopelow, M.L. (1991). The accuracy of standardized patient presentation. *Medical Education*, 25, 100–109.

The Macy Initiative in Health Communication Casebook (2003). Referenced in and available from the authors: Yedidia, M.J., Gillespie, C.C., Kachur, E., Schwartz, M.D., Ockene, J., Chepaitis, A.E., et al. (2003). Effect of communications training on medical student performance. *The Journal of the American Medical Association*, 290, 1157–1165.

van der Vleuten, C.P.M. (1996). The assessment of professional competence: Developments, research, and practical implications. *Advances in Health Sciences Education*, 1, 41–67.

van der Vleuten, C.P., & Schuwirth, L.W. (2005). Assessing professional competence: From methods to programmes. *Medical Education*, 39, 309–317.

van der Vleuten, C.P., & Swanson, D.B. (1990). Assessment of clinical skills with standardized patients: State of the art. *Teaching and Learning in Medicine*, 2, 58–76.

Vu, N.V., Marcy, M.M., Colliver, J.A., Verhulst, S.J., Travis, T.A., & Barrows, H.S. (1992). Standardized (simulated) patients' accuracy in recording clinical performance check-list items. *Medical Education*, 26, 99–104.

Wallace, P. (1997). Following the threads of an innovation: The history of standardized patients in medical education. *CADUCEUS*, 13(2): 5–28.

Wallace, P. (2007). *Coaching standardized patients, for use in the assessment of clinical competence.* New York: Springer Publishing Company.

Welch, C. (2006). Item and prompt development in performance testing. In S.M. Downing & T.M. Haladyna (Eds.), *Handbook of test development* (pp. 303–328). Mahwah, New Jersey: Lawrence Erlbaum Associates.

William, R.G., Klaman, D.A., & McGaghie, W.C. (2003). Cognitive, social, and environmental sources of bias in clinical performance ratings. *Teaching and Learning in Medicine*, 15(4), 270–292.

Wind, L.A., Van Dalen, J., Muijtjens, A.M., & Rethans, J.J. (2004). Assessing simulated patients in an educational setting: The MaSP (Maastricht Assessment of Simulated Patients). *Medical Education*, 38(1), 39–44.

Yudkowsky, R., Downing, S., Klamen, D., Valaski, M., Eulenberg, B., & Popa, M. (2004). Assessing the head-to-toe physical examination skills of medical students. *Medical Teacher*, 26, 415–419.

Yudkowsky, R., Downing, S.M., & Sandlow, L.J. (2006). Developing an institution-based assessment of resident communication and inter-personal skills. *Academic Medicine*, 81, 1115–1122.

Yudkowsky, R., Bordage, G., Lowenstein, T., & Riddle, J. (2007, November). Can 4th year medical students anticipate, elicit, and interpret physical findings in a hypothesis-driven physical exam? [Abstract] *Annual Meeting of the Association of American Medical Colleges*, Washington D.C.

Ziv, A., Rubin, O., Moshinsky, A., & Mittelman, M. (2007). Screening of candidates to medical school based on non-cognitive parameters using a simulation-based assessment center. *Simulation in Healthcare*, 2(1), 69.

10

SIMULATIONS IN ASSESSMENT

WILLIAM C. McGAGHIE AND S. BARRY ISSENBERG

This chapter addresses the role of simulations in the assessment of health professionals. It amplifies, but does not duplicate, the lessons of Chapter 8 on Observational Methods and Chapter 9 covering Performance Examinations. Those chapters laid down an assessment foundation by describing methods including faculty ratings and simulated clinical encounters using standardized patients (SPs) as approaches to learner assessment. Here we focus on the utility of other health care simulation devices and procedures to contribute to personnel evaluation. In general, health care simulations aim to imitate real patients, anatomic regions, or clinical tasks, or to mirror the life situations in which care is delivered. These simulations range from static anatomic models and single task trainers (e.g., venipuncture arms and intubation mannequin heads) to dynamic computer-based systems that can respond to user actions (e.g., full body anesthesia simulators); from individual trainers for a single user to interactive role playing scenarios involving groups of people; and from low tech SP encounters to high tech virtual reality surgical simulators. All of these technologies *simulate* clinical contacts between health care providers, patients, and even patients' families with varying degrees of realism. This chapter is about how to choose and use these simulated encounters as tools to assess learner competence.

Simulations have a seductive allure in health professions education. They offer context in assessment settings by engaging learners in professional situations that resemble "in vivo" conditions. Simulations can be used in a variety of ways to evaluate individuals and health care teams including: (a) procedural skills; (b) critical thinking and responses to changing circumstances; (c) behavior under stress; and (d) teamwork. However, even high-fidelity simulations are never identical to real life. The idea is to use simulations as learner assessment tools that resemble patient care problems. Solutions to the simulated patient problems should match faculty evaluation goals for learners.

This chapter has seven sections. The first three sections are short and discuss key background matters: (a) What is a simulation? (b) The learner assessment skill set needed by simulation users [individuals or teams] from prior reading, or from practical experience; and (c) practitioner goals, being plain about assessment goals and how simulation tools can help you reach those goals. The next two sections give practical advice about designing a learner assessment plan grounded in clinical practice that features simulation technology. These sections include: (d) assessment design; and (e) measurement quality. The last two sections tackle tough issues that are now the focus of vigorous research and development. These are: (f) transfer of learning outcomes from the controlled simulation lab to the chaotic patient care clinic, and (g) present and future faculty development needs.

This chapter focuses on *assessment planning*, esp. the role of simulation as one of many tools for learner evaluation. The chapter is about *curriculum integration*, being sure that simulation used as an assessment tool matches educational goals. The importance of integrating simulation-based experiences into an overall curriculum plan is one of the key "lessons learned" from a 35-year systematic literature review on the features and uses of high-fidelity medical simulations that lead to effective learning (Issenberg, McGaghie, Petrusa, et al., 2005). The chapter differs from several other recent publications that address the use of simulations to evaluate health professionals (Dunn, 2004; Loyd, Lake, & Greenberg, 2004; McGaghie, Pugh & Wayne, 2007; Scalese & Issenberg, 2008). The differences are about emphasis and scope, not about the utility of simulation technology in personnel evaluation. For example, Dunn (2004) and Loyd, et al. (2004) give broad coverage to medical simulation for education and evaluation. McGaghie, et al. (2007) address simulation for assessing health professionals with an emphasis on educational research methods. Scalese and Issenberg (2008), by contrast, give detailed coverage to "bells and whistles" and technical features of an array of simulators now available in the health sciences.

What is a Simulation?

We begin this chapter with an operational definition of medical simulation given earlier (McGaghie, 1999).

> In broad, simple terms a simulation is a person, device, or set of conditions which attempts to present evaluation problems authentically. The student or trainee is required to respond to the problems as he or she would under natural circumstances. Frequently the trainee receives performance feedback as if he or she were in the real situation. Simulation procedures for evaluation and teaching have several common characteristics:
>
> - Trainees see cues and consequences very much like those in the real environment.
> - Trainees can be placed in complex situations.
> - Trainees act as they would in the real environment.
> - The fidelity (exactness of duplication) of a simulation is never completely isomorphic with the "real thing." The reasons are obvious: cost, [limits of] engineering technology, avoidance of danger, ethics, psychometric requirements, time constraints.
> - Simulations can take many forms. For example, they can be static, as in an anatomical model [for task training]. Simulations can be automated, using advanced computer technology. Some are individual, prompting solitary performance while others are interactive, involving groups of people. Simulations can be playful or deadly serious. In personnel evaluation settings they can be used for high-stakes, low-stakes, or no-stakes decisions (p. 9).

Health science simulations are located on a *continuum of fidelity* ranging from multiple-choice test questions (Boulet & Swanson, 2004) to more engaging task trainers (e.g., heads for intubation training) to full-body computer-driven mannequins that display vital signs and respond to drugs and other treatments (Issenberg & McGaghie, 1999). In most evaluation settings today's medical simulations rely on trained [faculty] observers to record learner response data, transform the data into assessment scores, and make judgments about trainees (e.g., pass/fail) from the scores. Some newer medical simulators automate data recording and scoring, which makes the process faster and less prone to observer error. However, in all situations the chain of events moves through a five step sequence: (a) stimulus presentation (e.g., simulator embedded patient problem or case); (b) examinee response; (c) data recording or capturing; (d) data transformation to a score; and (e) score judgment and interpretation. These are all parts of learner assessment. Our goal in this chapter is to show how medical simulation technology can make this cascaded enterprise efficient, effective, useful, fair, and feasible.

Two forms of medical simulation are not covered in this chapter. They are standardized patients (SPs) and computer games. Standardized patients are excluded because their use is covered extensively in Chapter 9 (Yudkowsky, this volume). Computer games are because at present time they have a limited role in the serious business of learner assessment in the health professions.

Learner Assessment Skill Set

We expect that health science educators who plan to use simulations for learner assessment have background knowledge in test development, administration, and use. For example, we anticipate that readers of this chapter have earlier covered the material in Chapter 1, Introduction to Assessment in the Health Professions. Readers should also have a good grasp of how written tests, observational methods, and performance examinations are developed and used from other chapters in this book. Familiarity with assessment principles given in these and other chapters will make it easier for educators to figure out the place of simulation in their assessment plans.

Practitioner Goals

Health science educators need to have one or more assessment goals clearly articulated before selecting and using simulation-based evaluation tools. *The goals–tools match is the most important message of this chapter.* A carpenter does not use a tape measure to pound nails. It's the wrong tool for the job. Similarly, educators should not acquire or build simulation devices for learner assessment without understanding their assessment goals, context, and consequences. Simulations are just one of many assessment options available to health science educators who are responsible for formative or summative trainee evaluation. Our aim is to help you match assessment goals and simulation tools to accomplish accurate and fair learner evaluations.

Table 10.1 presents 12 examples from the health professions of learner assessment goals matched with simulation assessment tools. All of the assessment goals in Table 10.1 are formative, i.e., in-progress tests and evaluations for the purpose of learner feedback and improvement. Of course, other assessment goals may be summative, i.e., final examinations or measures of professional competence like board examinations that have serious and lasting consequences or address selective professional school admission. The use of simulation technology for summative assessment in the health professions is currently rare but increasing gradually. Examples include the introduction of simulation into Israeli national board examinations in anesthesiology (Berkenstadt, Ziv, Gafni, & Sidi, 2006a, 2006b) and early feasibility research on the potential use of simulation combined with other modalities for high stakes medical testing in Canada (Hatala, Kassen, Nishikawa, et al., 2005; Hatala, Issenberg, Kassen, et al., 2007). Simulation technology has been used for selective medical school admission decisions in Israel where candidate interpersonal skills are evaluated using objective patient simulations rather than subjective letters of recommendation (Ziv, Rubin, Moshinsky, & Mittelman, 2007).

Table 10.1 is similar in purpose and format to Table 8.1 (McGaghie et al., Chapter 8, this volume) that addresses goals and tools for observational assessment. Education program directors and

Table 10.1 Simulation Based Assessment Goals and Tools

Assessment Goal	Example	Assessment Tool	Advantages	Limitations
Advanced Cardiac Life Support (ACLS)	Mastery assessment of medicine residents' responses to cardiac arrest scenarios (Wayne et al., 2006)	Simulated hospital "codes" in a laboratory setting using the METI life-size Human Patient Simulator (HPS®)	Very high-fidelity patient simulator and simulated "code" events. Assessment data are reliable and inferences about trainees are valid.	Simulator equipment and laboratory time are expensive and labor intensive.
Individual and Team Terrorism Training	"Assess individual and team skills acquired from an interactive training program to prepare emergency personnel to respond to terrorist acts" (Scott et al., 2006)	Scenario-based individual and team terrorist response exercises with faculty ratings of learning outcomes	Assessment data for individuals and teams are reliable and inferences about trainees are valid. EMT, paramedic, nurse, and physician trainees valued the training and assessment.	Individual and team training and assessment are time and labor intensive.
Anesthesia Acute Care	Assess acute care skills of anesthesiology residents and student nurse anesthetists (Murray et al., 2005)	Simulated acute care scenarios using the life-size patient mannequin developed by MEDSIM-EAGLE®	Acute care patient scenarios have very high realism. Assessment data are reliable and inferences about trainees are valid.	Simulator equipment and laboratory time are expensive.
Gynecological Laparoscopic Surgery	Evaluate basic laparoscopic surgical skills among three groups of gynecologic trainees based on surgical experience: novices, intermediate level, experts (Larsen et al., 2006)	Measurements of basic surgical skills were taken using the LapSimGyn virtual reality (VR) simulator	VR simulator provides a highly controlled, standardized measurement environment. Expected differences due to expertise groups were obtained.	Simulator-based assessment is costly yet very effective. Simulator training and assessment needs to be integrated into the surgical curriculum.
Pediatric Acute Care	Assess acute care management skills among pediatric residents using four simulated case scenarios: apnea, asthma, supraventricular tachycardia, sepsis (Adler et al., 2007)	METI high fidelity PediaSIM® mannequin human patient simulator with unweighted checklist data recorded by trained faculty raters	Controlled environment and rigorous rater training produced highly reliable data. Resident group differences due to clinical experience were found as expected.	Four simulated pediatric case scenarios are an insufficient sample for comprehensive resident assessment.

Topic Area	Study Description	Method	Findings	Limitations/Future Directions
Nursing: General Introduction	"This qualitative study examined the [assessment] experiences of students in one nursing program's first term of using high-fidelity simulation as part of its regular curriculum" (Lasater, 2007)	Computerized human patient simulator of unspecified origin. Students' reactions to simulation-based training experiences were assessed using focus groups	"Simulator served as an integrator of learning . . . theoretical, psychomotor, laboratory and clinical practice skills." All enhanced acquisition of clinical judgment.	Engineering limitations of the simulator mannequin (e.g., lack of nonverbal communication; no reflexes, swelling, or color changes) limit generalizability.
Respiratory Therapy: Bronchoalveolar Lavage	To "evaluate simulation-based education for training and competency evaluation [among respiratory therapists—RTs] of the mini bronchoalveolar lavage (mini-BAL) procedure, with an emphasis on patient safety and procedure performance standards" (Tuttle et al., 2007)	Laerdal SimMan® computer-based full body patient simulator with checklist data recorded by trained faculty raters	Simulation setting allowed controlled, standardized trainee assessments that produced highly reliable data. Simulation-based training greatly increased RT's mini-BAL competence scores and score retention.	Further research will better link RT's clinical skills performance in the simulation setting to performance in real patient care.
Nursing: Global Clinical Competence	Evaluate nursing students' clinical skills and competence using a 15 station OSCE grounded [in part] on simulation-based assessment exercises; study the effects of a simulation-based nursing curriculum (Alinier et al., 2006)	Fifteen OSCE stations measuring theory on safety in nursing practice, clinical knowledge, technical ability, and communication skills using observational ratings by trained faculty	OSCE assessments of nursing students are reproducible and yield reliable evaluation data. Intermediate fidelity simulation-based assessment and training is realistic and well received by students. Scores improved with practice.	"Students and [faculty] facilitators need to be adequately prepared for the use of patient simulators as a teaching [and assessment] tool." OSCE assessments require much faculty preparation.
Paramedic Endotracheal Intubation	To "determine whether the endotracheal intubation (ETI) success rate is different among paramedic students trained on a human patient simulator versus on human subjects in the operating room (OR)." (Hall et al., 2005)	Following simulation-based OR ETI training, paramedic students "underwent a formalized test of 15 intubations in the OR" with measurements of success rate and complications	Simulation-based ETI training produced results statistically identical to training results using real patients in the OR. This reduces patient risk and allows training under controlled conditions.	Blinding of faculty assessors to the training condition of the paramedic students would further increase the objectivity of the outcome data.

(Continued Overleaf)

Table 10.1 Continued

Assessment Goal	Example	Assessment Tool	Advantages	Limitations
Carotid Angiography Competence	Document performance improvement in carotid angiography (CA) skills, measured by metric-based procedural errors, due to a virtual reality (VR) simulation course (Patel et al., 2006)	The Vascular Interventional System Trainer (VIST)-VR simulator recorded trainee CA skills at procedure time (PT), fluoroscopy time (FT), contrast volume, and composite catheter handling errors (CE)	Data recorded by the VIST-VR simulator had high internal consistency and test-retest reliability. CA scores increased with simulator practice and experience.	The study enrolled a relatively small sample of interventional cardiologists (n = 20). Research on a broader sample of [simulated] cases is also needed.
Acute Care Nurse Practitioner (ACNP) Clinical Skills	Assess acute care nurse practitioner (ACNP) clinical skills using high-fidelity human simulation (HFHS) technology (Hravnak et al., 2007)	Laerdal SimMan® computer-based full body simulator with faculty evaluations completed in real time and from video recordings	ACNP training and evaluation conducted in controlled environment where patient safety is not a concern. Many opportunities for learner debriefing with a variety of clinical problems.	Mannequin-based clinical simulation is never a perfect reproduction of real patient care. Costs of money and faculty time can be high.
Medical Student Basic Clinical Skills	Evaluate and educate volunteer medical students at two procedure scenarios (urinary catheter insertion, wound closure) using inanimate models attached to simulated patients. Qualitative documentation of study outcomes (Kneebone et al., 2005)	Inanimate models for urinary catheter insertion and wound closure assessed by observers. "Live" simulated patients amplified the clinical encounters	Learners' overall impressions of the evaluation and training scenarios were very positive. Study revealed ways to improve the simulation technology and its links with simulated patients.	Study was limited due to the relatively small number of clinical procedures. Expansion to other clinical education centers is also needed.

faculty should consider the goals-tools match thoughtfully as simulation-based learner assessment plans are formulated.

Assessment Design

Systematic and thoughtful test planning is needed to create and use assessment tools that yield reliable scores that permit valid decisions about trainee achievement. The assessment design is a step-by-step plan that increases the odds that assessment goals and simulation tools are matched. We endorse a six step plan for assessment design drawn from several sources to create an assessment program's architecture (Downing, 2006; Newble, et al., 1994; Scalese & Issenberg, 2008). The stepwise plan is a practical, useful guide for busy teachers and program directors who aim to match educational assessment goals and simulation tools. This will promote curriculum integration of simulation technology in the health professions.

Table 10.2 lists the six assessment planning steps. The following discussion amplifies each step.

Content and Organization

The content coverage of a test is a sample of the material in a course or unit, just as a professional school curriculum is a sample of professional work. Health science educators can neither teach all relevant content and skills nor test every educational objective. Thus test planning, like curriculum planning, aims to include a representative sample of the cases or problems that health professionals see clinically. Case selection for trainee assessment is often governed by frequency (e.g., respiratory infection), urgency (e.g., myocardial infarction) or importance (e.g., secure an airway) (Raymond & Neustel, 2006). Thoughtful case selection produces better assessments and lowers the chances that tests will contain obscure "zebras."

Clinical tasks embedded within cases also warrant attention. Routine tasks that span clinical cases (e.g., blood pressure measurement) are candidates for assessment due to their frequency and importance for patient care. Rare but critical clinical tasks (e.g., needle

Table 10.2 Simulation Based Assessment Planning Steps

1. **Content and Organization**
   - Content definition and level of resolution
   - Problems or cases
   - Tasks within problems
   - Blueprint or test specifications (Table 10.3 Test Blueprint for Clinical Cardiology)

2. **Assessment Methods**
   - Select test methods
   - Appropriate to clinical problems and tasks
   - Problems and tasks dictate test methods
   - Recognize simplicity, limits, and practical constraints

3. **Standardize Test Conditions**
   - Fixed conditions: "patient," examiner, setting
   - Variable condition: trainee

4. **Assessment Scoring**
   - Turn trainee responses into numbers
   - Data quality

5. **Standard Setting**
   - Derive a minimum passing score (MPS)

6. **Consequences**
   - Anticipate assessment aftermath or sequelae

---

aspiration for tension pneumothorax) are also assessment priorities. Rare and trivial clinical tasks (e.g., cerumen removal) are a much lower assessment priority.

The content and organization of a simulation-based assessment is best captured by a blueprint or set of test specifications. A test blueprint identifies the cases, tasks, or other content to be included (and, by inference, excluded) in an assessment and how they will challenge the trainee. Challenges might include diagnosis, perform a procedure, formulate a plan, or know when to get help. A test blueprint is an operational definition of the purpose and scope of an assessment (Downing & Haladyna, Chapter 2, this volume).

Table 10.3 presents an *example* blueprint of a simulation-based assessment in clinical cardiology using the "Harvey" cardiology patient simulator (CPS) (Gordon & Issenberg, 2006). The example is for a test of second year internal medicine residents who are completing a four week cardiology rotation. This illustrative blueprint shows that recognition of the 12 cardinal cardiac auscultatory findings can be

Table 10.3 Test Blueprint for Clinical Cardiology Using the "Harvey" CPS

Cardinal Auscultatory Findings	Evaluation Goals				
	Identify finding	Identify finding and correlate it with underlying pathophysiology	Identify finding and correlate it with underlying disease process and differential diagnosis	Identify finding and correlate it with the severity of the underlying disease process and clinical management	TOTAL
1. Second Sound Splitting	10%		5%		15%
2. Third Sound		5%	5%		10%
3. Fourth Sound				10%	10%
4. Systolic Clicks		5%	5%		10%
5. Innocent Murmur	5%			10%	15%
6. Mitral Regurgitation		5%		5%	10%
7. Aortic Stenosis					0%
8. Aortic Regurgitation	5%		10%		15%
9. Mitral Stenosis		10%			10%
10. Continuous Murmur					0%
11. Tricuspid Regurgitation	5%				5%
12. Pericardial Rub					0%
TOTAL	25%	25%	25%	25%	100%

assessed against four separate and increasingly complex evaluation goals. They range from identify finding to identify finding and correlate it with the severity of the underlying disease process and clinical management. Tabular cell entries show the distribution of test content for this example. The cell entries and marginal totals indicate that assessment of second sound splitting, innocent murmur, and aortic regurgitation are emphasized over other options. Cells and marginals also show that identifying findings is weighted equally with the other three more complex evaluation goals. Other health professions education programs (e.g., nursing, pharmacy, physical therapy) and levels of testing (i.e., beginner to advanced) may have very different evaluation weighting schemes.

The point of Table 10.3 is that health science educators who use simulation technology for learner assessment must make conscious decisions about what the tests will cover (and not cover) and with what emphasis. This involves professional judgment and choice shaped by reason, experience, and anticipation about future professional practice needs of today's learners. Test blueprint development and use, combined with clinical educators' judgment and choice, contributes content-related validity evidence to learner assessment practices. As Chapter 2 points out, this is a basic building block of an assessment program that makes valid decisions about learner competence.

Assessment Methods

Many assessment methods are available to health science educators who use simulation for learner evaluation. However, there is no formula or set of rules that tell teachers which assessment methods to use. Instead, these decisions should be shaped by two factors: (a) the clinical problem or tasks being assessed, and (b) simplicity and practical constraints.

To illustrate, Table 10.1 points out a variety of assessment methods embedded in the evaluation "goals and tools" framework. The bottom line is simple: assessment goals shape decisions about assessment tools. Complex clinical skills like responding to ACLS events require equally rich assessment tools such as computer-driven mannequins in a simulation laboratory environment (Wayne et al., 2005a, 2006). Simpler clinical skills such as suturing, intubation, and arterial puncture can be assessed using basic task trainers (Issenberg & McGaghie, 1999).

Standardize Test Conditions

The conditions for simulation-based learner assessment, like other approaches to personnel evaluation, need to be standardized to yield best results. Standardization means the situation, setting, procedures, and apparatus used for assessment are uniform for all learners. These are "fixed" conditions: (a) patient (mannequin, SP); (b) trained examiner; (c) assessment forms (checklist, rating scale); (d) room or laboratory space; (e) time allocation; (f) clinical equipment (bags, masks, drugs, sterile tray, etc.); (g) prompts or instructions (signs, cue cards, verbal or video orientation); and (h) dress code. Fixed conditions do not vary. All learners who undergo assessment operate in the same environment.

By contrast, the only "variable" element in this situation is the examinee. We assume that individual differences in knowledge, skill, attitude, reasoning, or other learning outcomes are being expressed and measured by the assessment. The reliability (signal) of assessment data depends on ruling-out extraneous error (noise) by standardizing test conditions. There are two distinct types of assessment noise: random error or unreliability (Axelson & Kreiter, Chapter 3, this volume) and systematic error or construct-irrelevant variance (CIV), which is discussed in Chapter 2 (Downing & Haladyna, this volume). The goal, of course, is to reduce both types of noise and boost the signal in assessment score data.

Assessment Scoring

How can health science educators turn trainee responses to a simulation-based exam into scores (numbers) that are useful for assessment? How can the educators be assured that the scores are quality assessment data?

Scores can be derived from examinee responses to simulation technology in at least five ways:

1. Keyboard or written responses to standardized questions embedded in the simulator or its associated software as a scenario unfolds (Issenberg, McGaghie, Brown, et al., 2000; Issenberg, McGaghie, Gordon, et al., 2002) or on subsequent post-encounter tests about simulated events (Williams, McLaughlin, Eulenberg, et al., 1999).

2. Item-by-item behavioral responses (*process* data) recorded on a checklist by trained and calibrated observers (Murray, Boulet, Kras, et al., 2005; Wayne, Barsuk, O'Leary, et al., 2008; Wayne,

Butter, Siddall, et al., 2005a, 2006) that capture procedural correctness. Checklist process data can also be recorded automatically by embedded software, capturing actions (e.g., carotid pulse check) that were taken without being mediated by an observer (Albarran, Moule, Gilchrist & Soar, 2006).

3. Judgments about behavioral *products* created in a simulation environment (e.g., dental amalgam) by trained and calibrated observers (Buchanan & Williams, 2004).

4. Global judgments about trainee performance recorded by faculty on rating scales (Hodges, Regehr, McNaughton, et al., 1999; Regehr, Freeman, Robb, et al., 1999).

5. Trainee responses captured by haptic sensors embedded in or near a simulator (Pugh, Heinrichs, Dev, et al., 2001; Pugh & Rosen, 2002; Pugh & Youngblood, 2002; Minogue & Jones, 2006).

Each of these scoring methods has strengths and limitations shaped by situation of use, level of required evaluation detail, and faculty training and calibration. Practical realities in health science education programs such as simplicity, ease of use, and time requirements limit decisions about scoring methods. The idea is to get high quality assessment data with low cost and effort. This is often a difficult tradeoff.

Standard Setting

Standard setting is important because it encourages the faculty to specify the minimum passing score (MPS) [standard] for each exam in the curriculum. Standards express faculty expectations for students. They tell learners for each assessment exercise "how much is good enough." Very high standards, seen in rigorous exam MPSs, send a message that excellence is expected from all learners, that the faculty will not accept mediocrity. High standards assert faculty academic values. Assessment standards are usually set using "seat of the pants" methods based on faculty judgments. However, improved and more thoughtful approaches are being used increasingly (see Chapter 6).

Professional approaches to setting academic performance standards in the health professions have been described recently (Downing, Tekian, & Yudkowsky, 2006; Norcini & Guille, 2002). They all rely on systematic collection of expert judgments about expected learner performance. Experts are usually panels of experienced practitioners in a health profession—frequently teaching faculty. Systematic collection of experts' judgments involves engaging faculty panelists in exercises that focus decisions about expected learner behavior. Two of many possible examples are: (a) item-by-item judgments about test questions or performance checklist items (Angoff); or, (b) judgments about an entire assessment (Hofstee). Both approaches have strengths and weaknesses. Some clinical educators have averaged the results of Angoff and Hofstee standard setting methods to offset differences in MPS stringency (Wayne, Fudala, Butter, et al., 2005b; Wayne, Barsuk, Cohen & McGaghie, 2007).

Consequences

All educational assessments have consequences ranging from professional school admission decisions to formative feedback to final high stakes judgments. Health science educators should carefully consider the consequences of their assessment plans for learners, faculty, and the sponsoring educational program.

Assessment sequelae for learners are usually obvious: (a) school admission or rejection; (b) pass and move ahead; (c) performance below standard, more work and reassess; (d) failure, short-run or final. Faculty assessment sequelae include feedback about teaching effectiveness, the burden of remediating failing students, and recognizing curriculum strengths and weaknesses. Assessment consequences for educational programs include those for learners, faculty, and also matters of cost, efficiency, and student selection. The point is that health science educators should anticipate the consequences of educational assessments to minimize their costs and maximize their benefits.

Measurement Quality

Assessment scores from simulation technology that are employed as either formative or summative outcome measures must be sound technically. The scores must be dependable, trustworthy, before they can be used for any educational purpose. *Reliability* is the technical term used to describe the dependability of assessment scores. Score reliability is like a signal-to-noise ratio where the "signal" is good information and "noise" is measurement error. Reliable scores have high signal and low noise. *Validity* is the term used to describe the accuracy of actions or decisions that are made from assessment scores. Valid educational actions and decisions depend on reliable assessment scores.

High quality, i.e., reliable trainee assessment scores are essential for at least three reasons: (a) accurate learner feedback; (b) valid decisions about learner advancement, promotion, or certification; and, (c) rigorous research on simulation-based health professions education. Educators know that learner feedback is useless, simply cannot be done, without reliable performance scores. Evaluators know too that accurate promotion or certification decisions about learners are impossible without reliable data. Educational scholars understand that data reliability must be reported in all research studies as a basic quality assurance index.

How can health professions educators working in a simulation-based context take steps to boost the reliability of assessment scores and the validity of actions and decisions? Time spent refining and pilot testing measurement tools, training and calibrating faculty raters, and simplifying data recording and management is always a good investment. This is especially the case when assessment scores are derived from ratings by faculty observers, a common situation in simulation-based learner evaluation. Inter-rater reliability (agreement) is essential here and should be established routinely as a continuous quality control mechanism.

Measurement quality expressed as score reliability and the validity of actions and decisions are everyday issues in simulation-based assessment. Downing (2003, 2004) provides a thorough discussion about reliability and validity in a pair of journal articles.

Chapters 2, 3, and 4 of this volume present detailed and practical discussions of measurement quality issues including validity, reliability, and generalizability of assessments in health professions education.

Transfer of Training—Lab to Life

How can clinical educators be sure that educational outcomes measured and assessed in a controlled, simulation laboratory setting transfer to trainee behavior in the chaotic clinical environment? Such transfer of training is difficult to evaluate for a variety of scientific and ethical reasons. However, the question is still legitimate in the current era of evidence based clinical practice and best evidence medical education (BEME) (Issenberg, et al., 2005). How can we generalize simulation-based assessments of learning—knowledge, skills, attitudes—from laboratory to life (Bligh & Bleakley, 2006)?

On scientific grounds this is a problem in *generalized causal inference* (Shadish, Cook, & Campbell, 2002). The scientific solution requires a thematic and cumulative series of controlled studies featuring tight experimental designs and highly reliable data. While several small experimental studies have been published (e.g., Rosenthal, Adachi, Ribaudo, et al., 2006; Seymour, Gallagher, Roman, et al., 2002) a large body of educational science work on simulation in healthcare is unlikely to be done in the near future. Instead, the clinical education community will rely on reason, experience, and quasi-experiments (e.g., Wayne, Didwania, Feinglass, et al., 2008b) to make a convincing case that simulation-based learning and assessment has a "payoff" in clinical practice.

Critics should be mindful that few important clinical or life innovations are verified scientifically via randomized controlled trials (RCT). For example, a recent article in the *British Medical Journal* informed readers that there has never been a RCT to evaluate the safety and utility of parachutes (Smith & Pell, 2003). Finding volunteers for the control group has been difficult. The alternative in clinical education is to rely on good sense and new techniques like statistical process control (Diaz & Neuhauser, 2007) to demonstrate that the learning and assessment effects of simulation-based technologies are too great to be dismissed. There are occasions when it would be foolish to ignore obvious and consistent outcomes.

Faculty Development Needs

Faculty training and development about effective use of simulation technology to promote learner achievement and assess learning outcomes must become a priority training goal. This is a key message of the recent Colloquium on Educational Technology sponsored by the Association of American Medical Colleges (AAMC, 2007). Simple or sophisticated simulation technology will be ineffective or misused unless health professions faculty are prepared as simulation educators.

The faculty development agenda is shaped, in part, by a discussion about the "scope of simulation-based healthcare education" authored by Issenberg (2006). The author argues that the best practice of simulation-based healthcare education is a *multiplicative product* of (a) simulation technology [e.g., task trainers, mannequins], (b) teachers prepared to use the technology to maximum advantage, and (c) curriculum integration. Issenberg (2006) asserts that the major flaws in today's simulation-based healthcare education and assessment stem from a lack of prepared teachers and curriculum isolation, not from technological problems or deficits.

There are at least five priority areas where faculty development activities are needed to insure that simulation-based education and assessment are efficient and effective.

1. *Simulation operation*, fluid use of high and low fidelity simulation technologies to promote learner education and assessment.
2. *Curriculum integration*, inserting simulation-based learning and assessment experiences as required curriculum features including many opportunities for deliberate practice by trainees (Ericsson, 2004).
3. *Recognition of the strengths and limits of simulation technology* for education and assessment in the health professions. Simulation is not a panacea. Its best use depends on the goals-tools match discussed earlier.

4. In assessment, recognition that best use of simulation will engage learners in *dynamic testing* (Grigorenko & Sternberg, 1998). Dynamic testing occurs when assessments not only yield evaluative data about trainees but also fulfill teaching goals.
5. Faculty must learn to combine simulation modalities in their education and assessment plans (Kneebone, et al., 2005). Lifelike and effective simulation experiences can involve a collection of electromechanical, human, and inanimate parts.

Conclusion

This chapter has covered the use of a variety of simulation technologies for learner assessment in the health professions. The emphasis has been on assessment planning, achieving a goals–tools match, with the intent of rational integration of simulation technology into health science curricula. We argue that simulation is not a panacea for assessment or instruction. Instead, simulation is one of many sets of tools available to health professions educators. Thoughtful use of these tools will increase the odds that educators will reach their assessment goals.

Simulation technology is rapidly increasing in sophistication, fidelity, and educational allure. Health professions educators must become thoughtful and critical consumers of simulation in its many forms to be clear about its practical utility and resist seduction by flashy gizmos and gimmicks.

References

AAMC Colloquium on Educational Technology (2007). *Effective use of educational technology in medical education* [summary report]. Washington, D.C.: Association of American Medical Colleges.

Adler, M.D., Trainor, J.L., Siddall, V.J., & McGaghie, W.C. (2007). Development and evaluation of high-fidelity simulation case scenarios for pediatric resident evaluation. *Ambulatory Pediatrics*, 7, 182–186.

Albarran, J.W., Moule, P., Gilchrist, M., & Soar, J. (2006). Comparison of sequential and simultaneous breathing and pulse check by health care professionals during simulated scenarios. *Resuscitation*, 68(2), 243–249.

Alinier, G., Hunt, B., Gordon, R., & Harwood, C. (2006). Effectiveness of intermediate-fidelity simulation training technology in undergraduate nursing education. *Journal of Advanced Nursing*, 54, 359–369.

Berkenstadt, H., Ziv, A., Gafni, N., & Sidi, A. (2006a). Incorporating simulation-based objective structured clinical examination into the Israeli national board examination in anesthesiology. *Anesthesia & Analgesia*, 102, 853–858.

Berkenstadt, H., Ziv, A., Gafni, N., & Sidi, A. (2006b). The validation process of incorporating simulation-based accreditation into the anesthesiology Israeli national board exams. *Israeli Medical Association Journal*, 8(10), 728–733.

Bligh, J., & Bleakley, A. (2006). Distributing menus to hungry learners: Can learning by simulation become simulation of learning? *Medical Teacher*, 28(7), 606–613.

Boulet, J.R., & Swanson, D.B. (2004). Psychometric challenges of using simulations for high-stakes assessment. In W.F. Dunn (Ed.), *Simulations in critical care education and beyond* (pp. 119–130). Des Plaines, IL: Society of Critical Care Medicine.

Buchanan, J.A., & Williams, J.N. (2004). Simulation in dentistry and oral surgery. In G.E. Loyd, C.L. Lake, & R.B. Greenberg (Eds.), *Practical health care simulations* (pp. 493–512). Philadelphia: Elsevier.

Diaz, M., & Neuhauser D. (2007). Pasteur and parachutes: When statistical process control is better than a randomized controlled trial. *Quality and Safety in Health Care*, 14, 140–143.

Downing, S.M. (2003). Validity: On the meaningful interpretation of assessment data. *Medical Education*, 37, 830–837.

Downing, S.M. (2004). Reliability: On the reproducibility of assessment data. *Medical Education*, 38, 1006–1012.

Downing, S.M. (2006). Twelve steps for effective test development. In S.M. Downing & T.M. Haladyna (Eds.), *Handbook of test development* (pp. 3–25). Mahwah, NJ: Lawrence Erlbaum Associates.

Downing, S.M., Tekian, A., & Yudkowsky, R. (2006). Procedures for establishing defensible absolute passing scores on performance examinations in health professions education. *Teaching and Learning in Medicine*, 18, 50–57.

Dunn, W.F. (Ed.). (2004). *Simulations in critical care education and beyond*. Des Plaines, IL: Society of Critical Care Medicine.

Ericsson, K.A. (2004). Deliberate practice and the acquisition and maintenance of expert performance in medicine and related domains. *Academic Medicine*, 79(10, Suppl.), S70–S81.

Gordon, M.S., & Issenberg, S.B. (2006). *Instructor guide for Harvey the cardiopulmonary patient simulator*. University of Miami School of Medicine, Gordon Center for Research in Medical Education.

Grigorenko, E.L., & Sternberg, R.J. (1998). Dynamic testing. *Psychological Bulletin*, 124, 75–111.

Hall, R.E., Plant, J.R., Bands, C.J., Wall, A.R., Kang, J., & Hall, C.A. (2005).

Human patient simulation is effective for teaching paramedic students endotracheal intubation. *Academic Emergency Medicine*, 12, 850–855.

Hatala, R., Issenberg, S.B., Kassen, B.O., Cole, G., Bacchus, C.M., & Scalese, R.J. (2007). Assessing the relationship between cardiac physical examination technique and accurate bedside diagnosis during an objective structured clinical examination (OSCE). *Academic Medicine*, 82(10, Suppl.), S26–S29.

Hatala, R., Kassen, B.O., Nishikawa, J., Cole, G., & Issenberg, S.B. (2005). Incorporating simulation technology in a Canadian internal medicine specialty examination: A descriptive report. *Academic Medicine*, 80, 554–556.

Hodges, B., Regehr, G., McNaughton, N., Tiberius, R., & Hanson, M. (1999). OSCE Checklists do not capture increasing levels of expertise. *Academic Medicine*, 74, 1129–1134.

Hravnak, M., Beach, M., & Tuite, P. (2007). Simulator technology as a tool for education in cardiac care. *Journal of Cardiovascular Nursing*, 22, 16–24.

Issenberg, S.B. (2006). The scope of simulation-based healthcare education. *Simulation in Healthcare*, 1, 203–208.

Issenberg, S.B., & McGaghie, W.C. (1999). Assessing knowledge and skills in the health professions: A continuum of simulation fidelity. In A. Tekian, C.H. McGuire, & W.C. McGaghie (Eds.), *Innovative simulations for assessing professional competence* (pp. 125–146). Chicago: Department of Medical Education, University of Illinois at Chicago.

Issenberg, S.B., McGaghie, W.C., Brown, D.D., Mayer, J.W., Gessner, I.H., Hart, I.R., et al. (2000). Development of multimedia computer-based measures of clinical skills in bedside cardiology. In D.E. Melnick (Ed.), *The Eighth International Ottawa Conference on Medical Education and Assessment Proceedings. Evolving assessment: Protecting the human dimension*. Philadelphia: National Board of Medical Examiners, pp. 821–829.

Issenberg, S.B., McGaghie, W.C., Gordon, D.L., Symes, S., Petrusa, E.R., Hart, I.R., et al. (2002). Effectiveness of a cardiology review course for internal medicine residents using simulation technology and deliberate practice. *Teaching and Learning in Medicine*, 14(4), 223–228.

Issenberg, S.B., McGaghie, W.C., Petrusa, E.R. Gordon, D.L., & Scalese, R.J. (2005). Features and uses of high-fidelity medical simulations that lead to effective learning: A BEME systematic review. *Medical Teacher*, 27, 10–28.

Kneebone, R.L., Kidd, J., Nestel, D., Barnet, A., Lo, B., King, R., et al. (2005). Blurring the boundaries: Scenario-based simulation in a clinical setting. *Medical Education*, 39, 580–587.

Larsen, C.R., Grantcharov, T., Aggarwal, R., Tully, A., Sørensen, J.L., Dalsgaard, T., et al. (2006). Objective assessment of gynecologic laparoscopic skills using the LapSimGyn virtual reality simulator. *Surgical Endoscopy*, 20, 1460–1466.

Lasater, K. (2007). High-fidelity simulation and the development of clinical judgment: Students' experiences. *Journal of Nursing Education*, 46, 269–276.

Loyd, G.E., Lake, C.L., & Greenberg, R.B. (Eds.). (2004). *Practical health care simulations*. Philadelphia: Elsevier.

McGaghie, W.C. (1999). Simulation in professional competence assessment: Basic considerations. In A. Tekian, C.H. McGuire, & W.C. McGaghie (Eds.), *Innovative simulations for assessing professional competence* (pp. 7–22). Chicago: Department of Medical Education, University of Illinois at Chicago.

McGaghie, W.C., Pugh, C.M., & Wayne, D.B. (2007). Fundamentals of educational research using simulation. In R. Kyle & W.B. Murray (Eds.), *Clinical simulation: Operations, engineering, and management* (pp. 517–526). Philadelphia: Elsevier.

Minogue, J., & Jones, M.G. (2006). Haptics in education: Exploring an untapped sensory modality. *Review of Educational Research*, 76(3), 317–348.

Murray, D.J., Boulet, J.R., Kras, J.F., McAllister, J.D., & Cox, T.E. (2005). A simulation-based acute care skills performance assessment for anesthesia training *Anesthesia and Analgesia*, 101, 1127–1134.

Newble, D., Dawson, B., Dauphinee, D., Page, G., Macdonald, M., Swanson, D., et al. (1994). Guidelines for assessing clinical competence. *Teaching and Learning in Medicine*, 6(3), 213–220.

Norcini, J., & Guille, R. (2002). Combining tests and setting standards. In G.R. Norman, C.P.M. van der Vleuten, & D.I. Newble (Eds.), *International handbook of research in medical education* (pp. 811–834). Dordrecht, NL: Kluwer Academic Publishers.

Patel, A.D., Gallagher, A.G., Nicholson, W.J., & Cates, C.V. (2006). Learning curves and reliability measures for virtual reality simulation in the performance assessment of carotid angiography. *Journal of the American College of Cardiology*, 47(9), 1796–1802.

Pugh, C.M., Heinrichs, W.L., Dev, P., Srivastava, S., & Krummel, T.M. (2001). Use of a mechanical simulator to assess pelvic examination skills. *Journal of the American Medical Association*, 286(9), 1021–1023.

Pugh, C.M., & Rosen, J. (2002). Qualitative and quantitative analysis of pressure sensor data acquired by the E-Pelvis simulator during simulated pelvic examinations. *Studies in Health Technologies and Informatics*, 85, 376–379.

Pugh, C.M., & Youngblood, P. (2002). Development and validation of assessment measures for a newly developed physical examination simulator. *Journal of the American Medical Informatics Association*, 9, 448–460.

Raymond, M.R., & Neustel, S. (2006). Determining the content of credentialing examinations. In S.M. Downing & T.M. Haladyna (Eds.), *Handbook of test development* (pp. 181–223). Mahwah, NJ: Lawrence Erlbaum Associates.

Regehr, G., Freeman, R., Robb, A., Missiha, N., & Heisey, R. (1999). OSCE performance evaluations made by standardized patients: Comparing checklist and global rating scales. *Academic Medicine*, 74(10, Suppl.), S135–S137.

Rosenthal, M.E., Adachi, M., Ribaudo, V., Mueck, J.T., Schneider, R.F., & Mayo, P.H. (2006). Achieving housestaff competence in emergency airway management using scenario based simulation training. *Chest*, 129, 1453–1458.

Scalese, R.J., & Issenberg, S.B. (2008). Simulation-based assessment. In E.S. Holmboe & R.E. Hawkins (Eds.), *Practical guide to the evaluation of clinical competence* (pp. 179–200). Philadelphia: Elsevier.

Scott, J.A., Miller, G.T., Issenberg, S.B., Brotons, A.A., Gordon, D.L., Gordon, M.S., et al. (2006). Skill improvement during emergency response to terrorism training. *Prehospital Emergency Care*, 10, 507–514.

Seymour, N.E., Gallagher, A.G., Roman, S.A., O'Brien, M.K., Bansal, V.K., Andersen, D.K., et al. (2002). Virtual reality training improves operating room performance: Results of a randomized double-blinded study. *Annals of Surgery*, 236, 458–464.

Shadish, W.R., Cook, T.D., & Campbell, D.T. (2002). *Experimental and quasi-experimental designs for generalized causal inference*. Boston: Houghton Mifflin.

Smith, G.C., & Pell, J.P. (2003). Parachute use to prevent death and major trauma related to gravitational challenge: Systematic review of randomized controlled trials. *British Medical Journal*, 327, 1459–1461.

Tuttle, R.P., Cohen, M.H., Augustine, A.J., Novotny, D.F., Delgado, E., Dongilli, et al. (2007). Utilizing simulation technology for competency skills assessment and a comparison of traditional methods of training to simulation-based training. *Respiratory Care*, 52, 263–270.

Wayne, D.B., Barsuk, J.H., Cohen, E., & McGaghie, W.C. (2007). Do baseline data influence standard setting for a clinical skills examination? *Academic Medicine*, 82(10, Suppl.), S105–S108.

Wayne, D.B., Barsuk, J., O'Leary K., Fudala, M.J., & McGaghie, W.C. (2008a). Mastery learning of thoracentesis skills by internal medicine residents using simulation technology and deliberate practice. *Journal of Hospital Medicine*, 3(1), 48–54.

Wayne, D.B., Butter, J., Siddall, V.J., Fudala, M.J., Feinglass, J., & McGaghie, W.C. (2006). Mastery learning of advanced cardiac life support skills by internal medicine residents using simulation technology and deliberate practice. *Journal of General Internal Medicine*, 21, 251–256.

Wayne, D.B., Butter, J., Siddall, V.J., Fudala, M.J., Lindquist, L., Feinglass, J., et al. (2005a). Simulation-based training of internal medicine residents in advanced cardiac life support protocols: A randomized trial. *Teaching and Learning in Medicine*, 17, 210–216.

Wayne, D.B., Didwania, A., Feinglass, J., Fudala, M.J., Barsuk, J.H., & McGaghie, W.C. (2008b). Simulation-based education improves quality of care during cardiac arrest team responses at an academic teaching hospital: A case-control study. *Chest*, 133, 56–61.

Wayne, D.B., Fudala, M.J., Butter, J., Siddall, V.J., Feinglass, J., Wade, L.D., et al. (2005b). Comparison of two standard setting methods for advanced cardiac life support training. *Academic Medicine*, 80(10, Suppl.), S63–S66.

Williams, R.G., McLaughlin, M.A., Eulenberg B., Hurm, M., & Nendaz, M.R. (1999). The Patient Findings Questionnaire: One solution to an important standardized patient examination problem. *Academic Medicine*, 74, 1118–1124.

Ziv, A., Rubin, O., Moshinsky, A., & Mittelman, M. (2007). Screening of candidates to medical school based on non-cognitive parameters using a simulation-based assessment center. *Simulation in Healthcare*, 2(1), 69.

11

ORAL EXAMINATIONS

ARA TEKIAN AND RACHEL YUDKOWSKY

The oral examination, sometimes known as a *viva voce*, is character-
ized by a face-to-face interaction between an examinee and one or
more examiners. Test questions may be linked to a patient case, clinic
chart, or other clinical material; exam sessions can range from focused
five-minute probes to comprehensive "long cases" of up to an hour in
length.

The stated purpose of an oral examination is to explore an examinee's thinking in order to assess skills such as critical reasoning,
problem solving, judgment, and ethics, as well as the ability to express
ideas, synthesize material and think on one's feet. The potential
advantage of the oral exam over a constructed-response written exam
lies in the examiner's ability to follow-up with additional probes that
explore the examinee's response, and the ability to deepen or broaden
the challenge in order to better define the limits of the examinee's
abilities. The Accreditation Council for Graduate Medical Education
(ACGME) lists oral exams as a candidate method for the assessment
of competencies such as decision making, analytic thinking, use of
evidence from scientific studies, and sensitivity to contextual issues
such as age, gender, and culture (see also Chapter 1, this volume). Oral
examinations should not be used primarily to assess knowledge, which
is better assessed with a written exam, or to evaluate elements of
the patient encounter, better assessed with simulations, performance
exams or direct observational methods (see Figure 11.1).

Oral examinations are used both at undergraduate and postgraduate
levels, as well as in many certification and licensure examinations. Orals
were used as early as in 1917 with the foundation of the organized

specialty boards in the US (Mancall, 1995). As of 2006, fifteen of 24 American Board of Medical Specialties (ABMS) member boards use some sort of oral examination as part of their evaluation or certification process, as do most specialties of the Royal College of Surgeons and Physicians of Canada, dentistry boards in the US and Canada, the Royal College of General Practice in Great Britain, and other certification bodies around the world.

The many threats to the validity of the oral exam as well as its cost in faculty time have been a source of controversy and concern over the usefulness of orals as an assessment strategy (Schuwirth & van der Vleuten, 1996; Wass, Wakeford, Neighbour, & van der Vleuten, 2003; Davis & Karunathilake, 2005; Yudkowsky, 2002). In this chapter we review these threats and suggest some ways to address them, primarily by means of *structured* oral exams. We'll also look at some examples of how oral exams are used around the world.

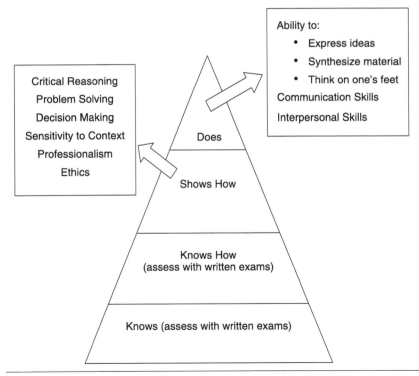

Figure 11.1 Miller's Pyramid (Miller, 1990): Competencies to Assess with Oral Exams.

Threats to the Validity of Oral Examinations

Concerns about the validity of traditional unstructured oral examinations have led to their gradual replacement by written tests, performance tests using simulations and standardized patients, and by structured oral exams, especially for high-stakes assessments. To understand this shift we will look at the vulnerability of oral exams to the two major threats to validity discussed in Chapter 2: construct underrepresentation (CU) and construct-irrelevant variance (CIV).

Construct underrepresentation (CU) or under-sampling is a major challenge for oral examinations. Like any other assessment, an oral exam must provide multiple data points that systematically sample the domain to be assessed. As with other tests of clinical skills, content specificity (Elstein, Shulman, & Sprafka, 1978) limits the ability to generalize from competency in one topic to competency in another. An oral exam that consists of questions about two or three topics or clinical scenarios is not likely to provide a broad and systematic sampling of the content domain (Turnball, Danoff, & Norman, 1996); an exam that assesses problem solving or clinical reasoning skills in only one or two scenarios is not sufficiently sampling that skill. Furthermore, if the oral exam is linked to encounters with real patients the content that can be assessed may be limited by patient availability, the patient's ability to cooperate, and his/her ability to consent to the exam (Yudkowsky, 2002). If learners are tested on different patients their tests may not be equivalent in either difficulty or content, compromising fairness and the ability to compare test scores across examinees.

Compounding the problem, early studies (Evans, Ingersoll, & Smith, 1996; McGuire, 1966) found that questions asked in oral examinations were not much different than questions in written examinations; Jayawickramarajah (1985) found that approximately two thirds of questions in an unstructured oral examination were simple recall. Regardless of the number of topics covered, these questions are not likely to elicit the higher-order thinking that is the appropriate focus of oral exams.

Construct irrelevant variance (CIV) refers to score variance due to factors that are irrelevant to the competency being assessed—for example, when characteristics such as politeness, demeanor, and dress impact the rating of clinical reasoning. CIV is a substantial threat to traditional oral examinations that use a small number of examiners per learner, since there are likely to be too few raters to compensate for stringency (hawk/dove) and bias effects (Linn & Zeppa, 1966; Schwiebert & Davis, 1993; Wass, et al., 2003, Weingarten, et al., 2000).

Construct-irrelevant variables that can impact the scores in oral examinations include mannerism and behavior, language and fluency, appearance and attractiveness (e.g., dress code—professional or non-professional), physical abnormalities/peculiarities or oddness, anxiety/stress level, and emotional status (Pokorny & Frazier, 1966). The level of confidence of candidates can have more influence on the score awarded by the examiners than what was actually said (Thomas, et al., 1992).

In an interesting experiment on the effect of communication style, Rowland-Morin and colleagues (1991) trained five actors and actresses to portray identical students with variations such as direct versus indirect eye-contact and moderate versus slower response rate. Examiners rated ten categories of performance (knowledge of facts, understands concepts, identified problems, integrates relevant data, makes proper decisions, is motivated, communicates effectively, is resourceful, has integrity, and is attractive in appearance). The study found that examiners were strongly influenced by the students' communication skills. Conversely, an examiners approving or disapproving facial expression can encourage or discourage an examinee's responses, introducing additional construct-irrelevant variance into the mix.

Structured Oral Examinations

The subjectivity, CU and CIV problems listed above led many educators to replace oral examinations with more objective and controllable methods such as written exams and performance tests using standardized patients and other simulations. Nonetheless, under controlled and standardized conditions as described below oral examinations can provide added value within a comprehensive assessment approach.

A *structured* oral examination offers significant benefits in combating CU and CIV. In a structured oral exam each examinee is exposed to the *same* or *equivalent tasks*, which are administered under the *same conditions*, in the *same amount of time*, and with *scoring as objective as possible* (Guerin, 1995). CU and CIV concerns can be addressed by assembling a series of oral exams, with careful blueprinting of the exam stations, standardization of questions and a rubric for scoring the answers; by utilizing multiple examiners with systematic training; by formal standard setting; and by systematic quality assurance efforts.

Structured oral examinations share many of the characteristics of performance tests such as standardized patient exams and Objective Structured Clinical Examinations (OSCEs) (Yudkowsky, Chapter 9, this volume). As with performance tests, increasing the number of tests or stations has a large impact on reliability/generalizability by increasing the sampling across content and raters, decreasing CU and allowing CIV to cancel out across tests/examiners. Daelmans, et al., (2001) investigated the effect of multiple oral examinations in an internal medicine clerkship, aiming for two 30-minute patient-based orals a day for five days. They found it would take ten 30-minute exams or about five hours of testing to reach a generalizability of 0.8, about comparable to the number of cases and time needed for a reliable OSCE (van der Vleuten & Swanson, 1990). Just as in OSCEs, increasing the number of exams with a single examiner at each "station" improves reliability more than doubling up examiners (Norman, 2000; Swanson, et al., 1995; Wass, et al., 2003).

Table 11.1 Characteristics of a Structured Oral Exam

- Multiple exam "stations"
- Content blueprinting
- Standardization of initial questions
- Rubrics to assist in scoring answers
- Multiple examiners
- Examiner training
- Formal standard setting
- Quality assurance efforts

Case Example 11.1: An Oral Exam "OSCE"

The McMaster University Admissions Multiple Mini-Interview (MMI) is a creative example of a structured oral (Eva, et al., 2004b). The traditional interview for admission to a health professions program can easily be conceptualized as an "oral examination"—a high stakes conversation between the interviewer and the applicant. The Multiple Mini-Interview is composed of an OSCE-like series of ten brief, structured interactions between students and faculty, community members and standardized "colleagues". Studies of the MMI confirm that applicant "performance" varied across interview contexts, and that the MMI predicted pre-clerkship and clerkship clinical performance better than did the traditional interview protocol (Eva et al., 2004a).

Blueprinting the Oral Exam

An exam blueprint ensures that the domain of interest is systematically and representatively sampled (Downing & Haladyna, Chapter 2, this volume; Haladyna, 2004; Downing & Haladyna, 2006). Use a specification table to identify the content area and skills to be assessed, and provide examples of questions to elicit the skills to be assessed (see Table 11.2 and the example in the MRCGP case study opposite).

Depending on the purpose of the exam, a variety of trigger materials may be used to provide a clinical context for the exam questions. An oral exam can be based on a live or simulated patient encounter, and serve as the probe for an OSCE station. At times the examiner himself may simulate a patient in order to assess a learner's data gathering or communication skills. In Chart-Stimulated Recall (CSR) (Maatsch, 1981) the examinee's own patients' charts serve as the trigger material for discussion with the examiner, allowing the examiner to probe deeply into the learner's clinical reasoning and decision making rationale in the context of care provided to his/her own patients.

Table 11.2 Blueprinting and Logistical Decisions

- Content domain and sub-domains to be sampled
- Skills/competencies to be assessed
  - o Decision making
  - o Patient management
  - o Diagnostic interpretations
  - o Sensitivity to contextual issues
  - o Communication and interpersonal skills
  - o Other
- Trigger materials (if any)
  - o Real patients
  - o Simulated patients
  - o Written vignettes
  - o Learner's own patient charts
  - o Lab results
  - o Examiner role play
- Desired breadth and depth of questions

Logistical Decisions:
- Number of oral exam stations
- Time/duration of each station
- Number of questions/cases per station
- Number of examiners per station

Case Example 11.2: Creative Blueprinting

The Examination for Membership in the Royal College of General Practitioners (MRCGP)

The MRCGP exam (United Kingdom) includes two consecutive 20-minute oral examinations, each conducted by a team of two examiners. Each candidate is assigned to two examiner teams linked as a quartet during a morning or afternoon session. To ensure a systematic sampling of candidate competencies, each quartet uses a blueprint grid to pre-plan ten topics that will be examined in all candidates that session. Topics are chosen that will enable candidates to demonstrate their decision-making skills in three competency domains (communication, professional values, and personal and professional development) and three contexts (patient care, working with colleagues, society and personal responsibility). For example, "Strategies for breaking bad news" is a topic that could assess the competency domain of "Communication" in the context of "Care of Patients"; the topic "Personal plans for re-accreditation" could assess the domain of "Personal and Professional Growth" in the context of "Society and Personal Responsibility" (Wass, et al., 2003). The three domains and contexts are the same for all examiner quartets. This somewhat unusual blueprint ensures that examiners focus their efforts on specific areas of interest to the RCGP that cannot easily be assessed in other ways.

The two examiners of each team alternate asking questions about one of the topics, spending no more than four minutes per topic, five topics per team. Each of the two examiners independently rates the candidate on all five topics using a nine-point categorical scale ranging from Outstanding through Bare Pass to Dangerous.

The RCGP is making a systematic effort to collect and disseminate validity evidence for their exam, resulting in a series of publications on the workings of a high stakes oral exam (RCGP website; Roberts, et al., 2000; Simpson & Ballard, 2005; Wakeford, et al., 1995; Wass, et al., 2003; Yaphe & Street, 2003).

Scoring and Standard Setting

Scoring issues for oral exams are similar to those for direct observation (McGaghie, et al., Chapter 8, this volume) and performance tests (Yudkowsky, Chapter 9, this volume), including instrument design for capturing and rating a performance and procedures for combining marks. Checklists and rating scales can encourage examiners to focus on the critical components of the exam, and behaviorally anchored scoring rubrics can help standardize ratings. As in performance tests, including global ratings helps to tap the unique judgment and experience of expert examiners.

Standard setting is a particular challenge for oral examinations. If left to the sole judgment of the individual examiner, pass/fail decisions could be legitimately attacked as both arbitrary and capricious. Pooling the judgments of several experts through a formal standard setting exercise will ensure that the cut scores are defensible and fair.

Any of the standard setting methods used for performance tests such as OSCEs can be adapted for structured oral exams with multiple "stations" and examiners. Examinee-based methods such as Borderline Group Method may be especially appropriate for oral exams in which different learners are questioned by different examiners. In this method the examiner scores or rates the examinee on several relevant items per the scoring rubric, and also provides a global rating ranging from definite pass to marginal pass to definite fail. The final pass/fail cut score is determined by the mean item score of all examinees with a "marginal pass" rating.

In an Angoff-type method, standards can be set either on the individual oral exam "station" level or on the test level. A panel of carefully selected judges reviews each item or exam station and each judge indicates the probability of the item or exam being successfully accomplished by a "borderline" examinee—an examinee just on the cusp of failure. The final cut score for the station or the test is the sum of the probabilities across items or stations.

See Chapter 6 (Yudkowsky, Downing, & Tekian, this volume) for a more complete discussion of standard setting issues, and Chapters 8 and 9 for discussion of scoring and standard setting in the context of observations and performance tests.

Preparation of the Examinee

Examinees taking an oral examination should know all the details involved in the process. Orient learners to the objectives, setting, duration, number of examiners, and the overall procedure in advance. Inform learners about the type of questions and criteria for passing, and provide opportunities to practice (particularly for high stakes examinations).

Selection and Training of the Examiners

Wakeford and colleagues (1995) suggest that selection criteria for examiners include appropriate knowledge and skills in the subject matter, "an approach to the practice of medicine and the delivery of health care that is within the limits of that acceptable to the examiners as a whole," effective interpersonal skills, demonstrated ability of a good team player, and being active in general practice. While selection of appropriate examiners is a critical step for any oral exam, one of the advantages of a structured oral exam is the opportunity to institute systematic training as well. For example, examiners can be trained to ask open-ended questions of higher taxonomic level, providing better assessments of the candidates' problem solving skills (Des Marchais & Jean, 1993). Frame-of-reference training, in which examiners practice rating exemplars of different levels of responses is an especially effective method for calibrating examiners to the rating scale (Bernardin & Buckley, 1981; and Yudkowsky (Chapter 9 this volume)). Newble, Hoare, & Sheldrake (1980) demonstrated that training tends to be ineffective for less consistent examiners, and suggested that inconsistent examiners and extremely severe or lenient raters be removed from the examiner pool. Systematic severity and leniency (but not inconsistency) can also be corrected by statistical adjustment of scores. Raymond, Webb, & Houston (1991) provide a relatively simple statistical procedure based on ordinary least squares (OLS) regression to identify and correct errors in leniency and stringency, resulting in a 6% change in the pass rate. In high-stakes exams, more complex statistical methods such as Many Faceted Rasch Measurement can help identify and correct for rater errors (Myford & Wolfe, 2003).

Quality Assurance

Quality assurance (QA) efforts can focus on preventing, checking for and remedying threats to the validity of the exam (Table 11.4), and on obtaining the five types of validity evidence described in Chapter 2. These might include activities such as reviewing the blueprint for content validity; ensuring that examiners' adhered to implementation

Table 11.3 Steps in Examiner Training for a Structured Oral Exam

1. Select examiners who are knowledgeable in the domain to be tested, familiar with the level of learners to be tested (e.g., 2nd year nursing students), and have good communication skills.
2. Orient examiners to the exam purpose, procedure, and consequences (stakes).
3. Explain the competencies to be assessed, types of questions to be asked and how to use any trigger material. Have examiners practice asking higher-order questions.
4. Review and rehearse rating and documentation procedures.
5. If possible, provide frame-of-reference training to calibrate examiners to scoring of different levels of responses.
6. Have new examiners observe an experienced examiner and/or practice via participation in a simulated oral examination.
7. Observe new examiners and provide feedback, after which an examiner is either invited or rejected. Examiners who are inconsistent or have clearly deviant patterns of grading (very lenient or very severe) should not be allowed to serve as examiners.
8. Continue ongoing calibration/fine-tuning of examiners, particularly in high stakes examinations.

Case Example 11.3: Assessing Examiners

The American Board of Emergency Medicine (ABEM) Oral Certification Exam

The ABEM five-hour oral certification examination (as of 2006) consists of seven structured oral simulations based on actual cases: five single-patient scenarios and two scenarios in which the candidate has to manage multiple patients concurrently. A single examiner scores each simulation, rating candidates on eight performance criteria based on critical actions relevant to that case. The examination blueprint (content specification) and pass/fail criteria can be found on the ABEM website: www.abem.org.

The ABEM expects their examiners to undergo six hours of training on case administration and scoring, achieving a high degree of inter-examiner agreement. Their examiners are monitored and evaluated on 17 criteria at each examination. Some of these are listed below.

- Established a comfortable tone of interaction with candidates

- Started cases on time
- Maintained control of case timing
- Finished cases on time
- Introduced cases according to guidelines
- Managed case material appropriately
- Administered cases according to agreed upon standards
- Played roles appropriately
- Cued appropriately
- Took comprehensive and readable notes

Examiners are assessed by senior examiners who rotate between rooms. Examiners who repeatedly deviate from training guidelines are not invited to return.

For more about the American Board of Emergency Medicine Exam see Reinhart, 1995 and Bianchi, et al., 2003.

guidelines for questions, scoring, and managing the exam; obtaining reliability indicators such as inter-rater reliability or generalizability estimates; investigating the relationship between scores on the oral exam and other assessments; and assessing the consequences of the cut-score standards set for the exam.

After the Exam

Planning for an oral examination includes consideration of post-examination issues common to all assessment methods. These include questions such as mechanisms for disseminating the results to examinees and other stakeholders; dealing with failing or marginal candidates, and whether there is an appeals process to review disputed scores.

Cost

There are many expenses involved in an oral exam: examination preparation and production cost (including item/case generation and scoring); costs associated with examiners' training, time and travel;

other reimbursements particularly if standardized or real patients are utilized; and venue/site expenses. The logistics of a structured oral exam are particularly complex, but are worth the extra cost and effort to be able to respond affirmatively to questions such as "Are we measuring what we intended to measure?" "Are the results reliable?" and "Is the exam worth the investment in time and money?"

Summary

Oral examinations remain the subject of debate and dispute, but when properly implemented orals can be credible contributors to the assessment toolbox. In the context of a low-stakes, formative assessment, an unstructured oral examination can provide an invaluable opportunity for faculty to engage in a conversation with learners, understand their thinking, and provide immediate feedback based on the encounter. In high-stakes settings, a structured, OSCE-like oral can provide a unique opportunity for in-depth probing of decision-making, ethical reasoning and other "hidden" skills.

When planning a structured oral examination, follow these evidence-based recommendations:

- Use multiple orals with multiple examiners
- Use a blueprint to guide question development
- Use a structured scoring system
- Select consistent, well-trained examiners
- Monitor the preparation, production, training, implementation, evaluation, and feedback phases of the examination process
- Use oral exams as one component of a comprehensive assessment system.

Table 11.4 Threats to Validity*: Oral Examinations

	Problem	Remedy
Construct Under-representation (CU)	Too few questions to sample domain adequately	Use multiple exams
	Unrepresentative sampling of domain	Blueprint to be sure exams systematically sample the domain
	Lower order questions (mis-match of questions to competencies)	Train examiners to use higher order questions
		Standardize the questions
		Use multiple examiners
	Too few independent examiners	Use one examiner per station
Construct-irrelevant Variance (CIV)	Flawed or inappropriate questions	Train examiners
	Flawed or inappropriate case scenarios or other prompts	Standardize questions
		Pilot test cases and prompts
		Provide scoring rubric
	Examiner bias	Train examiners to use rubric
	Systematic rater error:	
	Halo, Severity, Leniency, Central tendency	Frame of reference training for examiners
	Question difficulty inappropriate (too easy/too hard)	Train examiners
		Standardize questions
	Bluffing of examiners	Train examiners
	Language/cultural bias	Train examiners
	Indefensible passing score methods	Review and revise questions
		Use formal standard setting procedures
Reliability Indicators		Generalizability
		Inter-rater reliability
		Raterconsistency

Note: * For more about CU and CIV threats to validity, see Downing & Haladyna, Chapter 2, this volume.

References

Bernardin, H.J., & Buckley, M.R. (1981). Strategies in rater training. *The Academy of Management Review*, 6(2), 205–212.

Bianchi, L., Gallagher, E.J., Korte, R., & Ham, H.P. (2003). Interexaminer agreement on the American Board of Emergency Medicine Oral Certification Examination. *Annals of Emergency Medicine*, 41, 859–864.

Daelmans, H.E.M., Scherpbier, A.J.J.A., van der Vleuten, C.P.M., & Donker, A.B.J.M. (2001). Reliability of clinical oral examination re-examined. *Medical Teacher*, 23, 422–424.

Davis, M.H., & Karunathilake, I. (2005). The place of the oral examination in today's assessment systems. *Medical Teacher*, 27(4), 294–297.

Des Marchais, J.E., & Jean, P. (1993). Effects of examiner training on open-ended, higher taxonomic level questioning in oral certification examinations. *Teaching and Learning in Medicine*, 3, 24–28.

Downing, S., & Haladyna, T. (2006). *Handbook of test development*. Mahwah, NJ: Lawrence Erlbaum Associates.

Elstein, A., Shulman, L., & Sprafka, S. (1978). *Medical problem solving: An analysis of clinical reasoning*. Cambridge, MA: Harvard University Press.

Eva, K.W., Reiter, H.I., Rosenfeld, J., & Norman, G.R. (2004a). The ability of the multiple mini-interview to predict preclerkship performance in medical school. *Academic Medicine*, 79 (10 Suppl), S40–S42.

Eva, K.W., Rosenfeld, J., Reiter, H.I., & Norman, G.R. (2004b). An admissions OSCE: The multiple mini-interview. *Medical Education*, 38 (3), 314–326.

Evans, L.R., Ingersoll, R.W., & Smith, E.J. (1996). The reliability, validity, and taxonomic structure of the oral examination. *Journal of Medical Education*, 41, 651–657.

Guerin, R.O. (1995). Disadvantages to using the oral examination. In E.L. Mancall & P.H. Bashook (Eds.), *Assessing clinical reasoning: The oral examination and alternative methods* (pp. 41–48). Evanston, IL: American Board of Medical Specialties.

Haladyna, T. (2004). *Developing and validating multiple-choice test items*, (3rd ed.). Mahwah, NJ: Lawrence Erlbaum Associates.

Jayawickramarajah, P.T. (1985). Oral examinations in medical education. *Medical Education*, 19, 290–293.

Linn, B.S., & Zeppa, R. (1966). Team testing—One component in evaluating surgical clerks. *Journal of Medical Education*, 41, 28–40.

Maatsch, J.L. (1981). Assessment of clinical competence on the Emergency Medicine Specialty Certification Examination: The validity of examiner ratings of simulated clinical encounters. *Annals of Emergency Medicine*, 10, 504–507.

Mancall, E.L. (1995). The oral examination: A historic perspective. In E.L. Mancall & P.H. Bashook (Eds.), *Assessing clinical reasoning: The oral examination and alternative methods* (pp. 3–7). Evanston, IL: American Board of Medical Specialties.

McGuire, C.H. (1966). The oral examination as a measure of professional competence. *Journal of Medical Education*, 41, 267–274.

Miller, G. (1990). The assessment of clinical skills/competence/performance. *Academic Medicine*, 65 (Suppl.), S63–S67.

Myford, C.M., & Wolfe, E.W. (2003). Detecting and measuring rater effects using many-facet Rasch measurement: Part I. *Journal of Applied Measurement*, 4(4), 386–422.

Newble, D.I., Hoare, J., & Sheldrake, P.F. (1980). The selection and training of examiners for clinical examinations. *Medical Education*, 14, 345–349.

Norman, G. (2000). Examining the examination: Canadian versus US radiology certification exam. *Canadian Association of Radiologist Journal*, 51, 208–209.

Pokorny, A.D., & Frazier, S.H. (1966). An evaluation of oral examinations. *Journal of Medical Education*, 41, 28–40.

Raymond, M.R., Webb, L.C., & Houston, W.M. (1991). Correcting performance-rating errors in oral examinations. *Evaluation and the Health Professions*, 14, 100–122.

Reinhart, M.A. (1995). Advantages to using the oral examination. In E.L. Mancall & P.H. Bashook (Eds.), *Assessing clinical reasoning: The oral examination and alternative methods* (pp. 31–39). Evanston, IL: American Board of Medical Specialties.

Roberts, C., Sarangi, S., Southgate, L., Wakeford, R., & Wass, V. (2000). Oral examinations equal opportunities, ethnicity, and fairness in the MRCGP. *British Medical Journal*, 320, 370–375.

Rowland-Morin, P.A., Burchard, K.W., Garb, J.L., & Coe, N.P. (1991). Influence of effective communication by surgery students on their oral examination scores. *Academic Medicine*, 66, 169–171.

Schuwirth, L.W.T., & van der Vleuten, C.P.M. (1996). Quality control: Assessment and examinations. Retrieved June 30, 2008 from http://www.oeghd.or.at/zeitschrift/1996h1-2/06_art.html

Schwiebert, P., & Davis, A. (1993). Increasing inter-rater agreement on a family medicine clerkship oral examination—A pilot study. *Family Medicine*, 25, 182–185.

Simpson, R.G., & Ballard, K.D. (2005). What is being assessed in the MRCGP oral examinations? A qualitative study. *British Journal of General Practice*, 55, 420–422.

Swanson D.B., Norman G.R., & Linn R.L. (1995). Performance-based assessment: Lessons learnt from the health professions. *Educational Researcher*, 24, 5–11.

Thomas, C.S., Mellsop, G., Callender, K., Crawshaw, J., Ellis, P.M., Hall, A., et al. (1992). The oral examination: A study of academic and non-academic factors. *Medical Education*, 27, 433–439.

Turnball, J., Danoff, D., & Norman, G. (1996). Content specificity and oral certification examinations. *Medical Education*, 30, 56–59.

van der Vleuten, C.P.M., & Swanson, D.B. (1990). Assessment of clinical skills with standardized patients: State of the art. *Teaching and Learning in Medicine*, 2, 58–76.

Wakeford, R., Southgate, L., & Wass, V. (1995). Improving oral examinations: Selecting, training, and monitoring examiners for the MRCGP. *British Medical Journal*, 311, 931–935.

Wass, V., Wakeford, R., Neighbour, R., & van der Vleuten, C. (2003). Achieving acceptable reliability on oral examinations: An analysis of the Royal College of General Practitioners membership examination's oral component. *Medical Education*, 37, 126–131.

Weingarten, M.A., Polliack, M.R., Tabenkin, H., & Kahan, E. (2000).

Variations among examiners in family medicine residency board oral examinations. *Medical Education, 34,* 13–17.

Yaphe, J., & Street, S. (2003). How do examiners decide? A qualitative study of the process of decision making in the oral examination component of the MRCGP examination. *Medical Education, 37,* 764–771.

Yudkowsky, R. (2002). Should we use standardized patients for high stakes examinations in psychiatry? *Academic Psychiatry, 26*(3), 187–192.

12

ASSESSMENT PORTFOLIOS

ARA TEKIAN AND RACHEL YUDKOWSKY

The word portfolio comes from the Latin word *portare* (to carry) and *folium* (leaf, sheet). The Webster Dictionary's definition of portfolio is "a flat, portable case for carrying loose papers [and] drawings" (Webster's Encyclopedia, 1996). In health professions education, a portfolio is a collection of evidence documenting progress, accomplishments and achievements over time. Unlike written exams and performance tests, whose scope is limited to behaviors and characteristics that can be observed and measured at a single point of time, portfolios provide a means to assess competencies such as self directed learning, which are demonstrated over the course of months or years. Portfolios also comprise a vehicle for the longitudinal, multi-method, multi-source assessment of learner achievement. While portfolios can be used for both instruction and assessment purposes, our focus will be on the use of portfolios for assessment. In this chapter we will describe both single-competency and multi-source or "omnibus" assessment portfolios, and focus on the challenge of using portfolios to obtain valid and reliable scores.

Portfolios and Reflection

A portfolio in the health professions is not simply a collection of work samples or a record of activities; the distinctive aspect of a portfolio is the reflective component, an opportunity for the learner to provide a commentary on the included items and explicate their meaning to the reader. As such it is a unique and individual creation and a dynamic record of personal and professional growth.

A portfolio can serve as both a *vehicle* to promote reflective learning and as *evidence* of that reflection and of other learning. The use of portfolios to facilitate learning is based on the experiential/reflective learning models of Kolb (1984) and Schön (1987) (Figure 12.1). These models emphasize the need to reflect on an experience, often together with a coach or mentor, in order for the experience to be incorporated effectively as new learning. The process of portfolio development promotes this reflection: writing about experiences is itself a tool that forces thinking, structuring thoughts and reflection, thus supporting professional development (Pitkala & Mantyranta, 2004).

Types of Portfolios and their Contents

The contents of a portfolio depend on its purpose. As a vehicle to promote reflection, a formative or learning portfolio may include private, reflective responses to learning experiences, including reflection on errors and mistakes. These reflections may be reviewed and discussed with a mentor, tutor or peers for the purpose of formative assessment and feedback. Summative or assessment portfolios, on the other hand, consist of a public compilation of evidence of learning and/or work samples, often reflecting a learner's best work, most typical work, or work on a theme (Davis, et al., 2001b; O'Sullivan, et al., 2004; Paulson, Paulson, & Meyer, 1991; Rees, 2005). While an assessment portfolio may include selected entries from the learning portfolio, the different purposes should be explicit, and the selection

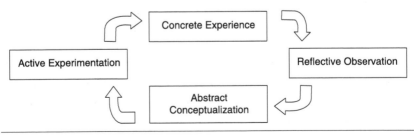

Figure 12.1 Kolb's Experiential Learning Cycle.*

Source: *Adapted from Kolb (1984).

of reflective entries to be made public should be left to the learner (Pinsky & Fryer-Edwards, 2004; Pitts, 2007).

A portfolio can serve to document the accomplishment of a single curricular objective or competency such as self-directed learning. Portfolios are especially suited to providing evidence for the achievement of competencies that are difficult to observe directly in controlled circumstances at a single point in time. By providing an annotated, reflective record of activities over time, portfolios can afford indirect observation of complex competencies such as practice-based learning and improvement or system-based practice. In addition, the process of selecting and justifying "best work" for an assessment portfolio allows the learner to demonstrate aspects of professionalism such as the ability to reflect on and self-assess one's own work, and implies a deep understanding of the characteristics and criteria that determine the quality of the work (Pinsky & Fryer-Edwards, 2004).

Portfolios can also complement single-source, single-competency assessment by providing a rich multidimensional description of the learner's accomplishments over time and verifying the achievement of multiple and complex learning objectives. An "omnibus" assessment portfolio is a compilation of evidence from a variety of methods and sources. The omnibus portfolio can include entries across the spectrum of Miller's pyramid from "knows" to "does" (Downing & Yudkowsky, Chapter 1, this volume and Figure 12.2). Entries can continue to accumulate in the portfolio until the evidence is sufficient for the decision required. As faculty gain experience with assessment portfolios, patterns of exceptional or dysfunctional learning, like "growth charts," can provide an opportunity for early intervention and remediation.

Scoring the Portfolio

The primary challenge of assessment portfolios is how to move from a collection of evidence to a single summative score or decision. As an example, imagine an omnibus portfolio consisting of four components: annual written exam scores, annual performance test (OSCE) scores, monthly end-of-rotation clinical evaluations, and semi-annual reflections by the learner. Some possibilities for scoring the portfolio are:

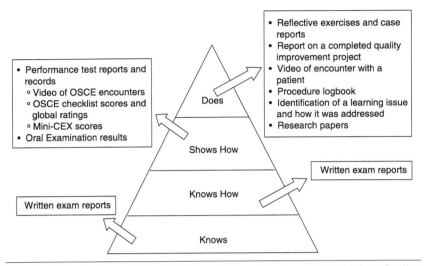

Figure 12.2 Miller's Pyramid (Miller, 1990): Sample Elements that can be Included in an Omnibus Assessment Portfolio.

- Score each component separately, and average the scores across components for the final portfolio score (*compensatory scoring*). In such situations, good performance on one or more components will compensate for the poor performance on other components. For example, if a student performs poorly on the monthly end of rotation clinical evaluation, good performance on the other three components will compensate for poor performance on this component. In a compensatory system, it is difficult to give feedback about each component, because the score is an aggregate of several components.

- Score each component separately; the learner must reach a minimum standard in each component in order to pass (*conjunctive scoring*). A student performing poorly on the monthly end of rotation clinical evaluation will not get a passing score irrespective of good performance on the other three components, because the scores for each component do not compensate for each other. (For more on conjunctive vs compensatory scoring see Chapter 6 in this volume.)

- Rate the portfolio-as-a-whole using an analytic or primary trait rating rubric (see Chapters 7 and 9). For example, the portfolio-as

-a-whole could be rated on characteristics such as organization, completeness, or quality of reflection. Alternatively the portfolio-as-a-whole could be rated on the quality of evidence provided for each of several individual competencies such as communication, knowledge, or professionalism.

- Rate the portfolio-as-a-whole using a single global rating rubric—for example, a five-point scale ranging from definite pass to definite fail.

Optional steps include an oral "defense" of the portfolio to allow examiners to probe for additional information and understanding; discussions between examiners to reach a consensus grade; and requesting additional information and/or rating by additional examiners for marginal or borderline students.

Designing a Portfolio System: Addressing Threats to Validity

Portfolios face the same threats to validity as other assessment methods (Downing & Haladyna, Chapter 2, this volume and Table 12.1). Because of these challenges, portfolios are best used as part of a comprehensive assessment system that can triangulate on learner competence (Webb, et al., 2003; Melville, et al., 2004).

The contents of the portfolio should systematically sample the learning objectives to be assessed. A portfolio intended to assess the self-directed learning of nurse practitioners, whose entries include only a log of textbook reading, is an example of a *construct under-representation* (CU) or under-sampling validity challenge (see Chapter 2). CU can be avoided by providing learners with a portfolio structure and guidelines that specify the learning objectives to be documented, the types of desirable evidence, and the amount of evidence required, systematically sampling work *over time* and *over tasks*. For example, guidelines for a portfolio intended for the assessment of self-directed learning might specify including:

- An explanation of five new learning objectives initiated by critical incidents
- Learning plans to achieve these objectives

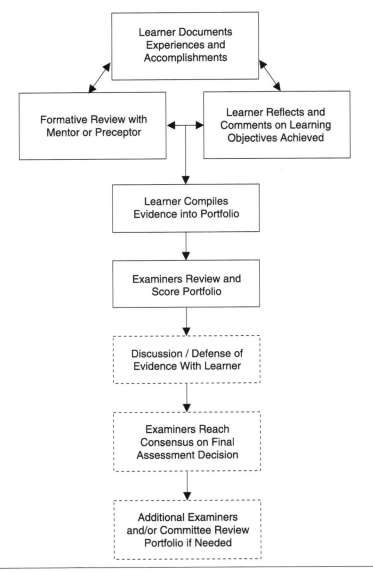

Figure 12.3 Assessment Portfolio Steps.

- A description of the educational activities undertaken
- A reflective self-appraisal of learning showing that growth and professional development is taking place.

Construct irrelevant variance (CIV) occurs when scores inadvertently include elements other than the ability to be assessed. These irrelevant elements ("noise" in the scores) can be due to either learner or rater factors. Learners may contribute to CIV when they are reluctant to reflect honestly on errors or to expose their weaknesses in the context of an assessment. Separating the reflective (formative) and assessment (summative) functions of the portfolio, and allowing learners to select the "best work" or "best evidence" entries to make public in the assessment portfolio can help minimize this problem (Pinsky & Fryer-Edwards, 2004).

Portfolio raters are subject to the same biases and errors as raters for oral exams and performance exams (see Table 12.1) (Roberts, Newble, & O'Rourke, 2002; Ward, Gruppen, & Regehr, 2002). One approach to the rater (dis)agreement challenge is to standardize the contents of the portfolio and to use multiple raters whenever possible – parallel to the approach for standardizing essay, oral and performance exams. An example would be to have various portfolio entries scored by different raters, resulting in multiple "observations" by multiple raters. Another tactic is to include portfolio entries such as OSCE or MCQ results with known high reliability; the portfolio as a whole partakes of the reliability of its component parts. As with other subjective judgments, benchmarks for acceptable entries, frame-of-reference rater training and rater consensus through discussion can improve rater agreement (McGaghie, et al., Chapter 8, this volume; O'Sullivan, et al., 2002, 2004; Pitts, et al., 2002; Rees & Sheard, 2004).

Reliability of Portfolios

Nonetheless, the ability of portfolio ratings to achieve acceptable levels of psychometric reliability is still at issue. Gadbury-Amyot, et al. (2003) had seven faculty raters score 20 portfolios of baccalaureate dental hygiene students using a scoring rubric based on primary trait analysis: faculty rated the portfolio on seven subscales such as "growth and development," "competencies," "lifelong learning," and "communication" using a four-point Likert scale where 1 = no evidence of the trait and 4 = complete evidence of the trait. A generalizability analysis D-study (see Kreiter, Chapter 4, this volume) established that three raters, each scoring the portfolio on ten subscales, would provide an acceptable phi coefficient (reliability) of 0.83. On the other hand, several studies have concluded that low inter-rater reliability precludes the use of portfolios for a high stakes, summative assessment (Melville, et al., 2004; Pitts, Coles, & Thomas, 1999 and 2001). For example, in a series of studies, Pitts et al. trained experienced general practice trainers to rate the portfolios of participants in a Trainers Course and assessed their level of agreement. Using a six-point scale, the portfolio-as-a-whole was rated on six characteristics such as "reflective learning process," "awareness of educational resources" and "recognition of effective teaching behaviors." To assess the reliability of pass/fail decisions the scale was collapsed to a dichotomous score of "pass" or "refer." The study found only slight to fair agreement between raters, with kappas ranging from 0.05 to 0.36 for eight independent assessors. While they were able to achieve "moderate" agreement after discussion between pairs of examiners, they concluded that "despite explicit instructions to compilers [learners], considerable investment in assessor training, and the negotiation, agreement and publication of overt criteria, individual assessments . . . show only fair inter-rater reliability and are untrustworthy in high-stakes assessment" (Pitts, et al., 2002).

Disaggregating the portfolio and scoring the components independently increases psychometric reliability, but at the expense of the holistic, developmental view of the learner that is the portfolio's raison d'etre. An alternative approach to the reliability problem is to use qualitative research methodology to assure the appropriate evaluation of the portfolio-as-a-whole (Driessen, et al., 2005; McMullan, et al., 2003, Webb, et al., 2003). This approach emphasizes establishing the credibility and dependability of the portfolio rating, rather than using traditional psychometric measures of reliability. How credible is the final decision, and how much can I depend on it? The *credibility* of an assessment is improved by employing triangulation (combining different information sources—analogous to multiple raters), prolonged engagement (e.g., multiple formative reviews of the portfolio over time—analogous to multiple observations), and member checking (reviewing and discussing the assessment with the student). *Dependability* is enhanced by audit (quality assurance procedures with external

Table 12.1 Threats to Validity: Portfolios

	Problem	Remedy
Construct under-representation (CU)	Not enough evidence of learning is presented	Provide learners with guidelines for type and quantity of evidence needed; Formative review with preceptor
	Evidence is not presented for all learning objectives	Specify portfolio structure based on blueprint of learning objectives; Formative review with preceptor
Construct-irrelevant variance (CIV)	Examiner bias	Provide scoring rubric Train examiners to use rubric Rater consensus discussion
	Systematic rater error: Halo, Severity, Leniency, Central tendency	Benchmarks, frame of reference training for examiners Rater consensus discussion
	Ability to reflect may be confounded with writing ability	Oral discussion/defense of portfolio Formative review of portfolio for correct writing and presentation before official submission
	Insincere reflective entries because of confidentiality and privacy concerns	Separate formative and summative functions of portfolio Give learners control over which reflective entries to include
Reliability indicators	Generalizability Inter-rater reliability or agreement Reproducibility of pass/fail decisions Credibility Dependability	

auditors) and audit trail (documentation of the assessment process to enable external checks). These qualitative approaches to the assessment and quality assurance of the portfolio-as-a-whole can help avoid reductionism and preserve an integrated, holistic view of the learner as a unique individual developing over time.

Case Examples

The following case studies illustrate three creative adaptations of portfolios for the assessment of learners in the health professions.

Case Example 12.1: A High-Stakes Omnibus Portfolio Assessment to Establish Readiness for Graduation (Davis, et al., 2001a, b)

After moving to outcome-based education in 1996–1997, Dundee medical school redesigned its final examinations to meet the needs of the new curriculum. The final examinations occured in two parts. At the end of Year-4, knowledge, problem solving and clinical skills were assessed by means of written tests and an OSCE. At the end of Year-5, faculty members evaluated overall progress towards all 12 of the desired learning outcomes, including personal and professional development, by means of an omnibus portfolio. All three of the examination components—written tests, OSCE, and portfolio—had to be passed for graduation.

The portfolio included entries such as:

- Pre-marked samples of student work
  - Ten short patient presentations
  - Seven case discussion reports
  - One Year-4 project report
- Procedure log, signed by faculty
- Faculty assessment forms from Special Study Modules and electives
- Learning contracts from medicine and surgery apprenticeships with grades awarded for each learning outcome
- The student's personal summary of progress towards each of the 12 learning outcomes, reflecting on and justifying his or her accomplishments.

Scoring the Portfolio

Two examiners independently read and graded each of the 12 outcomes, based on the evidence presented in the portfolio. They discussed their ratings and agreed on areas of strength and weakness to be explored with the student during the oral review.

After a 40-minute oral review and defense of the portfolio, the examiners again independently assigned grades for each outcome based on the student's performance during the oral review. They then reached consensus on a final set of grades, on which pass/fail decisions were based.

Students who received consensus grades of "marginal fail" on at least two outcomes, or definite fail on one outcome, proceeded to remediation and/or further examination by OSCE and an additional review of the portfolio.

Year 1 studies demonstrated a 98% pass/referred agreement between two independent pairs of examiners.

Case Example 12.2: Showcase or "Best Work" Portfolios for Psychiatry Residents (O'Sullivan, et al., 2002 and 2004)

Psychiatry residents were asked to exhibit their "best work" in five of 13 essential topic areas each year, including topics such as initial evaluation and diagnosis, treatment course, self directed learning, working with teams, crisis management, legal issues, and presentation/teaching skills. Four of the topics were freely selected by residents; an entry in the area of bio/psycho/social formulation was mandatory. Resident guidelines specified the meaning of each topic, what to include in the entry, and the rubric showing how the entry would be evaluated. For each entry, residents selected a case or experience to showcase their "best work" in that topic. Entries were not developed specifically for the portfolio. Residents submitted copies of (de-identified) patient documentation that they had produced, and wrote a brief reflective self-assessment explaining how this case and the supporting documentation demonstrated their competency.

Scoring the Portfolio

Program faculty developed topic-specific, six-point scoring rubrics in which the low end indicated a lack of knowledge or skill that could place patients at risk and the high end indicated an ability to deal with complex problems effectively and creatively. Two external examiners who were unfamiliar with the residents and their patients scored each of the portfolio entries. Portfolio entries were sorted by topic, and raters scored all entries within a given topic (across residents) before moving to the next topic. Raters were trained by scoring benchmark entries.

Overall portfolio scores tended to increase with year of training. Scores were moderately correlated with a national, in-training written exam, but not with clinical rotation ratings. A generalizability analysis and D-study showed that five entries scored by two raters provided sufficient reliability for norm-referenced (relative) decisions with $G = 0.81$, and that five entries scored by three raters or six entries scored by two raters would provide sufficient reliability for criterion referenced (absolute) decisions.

As an unintended consequence, the portfolios identified poor performance across residents in certain topic areas, resulting in an almost immediate change in the curriculum.

Case Example 12.3: A Clinical Portfolio for Baccalaureate Nursing Students (Lettus, Moessner, & Dooley, 2001)

Regent's College created a portfolio assessment option to meet the needs of experienced registered nurses returning to school to obtain their Baccalaureate degree. The portfolio allowed these senior nurses, who were not always providing traditional hands-on nursing care, to document clinical competencies essential to nursing practice. Students developed their portfolios individually and at their own pace, based on a detailed portfolio development guide provided by the college.

The portfolio included three sections:

- Section 1 consisted of a resume that identified educational and professional experiences such as formal and continuing education and professional committee work, and reflected on the learning gained from these experiences. As a capstone for this section, the student identified an area of professional growth, engaged in a professional activity in this area, and wrote a scholarly paper about the learning attained.
- Section 2 was structured around competency objectives. The student developed a learning statement for each objective, describing and documenting his or her accomplishment of the objective; each statement had to be accompanied by two to four pieces of supportive evidence such as a course description, performance review, or letter from a supervisor.
- Section 3 of the portfolio was a case study that demonstrated the student's ability to care for a patient/client over time, making clinical decisions supported by the nursing literature.

A series of three one-hour telephone conferences for six to eight students and a nurse educator provided a formative, supportive opportunity to discuss the meaning and content of the portfolios.

Scoring the Portfolio

The portfolio development guide included examples of acceptable responses to each objective and acceptable documentation; sample case studies; and the scoring criteria for the learning statements and case study.

To avoid confounding clinical competencies with writing skills, the portfolio was reviewed for grammar, spelling, and errors in structure and format, and returned for revision before being submitted for scoring. A random sample of the documentation was verified to prevent fraud.

Examiners participated in a two-day training session to review the guidelines and to rate and discuss sample portfolios. Three raters scored each portfolio independently; the final pass/fail decision was reached by consensus. If a section was failed students repeated that section only.

Summary

Portfolios can provide a useful structure for gathering multi-method, multi-source, reflection-annotated evidence about the achievements of learners over time, but are open to the same threats to validity as other qualitative or holistic assessments. Portfolios have been used extensively for learning and assessment in nursing education and increasingly in undergraduate, graduate, and continuing medical education; with learners in dentistry, occupational therapy, physical therapy, and other health professions; and for faculty promotion and tenure (Table 12.2). With increases in Internet technology, educators are also experimenting with computer-based, web-based and e-portfolio structures (Carraccio & Englander, 2004; Dornan, Lee, & Stopford, 2001; Parboosingh, 1996; Rosenberg, et al., 2001). Table 12.3 provides a summary of guidelines for the successful implementation of assessment portfolios in the health professions.

Table 12.2 Portfolios in the Health Professions

Nursing	Jasper, 1995
	Wenzel, et al., 1998
	Gallagher, 2001
	Lettus, et al., 2001
Medicine	Challis, 1999
	Mathers, et al., 1999
	Pinsky & Fryer-Edwards, 2001
	Wilkinson, et al., 2002
	O'Sullivan, et al., 2002 and 2004
	Driessen, et al., 2003
	Gordon, 2003
Dentistry	Chambers, 2004
Dental Hygeine	Gadbury-Amyot, et al., 2003
Occupational Therapy	Zubizarreta, 1999
Physical Therapy	Paschal, et al., 2002
Faculty Promotion and Tenure	Hafler & Lovejoy, 2000

Table 12.3 Practical Guidelines for Assessment Portfolios

Introducing the portfolio
- Introduce portfolios slowly with input and feedback from learners and faculty
- Clarify goals
- Separate working (formative) and summative (performance) portfolio functions
- Provide support and training in the use of portfolios for both learners and faculty

Implementing the portfolio
- Provide learners with a standard structure and guidelines for the type and quantity of material to be included in the portfolio
- Sample learners' work over tasks and over time
- Provide frequent formative feedback in a supportive educational climate
- Provide time for creating portfolio entries within the structure of existing activities

Assessing the portfolio
- Provide benchmarks and frame-of-reference training to raters
- Allow raters to discuss scores and reach a consensus
- Use both qualitative and quantitative approaches to assessment and quality assurance
- Triangulate the results of the portfolio assessment with other assessment methods

References

Carraccio, C., & Englander, R. (2004). Evaluating competence using a portfolio: A literature review and web-based application to ACGME competencies. *Teaching and Learning in Medicine*, 16, 381–387.

Challis, M. (1999). AMEE Medical Education Guide No. 11 (revised) Portfolio-based learning and assessment in medical education. *Medical Teacher*, 21, 370–377.

Chambers, D.W. (2004). Portfolios for determining initial licensure competency. *Journal of American Dental Association*, 135(2), 173–184.

Davis, M.H., Friedman Ben–David, M., Harden, R.M., Howie, P., Ker, J., McGhee, C., et al. (2001a). Portfolio assessment in medical students' final examination. *Medical Teacher*, 23: 357–366.

Davis, M.H., Friedman Ben-David, M., Harden, R.M., Howie, P., Ker, J., McGhee, C., et al. (2001b). AMEE Medical Education Guide # 24: Portfolios as a method of student assessment. *Medical Teacher*, 23, 535–551.

Dornan, T., Lee, C., & Stopford, A. (2001). SkillsBase: A web-based electronic learning portfolio for clinical skills. *Academic Medicine*, 76, 542–543.

Driessen, E., Schuwirth, L., Van Tartwijk, Vermont, J., & van der Vleuten, C. (2003). Use of portfolios in early undergraduate medical training. *Medical Teacher*, 25, 18–21.

Driessen, E., van der Vleuten, C., Schuwirth, L., Van Tartwijk, J., & Vermont, J. (2005). The use of qualitative research criteria for portfolio assessment as an alternative to reliability evaluation: A case study. *Medical Education*, 39, 214–220.

Gadbury-Amyot, C.C., Kim, J., Palm, R.L., Mills, G.E., Noble, E., & Overman, P.R. (2003). Validity and reliability of portfolio assessment of competency in a baccalaureate dental hygiene program. *Journal of Dental Education*, 67(9), 991–1002.

Gallagher, P. (2001). An evaluation of a standards based portfolio. *Nurse Education Today*, 21, 409–416.

Gordon, J. (2003). Assessing students' personal and professional development using portfolios and interviews. *Medical Education*, 37, 335–340.

Hafler, J.P., & Lovejoy Jr., F.H. (2000). Scholarly activities recorded in the portfolios of teacher-clinician faculty. *Academic Medicine*, 75, 649–652.

Jasper, M.A. (1995). The potential of the professional portfolio for nursing. *Journal of Clinical Nursing*, 4, 249–255.

Kolb, D. (1984). *Experiential learning: Experience as a source of learning and development*. Englewood Cliffs, NJ: Prentice Hall.

Lettus, M.K., Moessner, P.H., & Dooley, L. (2001). The clinical portfolio as an assessment tool. *Nursing Administration Quarterly*, 25, 74–79.

Mathers, N.J., Challis, M.C., Howe, A.C., & Field, N.J. (1999). Portfolios in continuing medical education—effective and efficient? *Medical Education*, 33, 521–530.

McMullan, M., Endacott, R., Gray, M., Jasper, M., Miller, C., Scholes, J., et al. (2003). Portfolio and assessment of competence: A review of the literature. *Journal of Advanced Nursing*, 41(3), 283–294.

Melville, C., Rees, M., Brookfield, D., & Anderson, J. (2004). Portfolios for assessment of pediatric specialist registrars. *Medical Education*, 38, 1117–1125.

Miller, G. (1990). The assessment of clinical skills/competence/performance. *Academic Medicine*, 65, S63–S67.

O'Sullivan, P.S., Cogbill, K.K., McClain, T., Reckase, M.D., & Clardy, J.A. (2002). Portfolios as a novel approach for residency evaluation. *Academic Psychiatry*, 26, 173–179.

O'Sullivan, P.S., Reckase, M.D., McClain, T., Savidge, M.A., & Clardy, J.A. (2004). Demonstration of portfolios to assess competency of residents. *Advances in Health Sciences Education*, 9, 309–323.

Parboosingh, J. (1996). Learning portfolios: Potential to assist health professional with self-directed learning. *Journal of Continuing Education in the Health Professions*, 16, 75–81.

Paschal, K.A., Jensen, G.M., & Mostrom, E. (2002). Building Portfolios: A means for developing habits of reflective practice in physical therapy education. *Journal of Physical Therapy Education*, 16, 38–53.

Paulson, F.L., Paulson, P.P., & Meyer, C.A. (1991). What makes a portfolio a portfolio? *Educational Leadership*, 48, 60–63.

Pinsky, L.E., & Fryer-Edwards, K. (2004). Diving for PERLS: Working and performance portfolios for evaluation and reflection on learning. *Journal of General Internal Medicine*, 19, 582–587.

Pitkala, K., & Mantyranta, T. (2004). Feelings related to first patient experiences in medical school: A qualitative study on students' personal portfolios. *Patient Education and Counseling*, 54, 171–177.

Pitts, J. (2007). Portfolios, personal development and reflective practice. *Understanding Medical Education Series*. Edinburgh, Scotland: Association for the Study of Medical Education.

Pitts, J., Coles, C., & Thomas, P. (1999). Educational portfolios in the assessment of general practice trainers: Reliability of assessors. *Medical Teacher*, 33, 515–520.

Pitts, J., Coles, C., & Thomas, P. (2001). Enhancing reliability in portfolio assessment: "Shaping" the portfolio. *Medical Teacher*, 23, 351–355.

Pitts, J., Coles, C., Thomas, P., & Smith, F. (2002). Enhancing reliability in portfolio assessment: Discussions between assessors. *Medical Teacher*, 24(2), 197–201.

Rees, C. (2005). The use (and abuse) of the term "portfolio". *Medical Education*, 39, 436–437.

Rees, C., & Sheard, C. (2004). The reliability of assessment criteria for undergraduate medical students' communication skills portfolios: The Nottingham experience. *Medical Education*, 38, 138–144.

Roberts, C., Newble, D., & O'Rourke, A. (2002). Portfolio-based assessments in medical education: Are they valid and reliable for summative purposes? *Medical Education*, 36, 899–900.

Rosenberg, M.E., Watson, K., Paul, J., Miller, W., Harris, I., & Valdivia, T.D. (2001). Development and implementation of a web-based evaluation system for an internal medicine residency program. *Academic Medicine*, 76, 92–95.

Schön, D.A. (1987). *Educating the reflective practitioner: Toward a new design for teaching and learning in the professions.* San Francisco, CA: Jossey-Bass.

Ward, M., Gruppen, L., & Regehr, G. (2002). Measuring self-assessment: Current state of the art. *Advances in Health Sciences Education: Theory and Practice,* 7, 63–80.

Webb, C., Endacott, R., Gray, M.A., Jasper, M.A., McMullan, M., & Scholes, J. (2003). Evaluating portfolio assessment systems: What are the appropriate criteria? *Nursing Education Today,* 23, 600–609.

Webster's Encyclopedic Unabridged Dictionary of the English Language (1996). New York: Gramercy Books, Random House Value Publishing, Inc.

Wenzel, L.S., Briggs, K.L., & Puryear, B.L. (1998). Portfolio: Authentic assessment in the age of the curriculum revolution. *Journal of Nursing Education,* 37, 208–212.

Wilkinson, T.J., Challis, M., Hobma, S.O., Newble, D.I., Parboosingh, J.T., Sibbald, R.G., et al. (2002). The use of portfolios for assessment of the competence and performance of doctors in practice. *Medical Education,* 36, 918–924.

Zubizarreta, J. (1999). Teaching portfolios: An effective strategy for faculty development in occupational therapy. *American Journal of Occupational Therapy,* 53, 51–55.

List of Contributors

Steven M. Downing, PhD, Associate Professor, University of Illinois at Chicago, College of Medicine, Department of Medical Education.

Steven M. Downing received a PhD from Michigan State University (MSU) in Educational Psychology, specializing in educational measurement. He has more than 25 years' experience in working with high-stakes testing programs in medicine and the professions.

In 2001, Dr. Downing joined the faculty of the University of Illinois at Chicago, Department of Medical Education. He teaches courses in all areas of testing and assessment for the Masters of Health Professions Education (MHPE) program and advises students with interests in educational measurement in the health professions. Formerly, he was Director of Health Programs and Deputy Vice President at the National Board of Medical Examiners (NBME), Senior Psychometrician at the American Board of Internal Medicine (ABIM), and Director of Psychometrics and Senior Program Manager for the Institute for Clinical Evaluation (ICE) at the American Board of Internal Medicine. Dr. Downing consults with various national and international testing programs in all areas of test development and psychometrics, with particular interests in selected-response formats, test validity issues, testing program evaluation, and computer-based testing.

Dr. Downing's research interests in educational measurement and assessment in medical education have resulted in more than 100 research papers, book chapters, and presentations at national and international professional conferences. Dr. Downing is the senior editor for a comprehensive book on test development, *Handbook of Test Development*, published by Lawrence Erlbaum in January 2006.

Rachel Yudkowsky, MD, MHPE, Assistant Professor, University of Illinois at Chicago, College of Medicine, Department of Medical Education.

Rachel Yudkowsky received her MD from Northwestern University Medical School in 1979, and is Board Certified in Psychiatry. She served as medical student psychiatry clerkship director, psychiatry residency program director, and director of education for the Evanston Hospital Department of Psychiatry, and as associate director of graduate medical education for the Department of Psychiatry and Behavioral Sciences of Northwestern University Medical School. She received a Masters degree in Health Professions Education (MHPE) in 2000.

Dr. Yudkowsky joined the Department of Medical Education of the University of Illinois at Chicago in 1999. She served as associate director of faculty development from 1999–2005, and has been director of the Dr. Allan L. and Mary L. Graham Clinical Performance Center since 2000, where she develops standardized patient and simulation-based programs for the instruction and assessment of students, residents, and staff. Her areas of research interest include performance assessment using standardized patients and setting passing standards for performance tests.

Dr. Yudkowsky is immediate past Chair of the Research and Grants Committee of the Association of Standardized Patient Educators, and serves on the Editorial Board of the journal Simulation in Healthcare. She teaches in the MHPE program and conducts workshops on HPE topics both nationally and internationally.

Thomas M. Haladyna, PhD—Chapter 2 (Validity)

Thomas M. Haladyna is Professor Emeritus at Arizona State University (ASU). Tom has been an elementary school teacher, a research professor, and a test director at American College Testing Program and faculty member in the College of Teacher Education and Leadership at ASU. He specializes in designing and validating testing programs, and he has worked in more than 50 national, regional, and state testing programs. His research has principally focused on issues affecting the validity of test score interpretations and how to better develop test items. He has authored or co-authored 12 books, more than 60 published journal articles, and hundreds of conference papers and technical reports. Currently, Tom co-edited the *Handbook of Test Development* with Steve Downing, and has several, ongoing research projects on testing.

Rick D. Axelson, PhD—Chapter 3 (Reliability)

Rick D. Axelson is Assistant Professor in the Department of Family Medicine and faculty consultant in the Office of Consultation and Research in Medical Education at the University of Iowa Carver College of Medicine. He received an MS in Statistics and a PhD in Sociology from the University of Arizona. Over the past 15 years, he has been involved with developing and implementing educational assessment systems at colleges and universities. In 2003, he and his colleagues founded the LearningAssessment@Listserv.cccnext.net to facilitate the development of effective assessment practices in the California Community College system. Most recently, he served as the Assistant Vice Provost for Institutional Research, Assessment, & Planning at the University of Missouri-Kansas City, where he worked with academic departments on enhancing their program review and outcomes assessment processes. His research interests include program evaluation (theory, methods, practice), learning outcomes assessment, learning communities, and the role of social and psychological factors in learning environments.

Clarence D. Kreiter, PhD—Chapter 3 (Reliability) and Chapter 4 (Generalizability)

Clarence D. Kreiter is Professor in the Department of Family Medicine and the Office of Consultation and Research in Medical Education at the University of Iowa Carver College of Medicine. Dr. Kreiter received his PhD in quantitative foundations of educational psychology from the University of Iowa. He serves on the editorial boards of two medical education research journals and has published on topics related to innovative cognitive and clinical skill assessments, selection methods for medical school admissions, evaluation of teaching, simulation, OSCE test design, Bayesian reasoning, generalizability analysis, and validity generalization. As a professor with the University of Iowa Carver College of Medicine, he consults on research design and statistics and teaches graduate-level medical education assessment courses.

Ara Tekian, PhD, MHPE—Chapters 6 (Standard Setting), 11 (Oral Exams) and 12 (Portfolios)

Ara Tekian, PhD, MHPE is Associate Professor and Director of International Affairs at the Department of Medical Education (DME), University of Illinois at Chicago. He joined DME in 1992 as Head of the International Programs and participates in teaching in the Master's of Health Professions Education (MHPE) program. Dr. Tekian teaches courses in curriculum development, assessment and instruction, and medical simulations; and has organized and conducted over 140 international workshops in more than 35 countries in different parts of the world. Dr. Tekian was the winner of the 1997 Teaching Recognition Program Award selected by the UIC Council for Excellence in Teaching and Learning. He was the 2006 Program Chair for Education in the Professions' Division of American

Educational Research Association (AERA), and serves on the *Educational Researcher* Editorial Board. He is the President Elect for 2009. He is the primary author of the book *Innovative Simulations for Assessing Professional Competence: From Paper-and-Pencil to Virtual Reality* published in 1999.

William C. McGaghie, PhD—Chapters 8 (Observational Assessment) and 10 (Simulations in Assessment)

William C. McGaghie is currently the Jacob R. Suker, MD, Professor of Medical Education and Professor of Preventive Medicine at the Northwestern University Feinberg School of Medicine. Dr. McGaghie received his PhD degree from Northwestern University. He has previously held faculty positions at the University of Illinois College of Medicine and the University of North Carolina School of Medicine. Dr. McGaghie has been a medical education scholar for 35 years, writing about topics including personnel and program evaluation, research methodology, medical simulation, attitude measurement, and faculty development. He serves on the editorial boards of six scholarly journals and consults with a variety of professional boards, agencies, institutes, and medical schools worldwide.

John Butter, MD—Chapter 8 (Observational Assessment)

John Butter is Assistant Professor of Medicine, Department of Medicine and Augusta Webster Office of Medical Education, Northwestern University Feinberg School of Medicine. Dr. Butter received his MD degree from Northwestern University and completed his residency at Beth Israel Hospital, in Boston. After serving on the faculty at Dartmouth Medical School, he joined the faculty of Northwestern University Feinberg School of Medicine. He co-directs the Clinical Education Center and has leadership positions in the clinical skills program at Northwestern. He has published on topics related to clinical skills development and competency based mastery learning. He also serves as Associate Program Director for the

Internal Medicine Residency and Associate Division Chief for Education in General Internal Medicine.

Marsha Kaye, RN, MSN—Chapter 8 (Observational Assessment)

Marsha Kaye is Director of Standardized Patient Programs at the Clinical Education Center of the Office of Medical Education and Faculty Development, Northwestern University Feinberg School of Medicine. She received her Masters of Science in Nursing at Yale University. She currently serves on the board of the Association of Standardized Patient Educators and has published articles on the use of standardized patients in teaching clinical skills to medical students. For the past ten years and now as Director of Standardized Patient Programs, she is responsible for the development and administration of the use of standardized patients in teaching, assessment and remediation of clinical skills to medical students at the undergraduate level. Before entering in the field of medical education, she was a Pediatric Nurse Practitioner.

S. Barry Issenberg, MD—Chapter 10 (Simulations in Assessment)

S. Barry Issenberg is Professor of Medicine, University of Miami Miller School of Medicine and the Gordon Center for Research in Medical Education. He received his MD degree from the University of Miami. Dr. Issenberg serves as Project Director for the technical and curricular research and development of Harvey, the Cardiopulmonary Patient Simulator and computer-based training and assessment system. In addition, Dr. Issenberg leads a national consortium of clinicians and medical educators from 14 medical centers. The consortium meets quarterly to develop curricula in cardiology, neurology and emergency medicine and to design its outcomes research studies. The consortium has designed, implemented and published the results of several multi-center studies that have shown the effectiveness of simulation technology to teach and assess clinical skills.

Index

Printed in Great Britain
by Amazon.co.uk, Ltd.,
Marston Gate.